EU Local Imprints

Josef Langer
Goran Vlašić
Božena Krce Miočić
(eds.)

EU Local Imprints

The Case of South Central Europe

PETER LANG
Frankfurt am Main · Berlin · Bern · Bruxelles · New York · Oxford · Wien

Bibliographic Information published by the Deutsche Nationalbibliothek
The Deutsche Nationalbibliothek lists this publication in the Deutsche Nationalbibliografie; detailed bibliographic data is available in the internet at http://dnb.d-nb.de.

Cover Design:
© Olaf Gloeckler, Atelier Platen, Friedberg

BM.W_F[a] Ministry of Science, Education and Sports

Editorial work on this book is financially supported by the *Bundesministerium für Wissenschaft und Forschung of the Republic of Austria* and the *Ministry of Science, Education and Sports of the Republic of Croatia*, through the bilateral project *EU-Integration: Gesellschaftliche Transformation in Kroatien*.

ISBN 978-3-631-60176-1

www.peterlang.de

Contents

Chapter III

Communication

Chapter IV

Tourism

Foreword

This book about European issues from a national and local perspective derived from a conference organized by the Department of Tourism and Communication Sciences at the University of Zadar (Croatia) and the Department of Sociology at the Alpen-Adria-Universität Klagenfurt, Austria. It contains proceedings from a stream of the 4th International Symposium on European Issues ("What will be? Analysis and Visions for Europe"), which was hosted at the University of Zadar and dealt with "Convergence/divergence in the Visions of Europe: Focus on Social Practice". The meeting took place on the 4th and 5th of September 2009 and assembled around two dozen scholars, experts and professionals. The book is meant as a counterpart to "Analysis and Visions for Europe" (2011) from the Klagenfurt thread of the same conference (25th and 26th of September 2009) which explores more macro-sociological aspects in the unfolding of the European Union. It also complements earlier publications such as "Euroregions – The Alps-Adriatic Context" (2007) and "Knowledge-Region: Alps-Adriatic Challenges" (2010) from previous conferences in this series. The emphasis of the book is on European Union local imprints in South Central Europe. It contains presentations from the symposium plus an introduction by the editors.

Here our thanks go to the University of Zadar, which provided the main material prerequisites for this stream of the symposium. Special thanks go to Karen Meehan from the Department of Sociology at the Alpen-Adria-Universität Klagenfurt, who supported the technical side of the editing work.

Klagenfurt and Zadar, December 2011

J. L., G.V. and B.K.

Introduction

Josef Langer – Goran Vlašić – Božena Krce Miočić

Introduction

This volume is the result of fruitful discussions on the ideas of integration. Given the continuing interest in political, economic, monetary, and other types of integration, the question this volume focuses on is this: how do these "traditional forms of integration" influence integrating mechanisms in more subtle areas of culture, communication and tourism? In the case of the European Union (EU) "membership presents an aspiration for a country in the process of accession". As such, it implies conflicts from, at least, two perspectives. First, on the part of the country that is being accepted for membership, there is a discrepancy between how things are expected to be done and local customs, which maintain old "undesirable" patterns. While, on the one side, there are such conflicts, at the same time clashes happen in the pursuit of the business interests of emerging market (EM) members who seek to benefit from the greater growth rates of accession countries. Therefore, some positive practices, though sought by an accession country, are supported only in theory, thus requiring that country's resourcefulness in solving these conflicting situations.

Contributions in this volume can be read individually, but jointly create a description of the interaction between the EU and accession states: both through positive and negative impacts. Authors provide perspectives on the impact of EU accession on culture, primarily in terms of risk perception, which was long viewed as highly undesirable in non-western countries; on education systems as important carriers of knowledge and culture; on communication and media, which serve as a basis for creating public opinion and therefore generating potential for positive changes; and on tourism as an important industry that has been subject to strong transformation processes as a result of successive EU enlargements.

The first set of contributions (Chapter I) focuses on managing cultural changes at different levels to adjust the values and norms of interacting parties. One such important aspect is the risk tolerance of a nation (but also at other levels), as conceptualized by Geert Hofstede. In an accession process, numerous risks arise, such as the unknown impacts of accession. However, risk exhibits an important impact on adjusting the culture to the market and entrepreneurial economy of the EU. As ALFIREVIĆ/PAVIČIĆ/VLAŠIĆ indicate, for such changes "some individuals, organizations, or even societies seem to have better starting positions '*to feign control over the uncontrollable*', i.e. to project and act upon the future-oriented insights". In their contribution they present management approaches that provide insights primarily at corporate levels: how to manage the future in the face of the uncertainties that accessions bring. In WITTINE/VLAŠIĆ's contribution, the discussion focuses on external perceptions of risk, i.e. on the perceptions of EU investors about political risks in Croatia. Although the author discusses great potential benefits from accession in terms of reducing political risks, he stresses that "in the end, it is important to point out that mere EU accession is not the panacea that would heal the problems the Croatian economy faces today. Structural economic, legal and social reforms behind the accession are the issues that matter and the ones that would bring the biggest benefit. "Although investments can have significant positive impacts on the local economy, there are numerous potential risks associated with different goals of partners from the EU and the accession countries.

In his contribution, ŠUBIĆ discusses the benefits and shortfalls of the vigorous privatization and internationalization of banking sector. While gaining direct benefits from capital inflows, but also knowledge inflows, the risks that the Croatian banking system incurred as a result of the greater control of international banks (primarily Italian and Austrian) required an adjustment of the Croatian National Bank to control their activities through a college of supervisors. Moreover, control has to transcend borders as many of the strategic decisions regarding Croatian banks are now made in EU countries. The deep integration of the Croatian banking system into the EU banking system created a solid infrastructure for the easier movement of capital to wherever the investment opportunities arise.

Besides the tolerance for risk and managing risk, culture has also changed in several other aspects. DRAŠKOVIĆ/GNJIDIĆ discuss consumer attitudes toward environmental issues and the adjustment of the Croatian environmental management policies to EU directives. This issue grows in importance with the elimination of borders, which will enhance movement of tourists. As EU directives provide more guidelines and minimum requirements, tourists make choices by changing locations: whether to maintain environmental consciousness and inform themselves about the local regulations, or to ignore such practices while not in their home country. One of the issues that authors discuss is this: who should be responsible for the development/maintenance of environmentally friendly behaviour: individuals or institutionalized efforts?

The contribution by BAKULA, the last in this section, provides a broader perspective on changes in attitudes of Croatian students between 1995 (when Croatians were expressing a relatively strong national identity cherishing their independence) and 2008, when the general aim of Croatia was to enter a new union: the EU. Comparing the indicators from 2008 with those from the 1995 study, the author concludes that "present-day students, on the average express less initiative and effort, they have a lower general knowledge level, and mostly seek 'cheap and on the spot forms of entertainment'."

Chapter II deals with the important area of education and how it works across borderless societies. HÖNIG provides a perspective on the impacts of Sorbonne, Bologna and Lisbon on European higher education. Her study provides a cross-time and cross-country comparison of impacts. While the goal of the Sorbonne Declaration was "to create a European area of higher education, where national identities and interests can interact and strengthen each other for the benefit of Europe of its students, and more generally of its citizens" (Sorbonne 1998), the Bologna Reform Process (Bologna 1999) focused more on applicability of knowledge thus linking it closely to business practice. Comparing "old-European" studies of sociology to "new-European" studies in Slovenia, the author concludes that in both contexts there are "observed continuing trends towards an enforced economization and standardization of higher education". A positive trend is toward the greater mobility of students, teachers, and administrative staff. However, "the *regional specialization* of departments in topics and approaches still prevails in its importance" therefore limiting mobility to an extent while ensuring diversity. The author stresses an important step to internationalization of European education: development of joint study programs.

ZEKANOVIĆ KORONA/FUČKO discuss opportunities of e-learning, distance learning, mobile learning and nano learning as types of constructive and collaborative learning. Perfecting these forms for educational purposes provides great opportunities for further elimination of borders and greater knowledge sharing, and thus greater knowledge development. The authors indicate these developments as trends in the EU and therefore as important to follow and implement in accession countries through the motivation of professors to incorporate such learning methods. However, these ideas need to be strongly marketed. Along these lines, in the contribution by MIHANOVIĆ/BUBALO/ VUČIĆ, the authors emphasise the importance of lifelong learning and of the integration of learning practices across borders. However, they argue that an important missing element in popularizing these is the marketing of educational institutions and programs. Marketing activities not only help the educational system to be more market oriented but at the same time they can get the market (both employers and current/potential employees) to recognize new competences that are likely to be important for success in the future integrated system of countries.

These marketing efforts require strong and well integrated media (Chapter III). The question is whether there are media houses or whether we are faced with content development agencies. PERIŠIN discusses the promises and perils of multi-platform media companies and the necessity for significant infrastructural investments into achieving cohesion. However, on these platforms it is not only media companies that compete: anyone can be a source of interesting content that seeks viewership. Following European directives, the Croatian TV market is turning completely digital in order to be able to offer greater benefits to its users. Radio, as a relatively old medium, is also facing important changes and turning digital. ZGRABLJIĆ-ROTAR/ŠOP indicate that, besides multi-platform media, radio must become multi-format media, with the ability to provide content in formats accessible from different devices, and allowing for non-linear broadcasting. If the media (in terms of content distribution) is converging and content is becoming the key, MALOVIĆ puts forth a discussion on his perspective on content specificities and the pursuit of profits in the Croatian media as it internationalizes.

With changes in media and different critiques that can be proposed, it is inevitable that social media is increasingly important where content is created and shared, depending on one's on-line network structure. In July 2011 Facebook had more than 750 million active members worldwide. Google recognized the importance of such a medium and in June 2010 it launched *Google plus,* which gained popularity in a short period of time (10 million users in two weeks, i.e. even before the official launch). FUDURIĆ/MANDELLI provide insights into how to measure success in these new media formats in which the content is not directly controlled by media or by companies, but rather these provide a platform for the democratic exchange of ideas.

The last chapter (Chapter IV) deals with tourism as an important industry, which, by its very nature, is likely to benefit from political and economic integration. KRCE-MIOČIĆ/ŽNIDAR/BAKIJA provide a perspective on the importance of nautical tourism, especially high end nautical tourism. ŠIMURINA/BOGUNOVIĆ/MARKOVIĆ offer an overview of the airline industry, as a supporting industry to tourism development in the face of integration: from the development of national carriers to low cost carriers connecting the EU to Croatia – the EU candidate country. These developments require investments into infrastructure, service, etc. However, investments, even when supported by the EU, are often not well directed and executed as local beneficiaries aim at short term returns. On the other hand, these differences create (and maintain) a potential for cultural tourism where, as PAVELIN claims, *the differences are what makes the difference.*

All contributions together serve as an overview of what is and what might become as a result of EU enlargements, from the perspective of accession countries in South Eastern Europe, particularly Croatia. In contrast to elites on both sides who usually paint EU membership in the brightest colours, the closer look into different smaller sectors and entities of society reveal more ambiguous processes and attitudes. The closer the view moves to the local issues, the more blurred and uncertain the question about advantages and disadvantages seems to become. A boilerplate in EU communication is the claim that enlargement is the most successful foreign policy of the Union. However, the benefit reversely explored from the position of different social fields in prospective member states appears much less conclusive. This poses a dilemma which can obviously only be solved by concrete future experience. Communication here and now can at most help to prepare a little for the journey. This book may serve to escort the reader, providing food for thought along the way.

Chapter I

Culture

Nikša Alfirević – Jurica Pavičić – Goran Vlašić

Future Insight as a Strategic Capability in the Regional and European Risk Society

"(...) So, first of all, let me assert my firm belief that the only thing we have to fear is fear itself – nameless, unreasoning, unjustified terror which paralyzes needed efforts to convert retreat into advance". (Franklin D. Roosevelt[1])

The Risk Society

In the middle ages, the very idea of risk could not be interpreted in the contemporary sense, since the faith in God's design made it impossible to construct rational expectations about the future. Only with the advent of capitalism and the rational-scientific paradigm, could time and future events be conceptualized as susceptible to analysis and prediction, which has been facilitated by the development of statistical methods and computing power. Such an association of time/future events with the calculation of probability created, according to Reith (2004), the contemporary notion of risk in the mid-17th century.

A significant step in conceptualizing the modernist notion of risk seems to be the viewpoint of its production by the Others – either of the same, or a different society – rather than by the will of God, or some other uncontrollable *force majeure* (Ewald[2], as cit. by Lupton 2005, p. 6). The rational view of controlling human behaviour, perceived as a potential source of risk, has created a major influence upon daily life in modern societies, although the development of modern technologies has not changed the psychological constraints for the rational assessment of risk (Gardner 2009). In addition, the developing complexity of both technology and its social consequences, make it increasingly difficult to reliably quantify the future outcomes/consequences of today's actions. According to Ulrich Beck (1986/1992), the high modernity has multiple significant consequences for the consideration of risk. Firstly, the societies of high modernity 'produce' major risks (such as different 'dirty' technologies, nuclear waste/disasters, genetic manipulation and human cloning, etc.), which have not been faced by humanity ever before. Out of the multiplicity of risks faced by the fragile humanity, some are 'picked up' and emphasized, especially by the general public, often regardless of the 'objective', i.e. scientific/expert

---

1 Franklin D. Roosevelt's inauguration speech, cited by Gardner (2009, p. 5).

2 Ewald (1993, pp. 221-228)

opinion. Such a 'cultural' approach to risk evaluation serves a dual purpose, as it enables laypeople to go on with their lives, while dealing with those sources of risk, which seem to be both manageable and compatible with the mainstream culture.

Therefore, a new dichotomy related to risk emerges (Beck 1992): on the one hand, massive bureaucracies seem to regulate each aspect of social life, in order to ensure that traditional (i.e. early modernity-based) risks are mitigated. This is used as an argument for the Foucauldian practices of surveillance/social control and other aspects of governments' behaviour (Linke/Smith 2009), but also as grounds for the emergence of 'fear entrepreneurs', who profit from the supply of security-enhancing products and services (Furedi 2007). On the other hand, new forms of risk, potentially leading to previously unseen consequences, are often undetected, due to the lack of regulation, lobbying by the corporate sector, high level of technical expertise required to understand their essence, etc. (Beck, op. cit.[3]).

The resulting *'culture of fear'* diverges from the pre-modern apocalyptic expectations, since the source of risk is ascribed to certain forms of human behaviour (such as terrorism, paedophilia, production of nuclear energy, genetically modified food, etc.), rather than to the will of God. Although the social production of fear through 'moral panics' is not a novelty (Goode/Ben-Yehuda 2009), Furedi (op. cit.) sees fear as a distinct feature of contemporary culture, constructed by the elites and communicated by mass media, which leads to the "[…] 'vulnerability' now seen as the natural state for most people […] As a label it is used to describe entire groups in society. […] We are all seen as being vulnerable in one way or another" (ibid.).

The idea of vulnerability should, probably, be viewed within the contingencies of specific social contexts, in which trajectories of 'vulnerable social actors' cross and interactions occur (see, e.g. Delor and Michel 2000, for a discussion in the context of HIV/AIDS research). Nevertheless, contemporary societies seem to accept the idea of vulnerability (and/or the minority status) as a *generic property* of such major groups, such as children. This can be illustrated by the emergence of over-protective 'helicopter parents', with the popular advice available (Skenazy 2009)[4], on how to reintroduce 'normal' parenting practices.

The argument of the higher level of risk being countered by treating individuals as increasingly vulnerable, i.e. as potential victims, may be viewed

---

3 Beck refers to the German translation of a 1982 volume by Charles Perrow *(Normale Katastrophen,* Campus, Frankfurt), with the original edition reprinted two years later as: Perrow, Charles (1984): *Normal Accidents: Living With High Risk Technologies,* Princeton University Press, Princeton.

4 Skenazy also writes a Weblog with stories on the topic of irrational fear(s) in parenting, available at: [http://freerangekids.wordpress.com], retrieved in April 2010.

as contradictory to Beck's and Giddens' other central concepts. Namely, their notions of *reflexivity/individualization* are also supposed to reflect the decline of confidence in the social structures, which were traditionally expected to manage risk (government, church, experts and scientists ...). Individuals are left to cope alone with the consequences of choices made in all aspects of life, as the very idea of reflexivity, defined by Giddens (1990) is related to appropriating new knowledge relevant for (re)adjusting both one's own identity, and the social processes related to one's environment. However, reflexivity entails *"continuous monitoring and surveillance"* (Ekberg 2007, in a discussion of Giddens, op. cit.) of the environment, which is also replicated at the level of the entire society.

Arguments for such a thesis could be found by many social practices performed by contemporary businesses and governments. They include consolidating and using data on citizen(s) by building centralized databases and using information technology approaches, such as *'data warehousing', 'data mining',* etc. (Garfinkel 2000; Hunter 2002); extensive usage of 'intelligent' tracking devices[5], which can be embedded into all kinds of products and other everyday objects (books, cars, personal identification documents, etc.) (Ohkubo/ Suzuki/Kinoshita 2005); tightened security measures for air travel and immigration since the 2001 terrorist attack on the US (Jensen/Draffan 2004), etc.

Maybe the most illustrative example of the willing submission to the surveillance can be found in the use of extremely popular *social networking Web sites,* such as *Facebook,* which has attracted more than 800 million members as at December 2011[6]. It should be noted that the site is becoming widely criticized, as it makes it quite difficult for its users to understand how their data are used and shared. For instance, it is becoming increasingly difficult to understand and use the 'privacy controls' on this social networking service, as well as to quit the service and delete personal data, once they have been submitted (Parliament of Canada 2010). The overall *Zeitgeist* related to the privacy of one's personal data in the Internet age is reflected by a quote by Facebook's founder Mark Zuckerberg, who believes that people may not be

---

5 The most commonly used devices of this kind are referred to as the 'Radio Frequency Identification (RFID) tags'. They may be embedded into consumer products, instead of a traditional bar code, in order to enable easier inventory tracking, transportation of goods, billing and contactless payment at the point of purchase. However, they may stay in an active state (i.e. transmitting data wirelessly, which can be read by using a special device) even after the purchase has been made. For more information on the topic, see the special edition of *Communications of the ACM* (Vol. 48, Issue 9, 2005).

6 See [http://www.facebook.com/press/info.php?statistics] retrieved in December 2011.

expecting the level of privacy to which they were once used[7]. This seems to be confirmed by the empirical research, which indicates that most social networking users either do not care about sharing their data, or have unrealistic expectations that they will remain private (Acquisti/Gross[8], as cited by Fuchs 2009).

By taking into account the popularity of social networking, it could be suggested that the average users are willingly opting for the convenience and 'fun' of the online experience, even if it increases the risks, still incomprehensible in the present. Some risks associated to the Internet by mass media, especially for the young, such as being exposed to an 'online predator' (Gardner, op. cit.), do not seem to be significant in this context. In line with the theory of the 'risk society', completely new forms of risk are being created by social networking, with their users even unaware of their existence.

For instance, personal data posted on electronic social networks creates new context(s) for abuse within the youth culture and 'offline' local communities, as suggested by Marwick[9] (as cited by Fuchs, op. cit.) for the case of the social networking Web site *MySpace.com*: "[…] Rather than focusing on nebulous 'predators,' it seems that parents, teachers, and social workers should emphasize identifying and preventing abuse in specific, local community settings […]". The public has already witnessed examples of 'hate groups', promoting racism and extremism[10], 'online extensions' of school bullying[11], including distribution of videos of humiliated victims, recorded by mobile phone cameras[12], etc.

In addition, the public display of risky behaviour on social networking Web sites, which has already been studied in the context of the safe use of the Internet, i.e. health-related intervention (Moreno et al. 2009), might have wider social consequences in the future career and life of such individuals. Namely, actors, such as future employers and credit rating agencies could be monitoring

---

7 See [http://www.guardian.co.uk/technology/2010/jan/11/facebook-privacy] retrieved on 20.4. 2010.

8 Acquisti/Gross (2006, pp. 36-58)

9 Marwick (2008)

10 See, e.g. *Facebook, YouTube Serving as Hot Spots for Hate Groups* [http://www.switched.com/2008/11/19/youtube-facebook-increasingly-being-used-by-hate-groups/]; *Report: Facebook A Haven For Hate Groups* [http://broadcast.oreilly.com/2009/09/report-facebook-a-haven-for-ha.html]; *Hate Groups And Social Networking* [http://blog.sherweb.com/hate-groups-and-social-networking] retrieved in April 2010.

11 See, e.g. [http://dnevnik.hr/vijesti/hrvatska/djevojcicu-zlostavljaju-u-skoli-i-putem-facebooka.html]; [http://dnevnik.hr/vijesti/hrvatska/facebook-kao-orudze-nasilja-nizu-zlostavljane-djece-nema-kraja.html]; [http://www.slobodnadalmacija.hr/Crna-kronika/tabid/70/articleType/ArticleView/articleId/95091/Default.aspx] (in Croatian only) retrieved in April 2010.

12 See, e.g. [http://www.youtube.com/watch?v=iwJiJiN5UhQ&feature=related] and associated Web links (in Croatian/Serbian only; retrieved in April 2010).

the social networking sites, in order to gain an impression of their (prospective) customers/employees, with a high danger of consulting irrelevant, obsolete, or even impartial data (Davis 2007). Several examples of such a new form of risk have already been exhibited, with the idea of the 'network reputation' being discussed by researchers (Solove 2007), who recognize the weaknesses of the current legal system in regulating this new area of social life.

The future-looking paradigm and the Risk Society

The 'open' paths of individual lives in high modernity imply individualization of risks, based on the assumption of individual decisions and responsibility for different forms of risk. However, a certain 'risk blindness', caused by media, experts and other sources of manipulation, predicted by Beck (1986/1992), is questioned by Tulloch and Lupton (2001). They find that risks in 'reflexive'/'personal' biographies of interviewed individuals are still perceived, explained and adjusted in terms of variables belonging to early modernity (including class, gender, race, age, ...). The capacity to look forward and plan for the contingencies of many risks, native to the age of high modernity, depends on the education and key skills individuals have acquired during the extended periods of their socialization. Not everyone has the same *habitus,* or the amount of cultural and other forms of capital (as conceptualized by Bourdieu), which are required for this task (Cooper 2008).

Hence, some individuals, organizations, or even societies seem to have better starting positions *"to feign control over the uncontrollable"* (Beck 2002), i.e. to project and act upon the future-oriented insights. In this context, the discourse of fear (including the associated mechanisms of social control) represents a closed and debilitating view of the future, concentrated on the maintenance of the status quo. Unfortunately, fear becomes a category of its own, the very centre of the discourse, which functions as an autonomous source of policies, with each and every risk being perceived in terms of a threat, worthy only of eliminating (Furedi, op. cit.). The social 'ideal type' (un)consciously presented by the proponents of such discourses/policies could be expressed in terms of identifying and acting upon all sorts of potential vulnerabilities, until *'everyone is a minority'* (of this, or that sort)[13]. We propose that the public policies and other elements of the public sphere in the societies of high modernity are developing a fixation on maintaining order and stability, in order to create an illusion of control. 'Real' control is, by and large, impossible, since

13 The phrase is used by Grant and Ogawa (1993), who idealistically reflect on the islands of Hawa'ii as a place/model of ultimate racial and cultural harmony/tolerance, or Stodghill and Bower, who reported for *Time Magazine* on the small town of Sequoia Way, located near Sacramento, California, as the racially most integrated place in the US. See [http://www.time.com/time/nation/article/0,8599,340694,00.html] retrieved in April 2010.

high modernity and, thus, reflexivity are based on fragmented and uncertain knowledge. Any form of 'structured denial' of this, widely accepted sociological postulate (Giddens 1990), may lead the individuals to become more susceptible to sacrificing their privacy, personal freedom(s), etc. to the promise of an increased security.

On the other hand, the risk society theory implies that significant vulnerabilities are not recognized by the mainstream social institutions. Their bureaucratic attention is mostly limited to the 'traditional' sources of risk, well-known from the early modernity period. This implies that the overall security cannot be enhanced by the institutions of the existing social order. Their behaviour, maybe even in line with the 'conspiracy theories' (Goertzel 1994), can be easily explained from the perspective of enhancing their position of power, with the possible future consequences vividly depicted by Orwell's popular novel *"1984"*. In this context, we propose that 'fixation' upon the objectives of eliminating 'lower' (easily perceptible) classes of risk may be a hazardous path of social development, which can be replaced by the development of individual and social competencies of future insight.

Development of foresight competence(s)

In the organizational context, business (and other related) risks have usually been addressed by the development of information systems, containing historic data, as well as providing analytical tools, which may be useful for a partial understanding of some future trends. Tools, such as Data Warehousing, enable organizations to structure the data previously stored in multiple and often incompatible databases, while Data Mining applies mathematical/statistical algorithms to detect patterns in the 'sea' of unconnected facts (Loshin 2003). Although such technologies – collectively known as *Business Intelligence (BI)* – help organizations to enhance the quality of their decision-making, Ranadivė (2006) argues that only the availability of real-time data and continuous analysis/adaption of business processes to new circumstances leads to better performance.

Although technology is usually created for the purpose of providing better control over natural, social and other processes, it does not seem to eliminate risks. Namely, technology only serves as a "[...] structural form for dealing with the contingent character of the modern world. It does so through the twin strategy of functional closure and simplification of the very processes it constructs and regulates" (Kallinikos 2007, p. 55, by referring to Luhmann[14]). In general, it does not provide a generic way to handle risks, as it only institutionalizes solutions for comprehensible problems and makes them available to a wider audience. In addition, information technology (IT) is in a

[14] Luhmann (1993)

specific position, since it can be viewed as a *'meta-technology',* i.e. the technology for managing other technologies (ibid.), with its failing possibly causing domino effect(s). High modernity, as the arena of the 'risk society', is highly dependent on multiple information systems, which are becoming interconnected and interdependent. Once again, in accordance with the risk society theory, this solves some problems and creates opportunities for enhanced control of predictable processes, but only with a price to be paid by a new sort of risk, related to the security of data and information systems, on which our societies have become highly dependent (Ciborra 2007).

The solution of this challenge might be found in the development of *'foresightful'* individuals and organizations, to use the term originally proposed by Tsoukas and Shepherd (2004). They differentiate forecasting, as a practice relying on past data to predict the value of a future event, from developing foresight, which could be described in terms of "[...] a sophisticated form of pattern recognition for discontinuities" (ibid, 6) and makes it possible to continue the existence of an organization even in a radically changed environment. Many of the constructs/theories from business studies can be associated to the notion of defying risks by developing future foresight capability.

For instance, the idea of *tacit knowledge,* introduced by Michael Polanyi some time ago, is intensively used in the field of Knowledge Management, to describe the forms of knowledge which are intrinsically tied to a human actor and cannot be easily formalized in terms of a document, computer system, etc. Authors, such as Nonaka (1994) have conceptualized knowledge production in contemporary organizations as a 'dialogue' between the tacit and more explicit form(s) of knowledge, depending on the effectiveness of converting one form of knowledge into another in a shared context ('ba') for knowledge growth (Nonaka/Toyama/Konno 2000). However, tacit knowledge is usually viewed as a one-dimensional term, describing the properties of a knowledgeable individual, which should be made more formal and accessible to the organizational/social knowing. Chia (2004) goes back to Polanyi's 1962 book *Personal Knowledge*[15], in which the primacy of tacit knowledge is affirmed. It is associated with the *'subsidiary awareness'* that makes it possible to be aware of multiple and partly related events, as well as open to new perceptions that may arise in the process.

Some concepts from the field of (business) strategy are also applicable to the foresight paradigm, especially Weick's (1995) idea of sense-making, i.e. adapting to the surprising conditions by 'picking up cues' from the environment and acting upon the interpretations of the emerging situation. In this context,

---

15 As opposed to the 1967 book, *The Tacit Dimension,* which is usually cited by authors in the field of business studies.

organizations are portrayed as continuously (re)negotiating their relationship(s) with the environment and (re)constructing the meaning for their existence. Similarly, the 'open path' of development for organizations can be traced to another popular approach from the field of business strategy, developed by Henry Mintzberg (1978)[16], usually referred to as the *emergent strategy.* It implies that the strategies, used by contemporary organizations, are quite often the results of a chance, having been simply 'stumbled upon' by the employees (or other members of the organization), who are well informed and open to learning. Within this theoretical school of thought, managers of an organization are not expected to be 'omnipotent' strategic leaders, who prescribe where the organization should go, but rather coaches and enablers of collective learning. Burgelman (1988) describes the strategy of such an organization in terms of a *"social learning process",* as it draws on the 'collective intelligence' and the social interactions of the organization's employees/members/stakeholders. Such a tacit theoretical consensus is even recognized by bestsellers on future insight. For instance, Surowiecki (2004), in his book on *Wisdom of Crowds,* suggested that, in most situations, the average/aggregated statistical response/decision of a group may have better effects than a decision made by the 'inner circle' of experts. The 'proliferation' of mass collaboration on the Internet can be cited as a powerful argument in favour of such claims, with the well-known Wiki-encyclopaedia[17] ('Wikipedia')[18], which is edited by its own readers, usually serving as a 'showcase'.

It is also important to note that the 'open path' of organizational development, implied by models from business studies, corresponds to the 'reflexive biographies' of the individuals in high modernity, as described by the theory of reflexive modernization. At different levels, they denote the same 'open-ended' future, shaped by the actors' own choices and, ultimately, their 'correct' evaluations of the risks associated with each of the choices available. In this context, the foresight competence models developed at the organizational level can be also applied on the individual, or even macro-sociological level(s), as generic modes of risk management.

There are many questions open for further research, of which we would like to emphasize the issue of social mechanisms for identifying and acting upon 'weak signals', i.e. events which 'signalize', although in a loosely structured manner, that a new form of risk may be arising, i.e. a discontinuity may be waiting 'around the corner' (see Ansoff[19], as cited by Seidl 2004). We propose

---

[16] See also Mintzberg/Waters (1985).

[17] *'Wiki'* is a technology enabling readers to change the content of a World Wide Web site, if they believe that information is incorrect and, thus, allowing for mass collaboration on the Internet. See [http://en.wikipedia.org/wiki/Wiki] retrieved in April 2010.

[18] See [http://www.wikipedia.org] retrieved in April 2010.

[19] See Ansoff (1975: pp. 21-33).

that future (sociological) research should be directed toward a description of such mechanisms and their effects. To this end, the multidisciplinary theoretical approach should be used, in order to accommodate findings from the fields of business and political studies. The other important aspect of this issue is to analyse and apply different models of future insights, be they market-based (Abramowicz 2007), founded on technology-enabled 'wisdom of masses', or any other feasible means.

References

Abramowicz, Michael (2007), *Predictocracy: Market Mechanisms for Public and Private Decision-Making,* Yale University Press, New Haven/London

Acquisti, Alessandro/Ralph Gross (2006), 'Imagined communities: Awareness, information sharing, and privacy on Facebook', in P. Golle/G. Danezis (eds.), *Proceedings of 6th Workshop on Privacy Enhancing Technologies,* Cambridge, pp. 36-58

Ansoff, H.I. (1975), 'Managing strategic surprise by response to weak signals', *California Management Review,* Vol. 18, pp. 21-33

Beck, Ulrich (1986/1992), *Risikogesellschaft – Auf dem Weg in eine andere Moderne,* Suhrkamp, Frankfurt a/M, with the English translation: *Risk Society: Towards a New Modernity,* Sage Publications, London

Beck, Ulrich (1992), 'From Industrial Society to the Risk Society: Questions of Survival, Social Structure and Ecological Enlightenment', *Theory, Culture & Society,* Vol. 9, pp. 97-123

Beck, Ulrich (2002), 'The Terrorist Threat: World Risk Society Revisited', *Theory, Culture & Society,* Vol. 19, No. 4, pp. 39-55

Burgelman, Robert A. (1988), 'Strategy Making as a Social Learning Process: The Case of Internal Corporate Venturing', *Interfaces,* Vol. 18, No. 3, pp. 74-85

Chia, Robert (2004), 'Re-educating Attention: What is Foresight and How is it Cultivated?', in H. Tsoukas/J. Shepherd (eds.) (2004), *Managing the Future: Strategic Foresight in the Knowledge Economy,* Blackwell Publishers, Oxford, pp. 21-37

Ciborra, Claudio (2007), 'Digital technologies and risk: a critical review', in O. Hanseth/C. Ciborra (eds.) (2007), *Risk, Complexity and ICT,* Edward Elgar, Cheltenham/Northampton, pp. 23-45

Cooper, Marianne (2008), 'The inequality of security: Winners and losers in the risk society', *Human Relations,* Vol. 61, No. 9, pp. 1229-1258

Davis, Donald C. (2007), *MySpace Isn't Your Space,* working paper 1943, The Berkeley Electronic Press (legal series), http://law.bepress.com/expresso/eps/1943 retrieved in April 2010

Ekberg, Merryn (2007), 'The Parameters of the Risk Society: A Review and Exploration', *Current Sociology,* Vol. 55, No. 3, pp. 343-366

Ewald, F. (1993), 'Two infinities of risk' in B. Massumi (ed.), *The Politics of Everyday Fear.* Minneapolis, University of Minnesota Press, Minnesota, pp. 221-228

François, Delor/Michel Hubert (2000), 'Revisiting the concept of "vulnerability"', *Social Science & Medicine,* Vol. 50, No. 11, pp. 1557-1570

Fuchs, Christian (2009), *Social Networking Sites and the Surveillance Society*, ICT&S Research Center of the University of Salzburg, Vienna/Salzburg, [http://fuchs.icts.sbg.ac.at/SNS_Surveillance_Fuchs.pdf] retrieved in April 2010.

Furedi, Frank (2007), 'The only thing we have to fear is the 'culture of fear' itself: How human thought and action are being stifled by a regime of uncertainty', *Spiked*, [http://www.spiked-online.com/index.php/site/printable/3053] (4. April 2007) retrieved in April 2010

Gardner, Dan (2009), *Risk – The Science and Politics of Fear*, Virgin Books/Random House, London

Garfinkel, Simson (2000), *Database Nation: The Death of Privacy in the 21st Century*, O'Reilly & Associates, Sebastopol

Giddens, Anthony (1990), *The Consequences of Modernity*, Polity Press, Cambridge

Goertzel, Ted (1994), 'Belief in Conspiracy Theories', *Political Psychology*, Vol. 15, No. 4, pp. 733-744

Goode, Erich/Ben-Yehuda Nachman (2009), *Moral Panics: The Social Construction of Deviance (2nd edition)*, Wiley-Blackwell, Oxford

Grant, Glen/Dennis M. Ogawa (1993), 'Living Proof: Is Hawaii the Answer?', *The Annals of the American Academy of Political and Social Science*, Vol. 530, No. 1, pp. 137-154

Hunter, Richard (2002), *World Without Secrets: Business, Crime, and Privacy in the Age of Ubiquitous Computing*, Gartner Press/John Wiley & Sons, New York

Jensen, Derrick/George Draffan (2009), *Welcome to the Machine: Science, Surveillance and the Culture of Control*, Chelsea Green Publishing, White River Junction

Kallinikos, Jannis (2007), 'Information technology, contingency and risk', in O. Hanseth/C. Ciborra (eds.), *Risk, Complexity and ICT*, Edward Elgar, Cheltenham/Northamp-ton, pp. 46-74

Levitas, Ruth (2000), 'Discourses of Risk and Utopia', in B. Adam/U. Beck/J. Van Loon (eds.), *The risk society and beyond: Critical issues for social theory*, SAGE Publications, London, pp. 198-210

Linke, Uli/Danielle Taana Smith (eds.) (2009), *Cultures of Fear: A Critical Reader*, Pluto Press, London

Loshin, David (2003), *Business Intelligence: The Savvy Manager's Guide*, Morgan Kaufmann/Elsevier, Boston

Luhmann, Niklas (1993), *The Sociology of Risk*, de Gruyter, Berlin

Lupton, Deborah (2005), *Key Ideas: Risk* (3rd Edition), Taylor & Francis/Routledge, New York

Marwick, Alice (2008), 'To catch a predator? The MySpace moral panic', *First Monday*, Vol. 13, No. 6

Mintzberg, Henry (1978), 'Patterns in Strategy Formation', *Management Science*, Vol. 24, No. 9, pp. 934-948

Mintzberg, Henry/James A. Waters (1985), 'Of Strategies, Deliberate and Emergent', *Strategic Management Journal*, Vol. 6, No. 3, pp. 257-272

Moreno, Megan A./Ann Van der Stoep/Malcolm R. Parks/Frederick J. Zimmerman/Ann Kurth/Dimitri A. Christakis (2009), 'Reducing At-Risk Adolescents' Display of Risk Behavior on a Social Networking Web Site: A Randomized Controlled Pilot Intervention Trial', *Archives of Pediatrics & Adolescent Medicine*, Vol. 163, No. 1, pp. 35-41

Nonaka, Ikujiro (1994), 'A Dynamic Theory of Organizational Knowledge Creation', *Organization Science*, Vol. 5, No. 1, pp. 14-37

Nonaka, Ikujiro/Ryoko Toyama/Noburu Konno (2000), 'SECI, Ba and Leadership: a Unified Model of Dynamic Knowledge Creation', *Long Rong Planning,* Vol. 33, No. 1, pp. 5-34

Ohkubo, Miyako/Koutarou Suzuki/Shingo Kinoshita (2005), 'RFID privacy issues and technical challenges', *Communications of the ACM,* Vol. 48, Issue 9, pp. 66-71

Parliament of Canada (2010), *Social Media: 3. Privacy and the Facebook Example (Background Paper),* Ottawa, http://www2.parl.gc.ca/Content/LOP/ResearchPublications/2010-06-e.pdf retrieved in April 2010

Ranadivė, Vivek (2006), *The Power to Predict: How Real-Time Businesses Anticipate Customer Needs, Create Opportunities, and Beat the Competition,* McGraw-Hill, New York/Chicago

Reith, Gerda (2004), 'Uncertain Times: The Notion of 'Risk' and the Development of Modernity', *Time & Society,* Vol. 13, No. 2/3, pp. 383-402

Seidl, David (2004), 'The Concept of 'Weak Signals' Revisited: A Re-description From a Constructivist Perspective', in H. Tsoukas/J. Shepherd (eds.), *Managing the Future: Strategic Foresight in the Knowledge Economy,* Blackwell Publishers, Oxford, pp. 151-168

Skenazy, Lenore (2009), *Free-Range Kids: Giving Our Children the Freedom We Had Without Going Nuts with Worry,* Jossey-Bass, San Francisco

Solove, Daniel J. (2007), *The Future of Reputation: Gossip, Rumor, and Privacy on the Internet,* Yale University Press, New Haven/London

Surowiecki, James (2004), *The Wisdom of Crowds: Why the Many are Smarter than the Few and How Collective Wisdom Shapes Business, Economies, Societies and Nations,* Doubleday/Anchor Books, New York

Tsoukas, Haradimios/Jill Shepherd (2004), 'Introduction: Organizations and the Future, From Forecasting to Foresight', in H. Tsoukas/J. Shepherd (eds.), *Managing the Future: Strategic Foresight in the Knowledge Economy,* Blackwell Publishers, Oxford, pp. 1-18

Tulloch, John/Deborah Lupton (2001), 'Risk, the mass media and personal biography: Revisiting Beck's "knowledge media and information society"', *European Journal of Cultural Studies,* Vol. 4, No. 1, pp. 5-27

Weick, Karl E. (1995), *Sensemaking in organizations,* SAGE Publications, Thousand Oaks

Zoran Wittine - Zoran Vlašić

The Impact of EU Accession on the Perception of Political Risk in Croatia

The motivation behind investments in foreign markets is generally stimulated by the existence of greater opportunities in non-domestic markets. There is a vast spectrum of factors that impact market attractiveness in relation to foreign direct investments (FDI). Since it has been proven that foreign direct investments positively affect many of the variables determining the welfare of any economy, it is in the best interest of any government to positively balance all the factors attracting FDI. Generally speaking, every factor that determines the attractiveness of a country as FDI host in a way influences prospects (i.e. rate) of returns on investment and/or their variability (i.e. risk). Some of the factors investors seek when entering foreign markets are cheaper labour force, greater labour force productivity, greater asset productivity, availability of advanced technologies, favourable legal framework, tax relief incentives, resource availability, lower cost of resources, etc. (Galán/González-Benito 2001). Following the same logic, investors will try to avoid factors that threaten to diminish potential investment returns or increase uncertainty regarding their realization. These factors include an unfavourable legal framework, political tensions and political instability, tariff and non-tariff barriers, perception of corruption, cultural implacability, weak market prospects and all other factors that put country risk on a relatively higher level.

In order to achieve a sustainable competitive advantage and conquer new markets companies spread their businesses to developing countries, especially to the fast-growing and fast-developing markets. In those developing markets political risk is often stressed as the most important factor influencing the decision of market entry versus non-entry (Pacek/Thorniely 2009). In other words, we can state that political risk significantly determines the market attractiveness of a country as an investment host. Political risk represents the possibility that political decisions or political or societal events in a country will affect the business environment in such a way that investors will lose money or not make as much money as they expected when the investment was made. Political risks can be very subtle and difficult to notice, but still as dangerous as the obvious ones. Companies that understand how to interpret political risks greatly improve their chances of operating profitably in emerging markets. An additional reason why political risks play a major role in developing markets is because they are always very closely related to the economic conditions of a country. Political and economic risks are thus closely related and intertwined. Political concerns inevitably influence economic policies and vice versa.

Knowing that the comprising elements of economic risk are the threat of unfavourable movements of foreign exchange, interest rates and commodity prices we can easily notice the unbreakable linkages between political and economic conditions.

Entering new markets

As stated previously, better market opportunities are the driving force of internationalization processes. In other words, companies are often more ready to accept greater risks in order to achieve greater investment returns. Some authors would thus argue that the motivation of companies is purely economic or financial. However, if we dig below the surface we discover that company motives are a bit more subtle. Economic, technological and strategic reasons are the main reasons why companies engage in international business i.e. enter foreign markets (Prasad 2006). When a firm desires to exploit economies of scale and/or economies of scope, or simply seeks greater investment returns (most frequently return on assets (ROA), return on capital employed (ROCE) or return on investments (ROI)) its motivation derives from economic factors. The essence of the technological reasons comes out from the fact that various products will be differently positioned on the product life cycle in different countries. Thus it will be possible for the same product to be in the introduction phase in one market, the maturity phase in another and in the decline phase in yet another.

Different positions on the product life cycle would help a firm to exploit its rent-seeking behaviour by its multiple presence in multiple markets. Strategic reasons can be numerous: to exploit the first mover advantage; to erect entry barriers preventing the future entry of competing firms; to negate the possibility of the development of generic substitutes etc. Besides the aforementioned, additional reasons include the possibility to amortize R & D costs more quickly, prompt new ideas for new product innovations, etc.

Once it has defined a clear set of motives, a company can determine the mode of market entry (or internationalization strategy) and the desirable set of attributes a market has to have. Internationalization strategies include exports, international leasing and licensing, franchising, foreign direct investments (greenfield as well as brownfield) and strategic alliances. The mode of market entry will be directly correlated with the risks the company will have to face. That is why in volatile and risky markets companies usually enter through direct or indirect exporting, while at the same time monitoring the market and preparing the field for the more complex (and more risky) internationalization strategies. Simpler modes of entry – while being less risky and offering lesser returns – enable companies to steadily gather enough market information and set a risk coping strategy.

Measuring political risk

Unfamiliarity with external market conditions inevitably leads to a greater exposure of the company to different business risks. Company success is therefore greatly dependent on its ability to manage these risks. In order to adapt to foreign market conditions, companies must use reliable sources of information (Matić/Wittine/Ćenan 2010). If large enough, they can establish their own risk management departments; otherwise they can use services of specialized agencies.

External market conditions in foreign markets are shaped by the forces of competition, as well as the political, economic and cultural environment in those markets. Although there is no universally accepted typology for categorizing risks in international business (Al Khattab 2006), the three aforementioned factors are often stressed as the most relevant components of international business risks i.e. country risk. Country risk is defined as "the unique risk faced by foreign investors when investing in specific country as compared to the alternative of investing in other countries" (Al Khattab).

All the above-mentioned elements of country risk (i.e. political, economic and cultural component) are very difficult to measure and quantify. Their aggregate value for the same country is often different and depends on the methodology, available data and knowledge, attitudes and motives of the subject making the analysis. The focus of this paper will be the possible changes in the perceived political risk of Croatia once it enters the European Union. The reason why the authors analyse solely political risk is because, as stated previously, it represents one of the most important influencing factors when companies consider entry or non-entry decisions in developing markets. Political risk analysis is plainly the analysis of political events and conditions that could cause loss to international business (Coplin/O'Leary 1998).

At least up to the financial crisis (2008), it had been assumed that countries that enter the European Union greatly improve their political and economic conditions. In most of the countries EU accession has led to a greater inflow of foreign capital, which in turn has stimulated domestic employment and production. The free flow of goods and capital has also enabled technology spillovers, which in turn facilitated shifts in asset efficiency and productivity in general leading to greater levels of competitiveness. Competitive companies that use modern technologies are capable of producing products and delivering services with greater added value, which in turn enables leaps to the greater levels of GDP per capita. To back-up the above-mentioned statements, researchers have shown that companies from countries that access the EU achieve greater business results once their country enters the EU (Erfani/Islam 2010).

But what is the main reason EU accession leads to greater results of companies and improved overall conditions of member states? Or in other words, why do countries become more desirable as investment targets once they become a EU member or at least move very close to that status? Besides legislation that substantially comes into harmony with the common EU law and guarantees the free flows of goods, capital and labour, countries that become a member of this great integration are often perceived as bearing a relatively lesser investment risk. Among others, the political element of country risk diminishes significantly in the eyes of investors. Whether cases like Greece will fundamentally alter this view, remains to be seen. Below, the authors will show the current political outlook of Croatia as rated by specialized agencies and will then try to derive in what way the perception of constituting factors of political risk could improve after its EU accession.

Changes in perception of political risk

The assessment of political risk requires the analysis of many factors, including the relationship of various groups in a country, the decision-making process in the government and the history of the country (Meldrum 2000). Any assessment of political risk should also take into consideration the state of independence of the judiciary and legal system, laws, customs and policies of foreign governments and the relationship of the analysed country with other countries (Price 2005). The analysis of those elements can illuminate the chances of, for example, selective interventions, restrictions on transfer of resources or capital, taxation inequalities, investment and operating restrictions etc. Corruption and nepotism are also considered to be major elements of political risk, specifically the way in which they are strongly intertwined with the existing culture.

Just a short glance at the elements constituting political risk is sufficient to establish that its assessment can be quite a tricky and ungrateful area. Even for the experts that are closely familiar with the political situation in a country it is very difficult to assess the likelihood of political changes and the possible effects this can bring to a company. In light of these problems a great deal of companies manages these risks simply by turning to proven and familiar markets.

Since political risk assessment is a very complex area and in order to avoid any subjective bias we will use indicators that are publicly published by eminent risk rating agencies to determine the current political risk level of Croatia.

The world's leading commercial publishers of country and political risk according to The Handbook of Country and Political Risk Analysis are:

- Bank of America World information Services
- Business Environment Risk Intelligence S. A.
- Control Risk Group (CRG)
- Economist Intelligence Unit (EIU)
- Euromoney Magazine
- Institutional Investor Magazine
- International Country Risk Guide (ICRG)
- Moody's Investor Service

- Political Risk Services
- S.J. Rundt/Associates
- Standard/Poor's Ratings Group

To determine level of political risk in Croatia we have chosen the risk measures and methodology of the International Country Risk Guide because of its transparent and comprehensive methodology. The Political Risk Rating used by ICRG includes twelve weighted components (and 15 sub-components) covering both political and social attributes and altogether a form political risk index which bears 100 points. Each component is assigned a maximum numerical value (risk points), with the highest number of points indicating the lowest potential risk for that component and the lowest number (0) indicating the highest potential risk.

Table 1 Political risk components and their respective sub-components

Components	Sub-components	Maximum Risk Value	Risk Value Croatia
Government Stability	Government Unity Legislative Strength Popular Support	12	6.5
Socioeconomic Conditions	Unemployment Consumer Confidence Poverty	12	6.5
Investment Profile	Contract Viability/Expropriation Profits Repatriation Payments Delay	12	9.5
Internal Conflict	Civil War/Coup Threat Terrorism /Political violence Civil Disorder	12	11.5
External Conflict	War Cross-border Conflict Foreign Pressures	12	10.0
Corruption		6	2.5
Military in Politics		6	5.0
Religious Tensions		6	5.0
Law and Order		6	4.5
Ethnic Tensions		6	5.0
Democratic Accountability		6	5.5
Bureaucracy Quality		4	3.0
Total		**100**	**74.5**

Source: The PRS group

The maximum number of points that can be awarded to any particular risk component is pre-set within the system and depends on the importance (weighting) of that component to the overall risk of a country. After a risk assessment (rating) has been awarded to each of the components, the components within each category of risk are added together to provide a risk rating category as a whole.
We will now more closely examine all the components and sub-components described in the table above[1].

Government Stability assesses both the government's ability to carry out its declared program(s) and its ability to stay in office. *Socioeconomic Conditions* assesses the socioeconomic pressures at work in society that could constrain government action or fuel social dissatisfaction. The risk rating assigned is the sum of three sub-components, each with a maximum score of four points and a minimum score of zero points. *Investment Profile* is an assessment of factors affecting the risk to investment that are not covered by other political, economic and financial risk components. *Internal Conflict* is an assessment of political violence in the country and its actual or potential impact on governance. The highest rating is given to those countries where there is no armed or civil opposition to the government and the government does not indulge in arbitrary violence, directly or indirectly, against its own people. *External Conflict* is an assessment both of the risk to the incumbent government from foreign action, ranging from non-violent external pressure (diplomatic pressures, withholding of aid, trade restrictions, territorial disputes, sanctions, etc.) to violent external pressure (cross-border conflicts to all-out war).

All the aforementioned components represent the sum of three sub-components, (actual sub-components can be seen in the upper table) each with a maximum score of four points and a minimum score of zero points. A score of four points equates to very low risk and a score of zero points to very high risk.

Corruption is an assessment of corruption within the political system. Such corruption is a threat to foreign investment for several reasons: it distorts the economic and financial environment; it reduces the efficiency of government and business by enabling people to assume positions of power through patronage rather than ability; and, last but not least, it introduces an inherent instability into the political process. *Military in Politics* even at a marginal level, is a diminution of democratic accountability. However, it also has other significant implications. The military might, for example, become involved in government because of an actual or created internal or external threat. Such a situation would imply the distortion of government policy in order to meet this threat, for example by increasing the defence budget at the expense of other

---

1 A detailed description has been taken from The PRS Group, available at [http://www.prs group.com/ICRG_Methodology.aspx].

budget allocations. In some countries, the threat of military take-over can force an elected government to change policy or cause its replacement by another government more amenable to the military's wishes. A military takeover or threat of a takeover may also represent a high risk if it is an indication that the government is unable to function effectively and that the country therefore has an uneasy environment for foreign businesses. *Religious Tensions* may stem from the domination of society and/or governance by a single religious group that seeks to replace civil law by religious law and to exclude other religions from the political and/or social process; the desire of a single religious group to dominate governance; the suppression of religious freedom; the desire of a religious group to express its own identity, separate from the country as a whole. *Law and Order* are assessed separately, with each sub-component comprising zero to three points. The Law sub-component is an assessment of the strength and impartiality of the legal system, while the Order sub-component is an assessment of popular observance of the law. Thus, a country can enjoy a high rating "3" in terms of its judicial system, but a low rating "1" if it suffers from a very high crime rate or if the law is routinely ignored without effective sanction (for example, widespread illegal strikes). *Ethnic Tensions* is an assessment of the degree of tension within a country attributable to racial, nationality, or language divisions. Lower ratings are given to countries where racial and nationality tensions are high because opposing groups are intolerant and unwilling to compromise. *Democratic Accountability* is a measure of how responsive government is to its people, on the basis that the less responsive it is, the more likely it is that the government will fall, peacefully in a democratic society, but possibly violently in a non-democratic one. *Bureaucracy Quality* – the institutional strength and quality of the bureaucracy is another shock absorber that tends to minimize revisions of policy when governments change. Therefore, high points are given to countries where the bureaucracy has the strength and expertise to govern without drastic changes in policy or interruptions in government services. In these low-risk countries, the bureaucracy tends to be somewhat autonomous from political pressure and to have an established mechanism for recruitment and training.

A political risk rating of 0.0 per cent to 49.9 per cent indicates a very high risk; 50.0 per cent to 59.9 per cent high risk; 60.0 per cent to 69.9 per cent moderate risk; 70.0 per cent to 79.9 per cent low risk; and 80.0 per cent or more a very low risk. As we can see in the last table column, Croatia had an aggregate political risk rating of 74.5 in 2009, which places it among the group of low risk countries. However, analysis by the authors, combined with the observations of what the impact of EU accession of peer countries was, shows that once Croatia enters the European Union components whose perception would be positively changed would include: Government Stability (because of the rise in Legislative Strength) by 0.5; Socioeconomic Conditions (it is logical to assume that all the components – Unemployment, Consumer Confidence and Poverty would positively change) by 1.5; Investment Profile (because of the positive changes in Contract Viability and Payment Delays sub-components) by 1; External Conflict by 0.5; Corruption by 1, Law and Order by 0.5 and Bureaucracy Quality by 0.5.

The authors assumed only the smallest positive changes in the short run, which could also improve far better in the long run. The authors also believe that Croatian EU accession would not have a negative impact upon any of the components. Therefore, it is evident that even the smallest changes in components determining political risk would change the political risk rating of the country and would move it into the cluster of countries bearing a very low political risk.

Conclusion

Croatia represents a rather small market, still struggling with the calamities of transition. One of the key leveraging factors that could boost the domestic economy are foreign investments. In order to attract these, investment risk needs to be diminished making investment returns more stable and uncertainty around them less volatile.

Through accession into the European Union Croatia would undoubtedly positively change its perceived political risk outlook. Since political risk in developing markets, as already stated "is often stressed as the most important factor influencing the decision of market entry vs. non-entry", it is logical to expect a greater inflow of foreign investments and benefits that go along with it.

In the end, it is important to point out that mere EU accession is not the *panacea* that would heal the problems the Croatian economy faces today. Structural economic, legal and social reforms behind the accession are the issues that matter and that would bring the biggest benefit.

References

Al Khattab, A. (2006), *Political Risk Assessment In Jordanian International Firms*, dissertation, University of Huddersfield

Coplin, W. D./M. K. O'Leary (1998), *Political Risk Yearbook*

Erfani, R./T. Islam (2010), 'The Financial Performance of Business Firms in the European Union: An Empirical Analysis', in *Proceedings of the EABR Conference*, Dublin

Galán, J.I./J. González-Benito (2001), 'Determinant factors of foreign direct investment: some empirical evidence', *European Business Review*, 13 (5), pp. 269-278

Howell, L. D. (2001), *The handbook of country and political risk analysis*. Yd ed. USA: Political Risk Services Group

ISO International Standards (2009), *Risk management – Principles and guidelines*

Matić, B./Z. Wittine/D. Ćenan (2010), 'Country Risk Management Practices – Evidence From Croatian Companies', *Proceedings of the EABR Conference*, Dublin

Meldrum, D. H. (2000), *Country Risk and Foreign Direct Investment*, Business Economics, pp. 33-40

Oetzel, J. M./R. A. Bettis/M. Zenner (2001), 'Country Risk Measures: How Risky Are They?', *Journal of World Business*, 36 (2), pp. 128-145

Pacek N./D. Thorniley (2004), *Emerging Markets*, Profile Books, London

Prasad A. (2006), 'Market Entry Decisions; Success and Failure Factors in International Business', *Journal of Management Research*, p. 6.

Price, T. (2005), 'Measuring political and economic risk', *Franchising World*, pp. 58-59

Vaughan, E./T. Vaughan (1988), *Rizici i upravljanje rizicima*, Poslovni savjetnik, Zagreb

Roman Šubić

EU Accession and the Croatian Banking System

Introduction

The on-going development of the Croatian economy has been accompanied by progressive movements in the financial sector. Taking a snapshot over the last decade in the financial sector positive changes could be observed in terms of deepening financial markets and widening the spectrum of products and services. However, a bank-oriented financial system still exists in Croatia, meaning that the financial system is dominated by the banking sector, although recent growth of the non-banking financial sector could also be noticed, with the development of various financial institutions.

In a period of transition, the banking system can play a pivotal role for growth and catching-up, but it can also be at the centre of fragility and collapse. Historical data shows that all transition economies have gone through more or less costly banking sector clean-up programs and only after these programs had been carried out did they achieve sustainable market-oriented economic expansion (Barisitz 2005, p. 58). In the case of Croatia, cyclical movements of the banking system could also be observed during its development from the period of socialism to today's era of EU-oriented banking system with a strong dependence on EU financial institutions. One of the assumptions in this paper is that in the last ten years the Croatian banking system has been highly influenced by foreign investments with many positive externalities brought up by the injection of foreign capital. Compared to the situation at the beginning of the century, the Croatian banking system has emerged as highly developed, becoming the leader among the countries in the region. Besides the complexity of the banking system, other areas of the financial system were simultaneously developed, but at this stage it seems that non-banking financial markets and institutions still require better organization and further extension.

Equivalently to the political strategy towards the EU integration, the Croatian banking system has already been integrated in global context of capital flows. As a brief introduction to the actual situation on the banking market, this contribution describes the development of the Croatian banking market from the period of abandoning the socialistic way of thinking and the foundation of the first capitalist financial institutions. Positive movements in the total assets of banks were accompanied by a decrease in the number of banks and a greater influence of foreign capital. The involvement of foreign banks could be explained by incentives to enter into the new emerging economy, and has resulted in changes of some indicators in the context of Croatia itself and compared with the countries in the region. Finally, emphasizing the importance of the banking market and possible spill-over effects on the whole economy, the role of banking supervision and its importance is explained, in special circumstances when the banking system is highly under the influence of foreign capital. This was the reason why supervision started to be more complex and why participating in the college of supervisors became necessary, respecting the memoranda of understanding on a bilateral basis.

Development of the Croatian banking system

In the first years of independence the banking market was highly regulated, lacking free market competition. At that time there were 26 commercial banks operating in the country, more than half of which were technically insolvent. This is why during last two decades the Croatian banking system has gone through deep restructuring. Bank privatization was slowly initiated at the beginning of 1990s, but produced no major result until 1993. Faced with this situation, as well as the chronic phenomenon of inflation, in October 1993 authorities embarked on a radical macroeconomic stabilization program which consisted of two key elements: first, restrictive monetary, fiscal and incomes policies and a strong orientation towards the exchange rate of the Croatian currency in order to achieve rapid disinflation, and secondly rehabilitation of banking sector. A new legal framework was also established, making legislation more suitable for the market economy. Basic market-oriented banking supervision regulations were issued, such as limits on lending to individual borrowers, capital adequacy, credit risk assessment and provisioning for non-performing loans. Further on, remaining limitations on private and foreign ownership of credit institution were removed, while licensing became quite liberal. As a result of these facts, the number of banks rose considerably, amounting to 60 at the end of 1998. However, the sector remained highly concentrated, with the two largest banks of the socialist period (the privatized Zagrebačka banka d.d., and the largely state-owned Privredna banka Zagreb d.d.) still dominating the market and accounting for about 42 per cent of total assets. Furthermore, at this time the banks' insolvency problem occurred again, requiring another intervention by the state in the process of restructuring and rehabilitation of banks. This sequence of events was not encouraging for foreign investors and only 6.7 per cent of banking assets were under foreign ownership in 1998.

On the other hand, the years after the banking crises in 1998-1999 and the second stabilization program witnessed strong economic expansion in Croatia, as well as regained confidence in the banking sector. This was the period of consolidation on the banking market, marked with the bankruptcies of some banks, as well as numerous mergers, acquisition and takeovers. The role of foreign investors in this process was crucial, and in only three years (1998-2001), the number of foreign banks climbed from 10 to 24, while their share in total bank assets increased even more, from 6.7 per cent to 89.3 per cent, due to the fact that the biggest market players were taken over by foreign owners. Firstly, in 1999, for the first time, the shares of the biggest bank in Croatia, Zagrebačka banka d.d. were in the majority ownership of foreign investors at the stock exchange, while the year after ownership structures of the second, third and fourth bank in the system were converted into dominantly foreign.[1]

The following years saw significant changes in bank ownerships, but without an important change of the foreign share in total bank assets, which amounted to 90.9 per cent at the end of 2009. During the whole period the number of banks decreased from 60 in 1998, to 34 at the end of 2009, while the number of banks in foreign ownership reached a peak of 24 banks at the end of 2001 and then started to decrease slightly to the number of 15 at the end of 2009. Regarding the indicator of total assets, the Croatian banking system has shown great improvement over the last ten years and the quantitative and qualitative development of the banking system could be observed in correlation with the presence of foreign banks. In this context the strong growth of bank assets was marked, which increased from 12.3 billion Euro in 1999 to 51.8 billion Euro at the end of 2009, as is shown in the following chart.

Figure 1 The development of the Croatian banking system 1998-2009

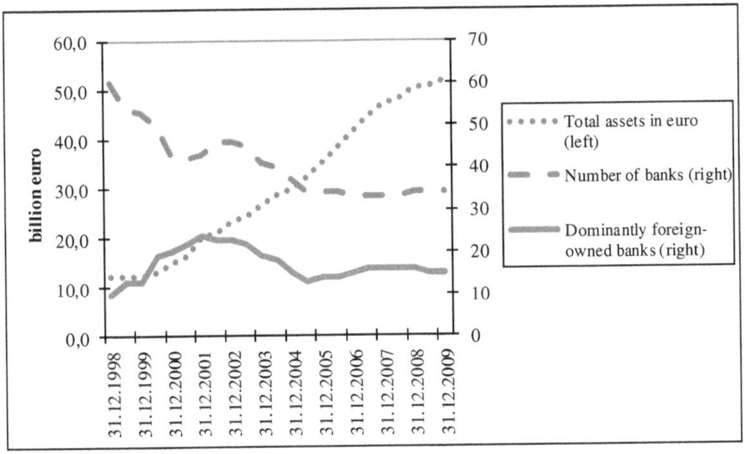

Source: Croatian National Bank

1 66.3% of shares of Privredna banka Zagreb d.d. were bought by the Italian Banca Comerciale Italiana S.p.A., 62.6% of shares of Splitska banka d.d. were bought by the Italian UniCredito Italiano S.p.A. and 59.9% of shares of Riječka banka d.d. were bought by the German Bayerische Landesbank AG.

Impacts of EU banks in Croatia

The continuous inflow of foreign capital into the ownership structures of Croatian banks was an important incentive for the change and development of the Croatian banking sector. Due to easier access to cheaper financial resources abroad (mainly through internal borrowings from their parent companies), foreign banks have provoked a lending boom in Croatia. Additionally, the presence of foreign banks has contributed to increasing the operational efficiency of Croatian banks. Further on, foreign banks were more willing to accept deposits and grant credits with a currency clause, or in foreign currency (especially in Euro, since EU-15 banks have a high ownership stake in Croatian banks), which led to Euroization of the Croatian market, which is an important precondition of Croatia's integration into the EU. Historical data shows that the major factors contributing to the development of financial systems and impacts of international capital on domestic market were technological advances, the globalization of the financial markets, enhanced supervision of credit systems and the creation of a single financial market with the significant role of the unique currency Euro (Asimakopoulos/Athanasoglou 2009, p. 5).

Concerning market concentration, the influence of foreign competition can also be noticed. Thus, the share of the market leader (Zagrebačka banka d.d.), decreased from 28.93 per cent at the end of 2000 to 25 per cent at the end of 2009. The CR2 concentration ratio which nearly approached the level of 50 per cent in 2000, declined to 41.73 per cent at the end of 2009. Opposite to this, the ratio CR5 experienced noticeable growth in this period, amounting to 75.39 per cent at the end of 2009 compared to 63.24 per cent in 2000. Only the two biggest banks maintained their positions during the whole period, while five other banks (mostly foreign) struggled for their positions among the top five (Société Générale – Splitska banka d.d., Erste & Steiermärkische Bank d.d., Raiffeisenbank Austria d.d., Hypo Alpe-Adria-Bank d.d. and Dubrovačka Banka d.d.).

Namely, several changes in ownership structures of these banks, as well as the acquisitions of other banks, made their market shares unsteady. Over the past years the general trend on the European level seems to be that the number of acquisitions is declining, while their total value is increasing and that frequently small banks are acquisition targets (Jansen/De Haan 2003, p. 2). The Herfindahl-Hirschman index, calculated for the Croatian banking market showed a moderate concentration level, despite modest growth in the monitored period, amounting to 1.367 points at the end of 2009.

Incentives of foreign banks to enter into the Croatian banking market

Besides the phenomenon of globalization, which allowed companies to do business globally and pushed an international flow of capital without restrictions, additional reasons, which made the Croatian market attractive to foreign investors could be detected. One of the most important incentives, which led foreign banks from the economic way of thinking, was the fact that higher profits could be gained on this new market than on their domestic markets. Although investing money in new, at that time scarcely developed markets carried higher risk, foreign banks recognized that the Croatian banking market is one of the emerging markets, which needed to be developed and because of its close relations with the real economy it was able to generate higher earnings. On the other hand, from the perspective of Croatian citizens, the presence of foreign-owned bank has strengthened the willingness of the banks' clients to put their money in a bank with a strong financial background so that in the event of unexpected shocks it can rely on its parent bank abroad (Gardo 2008, p. 76).

Besides the above-mentioned motive of higher profits and expansion in the emerging markets at a higher rate than in the domestic market, the incentives to foreign banks could be summarized in a few additional facts. The attractiveness of emerging markets could be combined with the willingness of the bank's management to experience the feeling of developing business and establishing a presence in several new countries. Another motivation was to help the customers of the bank in their domestic market to develop their business in new markets. For example, there were many Italian or Austrian banks whose financial support was crucial in terms of financing Italian or Austrian companies when they started or developed their business in Croatia. Furthermore, it could be noticed that Austrian banks played a crucial role in the development of the banking system through their ownership in Croatian banks and particularly through the financial support from the parent banks (Reininger/Walko 2005, p. 134). Achieving economies of scale and in some way economies of scope through the M & A were additional reasons why foreign investors chose the Croatian banking market instead of some other. Targeting the largest banks was more frequent than the acquisition of smaller banks, since large banks were expected to be more successful in creating fully or partly new banking products and services than small banks, due to the presence of economies of scale in product development (Bikker/Spierdijk/Finnie 2006, p. 18). When comparing the depth of the financial system and the spectrum of banking products in the period of the past ten years, it can be easily recognized that various products and services in the banking market were developed under the impact of foreign banks. Furthermore, foreign banks wanted to be first to introduce something new in the market and to set up some standards, which will be followed in the future. As in any other industry the advantage of being the first in the market is a great achievement and consequently there are clear differences between the banks that are trying to enter a market nowadays and the banks, which were already in the market many years before. In the case of Croatia, most of the foreign banks, which bought shares of domestic banks at the end of the 1990s or few years later are now market leaders and have the most important roles in the banking market.

Comparison to other countries from the region

In the last ten years the progressive development of banking systems could be noticed in all countries from the region, with foreign banks as one of the main drivers of changes and expansion on financial markets. The basis for this progress was the transformation of old banking structures, as well as market liberalization, thus opening access to foreign investment on these new, still undeveloped, but highly prospective markets. Due to this, a comparison between the countries in the region was made, putting an accent on the development of the banking system in terms of growing assets and changes of market participants as well as the impact of foreign banks. The countries that were included in the examination were the countries from the region that are candidates for full membership in the EU or that have started negotiations in the process of access to the EU.

The results of the study showed that in spite of many differences between the national economies, there were some similar trends with variable intensity. The scale of the total banking assets in national economies varied from 2.1 billion Euro in Kosovo to 389.2 billion Euro in Turkey and this is why, from a position of size, banking systems are not completely comparable. Nevertheless, research was conducted from which it could be concluded that the Croatian banking system is one of the most developed banking systems in the region. Comparing the ratio of total banking assets and country population the highest value of the indicator was marked in Croatia, while when comparing the number of banks and the size of population, the highest ratio is achieved in Montenegro.

Due to its size the Turkish banking market and the Turkish population are exceptions from the countries in the region, while a good comparison can be made between all other countries. When measuring the total assets of the banking system and the total assets of the biggest bank in the system it can be seen that banking in Croatia is the most developed. The results achieved by Croatian banks in the last ten years have encouraged the participants in the market to move forward and to reinvest more money, while consequently the system is being developed progressively over the whole period of time. The size of the total assets of the biggest bank, Zagrebačka banka d.d., with 12.7 billion Euro and the size of the system with 51.8 billion Euro have pushed Croatia to the top in terms of bank assets, while the remaining countries stayed far behind these figures. For example, the second position was held by the Serbian Banca Intesa a.d. with assets of 3.2 billion Euro, while the total assets of all 34 Serbian banks were 22.5 billion Euro. Previously mentioned facts are shown in the chart as follows.

Figure 2 Total assets of banking systems at the end of 2009

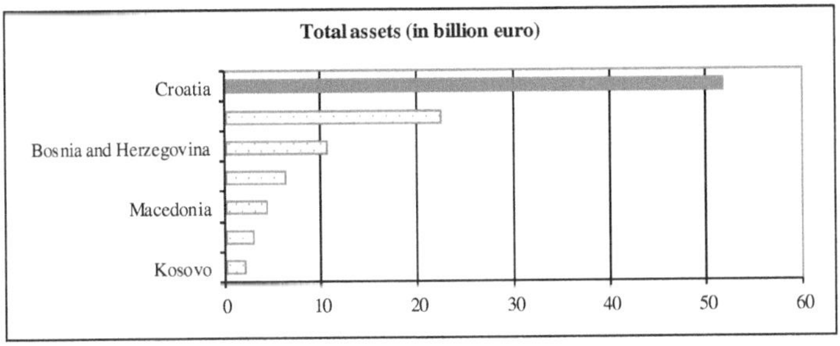

Source: Data from the Croatian National Bank and other supervisory bodies

From the aspect of foreign influence on domestic banks a significant contribution can be noticed, with more than 70 per cent of total assets in the ownership of foreign-owned banks in all observed countries, besides Turkey, which had only 14 per cent of foreign assets. 90.9 per cent of foreign assets in Croatia as at the end of 2009 has been a stable indicator for past 10 years and in comparison to the other countries it is not an outlier. Excluding Turkey, the lowest impact of foreign banks is noticed in Serbia (73.6%) and the highest influence of foreigners is seen in Bosnia and Herzegovina (94.5%). Altogether, it can be concluded that foreign banks have significantly influenced the ownership structure of the Croatian banking system, but also of all other banks in the region and consequently the output of their presence is difficult to measure, but could be seen in the development of the banking systems and the depth of financial products and services[2].

Supervising the foreign-owned banks

After a brief insight into the impact of foreign-owned banks on the domestic banking system, it is necessary to emphasize the importance of the effective supervision of banking institutions in systems that are more or less dependent on foreign capital. At the same time, the role of rigorous discipline between the market participants on the banking market is especially highlighted as there are numerous examples demonstrating how failures on the banking market can spill over onto the whole economy. The supervisory authorities for the banking system have a wide spectrum of instruments for regulating the behaviour of credit institutions on the market. In theory there are different known approaches of regulating credit institutions: a) theory of public interest, b) theory of capturing and c) theory of public choice. Concretely, according to the theory of

[2] For more about the banking system in SCE see Brkić/Salihović (2010).

public interest, the measures of the regulatory body are set up with the aim of maximizing profits for the whole society and the increase of total welfare. Opposite to that theory is the theory of capturing according to which strong regulation gives preferences to the institutions that are regulated, and from this kind of regulation society has no welfare at all. Combining the previous two theories, the theory of public choice equally emphasizes the advantages for the market competitors and for the society as well. The regulation, according the theory of public choice, will optimize the profits for the banks, which will be higher than potential profits on a market with perfect competition and lower than the profits achievable on a monopolistic market. (Miller/VanHoose 1997, p. 254) The most frequent case is the latter theory, which will enable both groups (banks and consumers) to maximize their profits through open market competition and the role of the supervisory body would be minor, limited to controlling the framework for effective competition.

However, the impact of the supervisory body on the behaviour of credit institutions should be strictly regulated and always prudential. It is questionable whether the supervisory body is capable of regulating all credit institutions on the market. This issue is especially interesting when the ownership structures of the banks are saturated with foreign-owned capital and when the business strategies of the banks can be coordinated from abroad. This dilemma of effective supervision of foreign-owned banks is also doubtful in periods of crisis, as was the situation in the past few years for example, when there were serious concerns whether the liquidity problems of parent banks would be subsequently transferred to their dependent companies in the banking groups. In this situation it is very important to have independent supervisory authority, which will strictly regulate the behaviour of all participants on the market and with the effective financial instruments to control the foreign affairs of the domestic banks.

In the case of Croatia, when the majority of the banks are owned by foreign capital, the Croatian National Bank obviously has a very important role that is seen through the financial instruments of monetary policy and on the other hand through the prudential regulation and supervision of the banking system. Stable monetary and foreign policy is one of the tasks of the Croatian National Bank and in order to achieve it, the central bank adopts measures and instruments necessary to regulate the credit activity and liquidity of banks and the money supply. There are numerous monetary policy instruments and measures and for the purpose of this paper the most important ones will be mentioned. Open market operations are used to increase the banking system's liquidity and are one of the most valuable tools of the central bank in the area of monetary policy. Another very important tool is reserve requirements, the purpose of which is to regulate the credit activity of credit institutions through ensuring sufficient liquid reserves of each participant on the market. Until October 2008 the measure of marginal reserve requirement was applied with the aim to limit strong foreign borrowing by banks through the obligation of depositing a part of funds borrowed abroad in a special account with the Croatian National Bank. This kind of instrument caused a significant increase of additional foreign exchange reserves accumulated with the central bank and, what is even more important, it affected the decrease of the external debt.

With the aim of slowing down fast credit growth, which was at times even several times faster than GDP growth, and with the purpose of ensuring macroeconomic and financial stability in the country, the central bank applied a limit to credit growth. However, in correlation with the effects of the financial crisis, in November 2009 the central bank decided to remove the obligation of banks to subscribe to bills of the central bank, which has consequently influenced the liquidity of the credit institutions.

Altogether, the main purposes of above mentioned monetary policy instruments and measures were directed at the control of the required liquidity of the banks and at the control of banking credit growth. And, of course, the no less important task should be to support the main objective of the Croatian National Bank, which is to maintain price stability.[3] The successful cooperation between the supervisory control of the banks and the instruments that the central bank applied to preserve the economy in the unstable period was especially visible in the last few years when the stable banking system was one of the anchors, which protected the Croatian economy from multiple effects of the global financial crisis.

Although the Croatian economy was affected by external influences either through the financial system or correlated with the real sector, the supervision of Croatian banks was strict enough to protect the economy from the spill-over effects from abroad. As the Croatian National Bank has established very good cooperation with other supervisory authorities through memoranda of understanding (MoUs), obvious positive effects could be seen. The formal framework for the cross-border cooperation of the Croatian supervisory authority is set up by the Credit Institution Act, which enabled the Croatian National Bank to conclude an agreement with one or more competent authorities of third countries for the purpose of exercising the supervision of branches of credit institutions, which have their registered offices in the Republic of Croatia and operate in third countries or branches of third-country credit institutions intending to provide services in the Republic of Croatia.[4]

In general, the basic principles and the contents of the MoUs are based on principles issued by the Basel Committee on Banking Supervision (BCBS) and the Committee of European Banking Supervisors (CEBS). Basically, the

3 Article 3 of the Act on the Croatian National Bank, Official Gazette 75/2008.
4 Article 226 (1) of the Credit Institution Act, Official Gazette 117/2008, 74/2009, 153/2009.

essential elements of the cooperation between the supervisory bodies should be defined on the arrangements for the sharing of information on all stages of banking supervision, starting with the authorization and licensing process to the off-site and on-site activities and to the situation of handling any problem institutions. Another part of cooperation is reflected through on-site inspections of cross-border banks carried out by home and host supervisor. In all the arrangements of the MoUs cooperation between supervisors of two countries should be promoted with a high level point of confidence in both directions so that the protection of information is totally preserved.

In the case of Croatia in the field of banking supervision several bilateral MoUs exist, which were signed with the countries correlated through the cross-border cooperation either as home supervisor or from the point of view of host supervisor. As one of the Croatian banks was in the ownership structure of the bank in Bosnia and Herzegovina an MoU was signed in November 2003 with the supervisory authorities of Bosnia and Herzegovina. Two years later the Croatian National Bank signed MoUs with Austrian and Hungarian supervisory authorities. Because of the great impact of Italian banks on the Croatian market there was a need to sign a MoU with Banca d'Italia and it was done in March 2006. Finally, two years later there were signed contracts on MoUs with Germany and with France. This process of signing MoUs and establishing closer cooperation with other supervisory authorities is still on-going and it is expected to lead to even closer relations between supervisors, not only between those in home-host correlation, but between the others as a clear demand of continuous supervision of credit institutions and collaboration between the supervisors on the global level has been recognized. From the political aspect of the Croatian accession to the EU, there was, as presented above, a spectrum of different cross-border relations in the financial market, which is reflected in the positioning of the supervisory standards that are applied in the Croatian banking market in line with European standards. Finally, taking into account previously mentioned facts and according to the assessment of international financial institutions, it could be concluded that the quality of supervision in the Croatian banking system has obviously increased during the past period through the fruitful cooperation with other supervisors in the field of exchanging information, knowledge and experiences.

Formation of the College of Supervisors

A topic closely correlated to the Memorandum of Understanding is the formation of the College of Supervisors. According to the definition by the Committee of European Banking Supervisors (CEBS), Colleges of Supervisors are permanent, although flexible, structures for cooperation and coordination among the authorities responsible for and involved in the supervision of the different components of cross-border groups, specifically large groups.[5] The aim of forming a College is the cooperation between different supervisory authorities involved in the supervision of cross-border banking groups. What is more, according to the principles of CEBS, the supervisors of the Member States are in that case obliged to form a College. In the banking sector Colleges may be organized as general Colleges or as core Colleges depending on the level of included supervisors. While general multilateral Colleges will involve all the competent authorities, a core multilateral Collage will concentrate only on a limited number of the most important supervisory authorities.

The benefits of organizing Colleges of Supervisors can be recognized through the effective and flexible cooperation and coordination among the supervisory authorities. Sharing of information on a confidential level between the home-host supervisors can be a very successful mechanism in the control of cross-border banking institutions. Very similar to the idea of Memorandum of Understanding, the aim of Colleges is to plan and coordinate supervisory on-site inspections, even organizing joint supervisory examinations and finally sharing the findings of these visits with the other supervisors participating in the College. Conceptually, it is desirable that the local supervisors who generally have a better understanding of the local market conditions can provide input to the decision-making of the lead supervisor. (European Financial Services Round Table 2004, p. 15) Except the information from on-site inspection the idea of College is to continuously share the information between related supervisors on the situation of the bank, recent developments, assessment of risk and so on. Closer cooperation in banking regulation offers clear advantages to all countries in the attempt to prevent future systemic problems. (Honohan 1997, p. 32) Over a period of cooperation it is expected that the supervisory authorities will better understand each other and establish better communications in order to more easily overcome the exceptions of each country's regulation.

From the perspective of Croatia, where the banking system is saturated with the foreign capital, it is expected that the Croatian National Bank should participate in several Colleges of Supervisors. According to their significance in the banking system the Colleges of Supervisors whose members are Croatian supervisors are listed: UniCredit Group, Intesa Sanpaolo Group, Erste Group, RZB Group, Hypo Group Alpe Adria, OTP Group, and Volksbank Group. UniCredit Group, the ultimate owner of the most important bank in Croatia, is supervised by the College of Supervisors established in 2006 whose home supervisor is Banca d'Italia and the host authorities are situated in 12 different EEA countries and 7 non-EEA countries. The second biggest bank in Croatia, owned by the Italian Intesa Sanpaolo Group, is supervised by the Banca d'Italia

[5] Committee of European Banking Supervisors: Colleges of Supervisors – 10 Common Principles, CEBS 2008 124, 27 January 2009

as well and by another 10 host authorities located in 5 EEA and 5 non-EEA countries. Other Colleges of Supervisors are organized in the same way and the Croatian National Bank is invited to actively participate as the host supervisor of the foreign banks.

The practical use of participating in Colleges of Supervisors from the perspective of the host supervisor is very obvious and can be summarized as the fluid exchange of information at different levels. The reports on on-site examinations, then reports on risk assessment systems, the confidential information on the banking business and many other facts are part of an information sharing package that is regularly shared between home and host supervisors. It should also be emphasized that colleges to be effective must remain flexible tools tailored to the needs of the individual groups and their families of supervisors. (British Bankers' Association 2008, p. 4) According to that, colleges have some general principles on how to be organized, but each has its own characteristics as well. In the context of Croatian EU accession from the banking point of view, it can be concluded that being part of a College of Supervisors is very useful because of the many above-mentioned advantages. It can be, not precisely speaking, said that this kind of cooperation between supervisors already represents one opportunity of Euro-integration, not from the political point of view, but surely from the position of doing banking business. In addition to that, participating in Colleges of Supervisors offers an ideal opportunity to harmonize the regulations and methodologies that have been used in the banking system of the host supervisor with the rules defined for the banking system of the home supervisor. Even the intention of EU regulators is to enhance the degree of harmonization between regulatory frameworks and at the same time to keep the national discretions regarding the local specificity of each country. Until now, the harmonization of the Croatian banking regulations and the adaptation with the EU framework has been carried out very well and the participation of the Croatian supervisors in EU banking integration is on a high level.

Conclusions

On the way to EU accession the Croatian economy has become increasingly dependent on international capital flows. The banking system has obviously become dependent on foreign-owned capital, as more than 90 per cent of total assets in the banking system have been acquired by banks, which are dominantly foreign-owned. This situation can be observed from different points of view, on the one hand, in the case of crisis domestic banks can rely on a capital injection from their parent banks, but on the other hand, it is also possible, as almost happened in recent years, parent companies could fall into problems in their own domestic markets, the consequences of which are then transferred to the companies in the group. Concerning the global financial crisis that has happened in past few years, the Croatian banking system has still remained stable enough to survive the external shocks. Due to the strict monetary policy of the Croatian National Bank, but also due to the well-organized supervision, the banking-system can be characterized as stable and prospective. Participation in the Colleges of Supervisors was another support, which gave the Croatian supervisory body an opportunity to exchange information, knowledge and ideas with the aim of protecting participants on the market from external shocks. After a short overview of the functioning of colleges it can be concluded that this is the right model for supervising and regulating banking groups, especially those, which are globally active.

The Croatian banking system can be characterized as moderately concentrated with a high involvement of foreign banks. The influence of foreign capital on the ownership structure of the domestic banks showed positive consequences on the Croatian market leading to the development of the banking products and services. Considering the continuing large number of smaller banks in the market, further market consolidation could be expected, either as a concentration of small institutions by itself or as consolidation driven by further inflow of foreign capital into the market.

References

Asimakopoulos, I./P.P. Athanasoglou (2009), 'Revisiting the merger and acquisition performance of European banks', *Working Paper No. 100*, Bank of Greece, August 2009

Barisitz, S. (2005), 'Banking in Central and Eastern Europe since the Turn of the Millennium', *Focus*, 02/05, OeNB

Bikker, J./L. Spierdijk/P. Finnie (2006), 'The Impact of Bank Size on Market Power', *Working Paper 120/2006*, De Nederlandsche Bank, December 2006

British Bankers' Association (2008), 'Colleges of supervisors', *BBA Report*, 10 June 2008

Brkić, N./A. Salihović (2010), 'Measuring Web Site Service Quality Using e-SQ and SDDA Criteria – Example of Central Banks in Southeast Europe', in J. Langer/N. Alfirević/G. Vlašić (eds.), *Knowledge Region: Alps.Adriatic Challenges, Volume II – Actors and Cases*, Peter Lang, Frankfurt/M & New York, pp. 77-91

Credit Institution Act, Official Gazette 117/2008, 74/2009, 153/2009

European Financial Services Round Table (2004), 'Towards a lead supervisor for cross border financial institutions in the European Union', June 2004

Gardo, S. (2008), 'Croatia: Coping with Rapid Financial Deepening', *Focus on European Economic Integration*, 1/2008

Honohan, P. (1997), 'Banking system failures in developing and transition countries: diagnosis and prediction', *Working Paper No. 39*, BIS, January 1997

Jansen, D./J. De Haan (2003), 'Increasing concentration in European banking: a macro-level analysis', *Research Memorandum WO No. 743*, De Nederlandsche Bank, September

Miller, R./D. VanHoose (2005), *Moderni novac i bankarstvo*, 3th edition, Zagreb, Mate, 1997

Reininger, T./Z. Walko (2005), 'Das kroatische Bankensystem', *Finanzmarktstabilitätsbericht*, OeNB

Nikola Draskovic – Vladimir Gnjidic

Tourism and Environment in Croatia: When a Tourist Meets Local Environmental Legislation

Introduction

Tourism plays an important role in the world economy. According to the World Travel and Tourism Council (WTTC) (2008), travel and tourism contributed directly and indirectly to the global economy in 2008 by generating 9.9 per cent of the Gross Domestic Product (GDP) and by the employment of 238.3 million people, which stands for 8.4 per cent of total employment. During the last few decades, tourism has undergone rapid growth. It was one of the fastest-growing industries in the second half of the 20th century and is often used as a key for economic growth in both developed and developing countries (Font/Ahjem 1999). Based on the World Tourism Organization (WTO) statistical data, Palmer and Riera (2003) concluded that trips abroad have multiplied by twenty-five since the 1950s, whilst in the year 2000 the income generated by these trips reached a figure two hundred times higher than that of 1950, concluding with the 4 per cent rise of the growth rate for trips abroad until the year 2011, with a subsequent increase in the tourist industry's share of international output and employment. Accordingly, the expenditure of international tourists increased from two billion to 425 billion US dollars between 1950 and 1996 (Mihalic 1999). The Croatian economy is even more dependent on tourism. According to the Croatian Ministry of Tourism (2010), tourism generates more than 20 per cent of the country's gross domestic product, while the majority of tourists come from the EU countries (Figure 1 below). Consequently, tourism is often referred to as probably one of the most important industry sectors in Croatia, which has positive effects on the wider industry (e.g. food and beverage industry, services, etc.), despite its relatively lower level of development compared to other more developed European countries (Bunja 2003).

There are also certain downsides related to the expansion of world tourism. It increasingly poses a threat to the environment – particularly if it is not well-planned and managed (Beladi et al. 2009). The environment is especially threatened in emerging countries where environmentally friendly practices in tourism are still undeveloped and environmental laws are not fully implemented. Therefore, the aim of this paper is to reveal possible issues of tourism and environmental legislation through empirical research and to develop guidelines for further research. Due to practical reasons, the focus of primary research is on Croatia and Croatia's packaging waste deposit system, which was introduced in 2005.

Figure 1 Foreign tourists in Croatia by country of origin (2008)

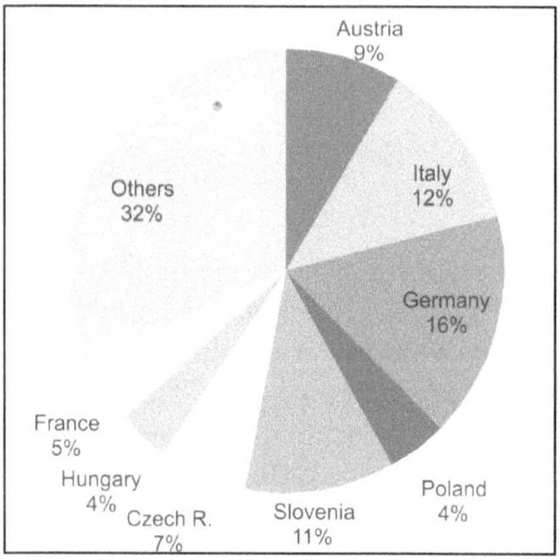

Source: Croatian Ministry of Tourism (2010)

Tourism, the environment and sustainability

Tourism is commonly considered as a threat for environment. Consequently, there is also growing public concern about the environmental damage provoked by tourism (The European Opinion Research Group for Directorate General Environment 2002). Liu, Sheldon, and Var (1987) analysed local residents' perceptions of the potential negative impacts of tourism and concluded that it is directly dependent on the ratio between the number of tourists and the number of residents. According to their study's results, growing pressure from tourism (with a higher ratio of tourists per resident, for instance) heightens perceptions of the environmental problems that tourism causes for the community. Negative environmental impacts of growing mass tourism could have many different results such as visual pollution, wastewater outflows (Logar 2009), declining of fish catches, the loss of biodiversity (Sawkar et al. 1998), solid waste disposal, loss of vegetation coverage, soil erosion, tree damage and root exposure, fresh water, land and air pollution etc. (Sasidharan et al. 2003)

One of the reasons for negative impacts of the growth in the amount of foreign tourism lies in the fact that the imported lifestyle and behaviour is not necessarily that of the host community. Aloj Totáro and Simeone (2001) emphasize the importance of taking into consideration individual's behaviour in order to achieve the goal of making economic growth compatible with environmental protection. In order to shape desirable tourist behaviour, the role of tourism marketing should revolve around the creation of awareness of the nature of a tourist resource and creation of the destination's image (Wheeler

1995). Probably one adequate tool for neutralizing negative effects from tourism could be education regarding the behaviour model of visiting tourists toward the packaging waste collection/disposal. As Davies and Cahill (2000, p. IX) underline: "Education can be used to support existing regulations, and to encourage environmentally responsible behaviour where no regulations exist [...] as tourists may be more receptive to educational efforts that focus on the environmental benefits of altering their behaviour than to regulatory prohibitions per se."

Obviously, the sector's growth is not exempt from certain costs that are, amongst others, arising from altering the ecological resources of host destinations. At the same time, tourism must recognize its responsibility to the environment, being a resource-dependent industry (Horobin/Long 1996). That is why tourism theoreticians have developed a concept of *sustainable tourism*[1] in which tourism is developed and maintained in a form such that it is viable over an indefinite period of time. Emphasizing more the social aspect of the concept, during the World Summit on Sustainable Development (2002) sustainable tourism has been defined as the kind that both now and in the future: (1) operate within natural capacities for the regeneration and future productivity of natural resources, (2) recognize the contribution that people and communities, customs and lifestyles, add to the tourism experience, (3) accept that these people must have an equitable share in the economic benefits of tourism, guided by the wishes of the local people and communities in host areas.

Saarinen (2006) emphasizes the academic concerns regarding the negative effects of tourism, as well as the idea of sustainable tourism. According to the author, negative impacts became evident fairly early in the mass destinations on the Mediterranean coast, threatening for the industry's viability and image. Davies and Cahill (2000) found that waste generated from tourists in hotel rooms would range from 40 pounds per room per month to 66 pounds per room per month. Accordingly, Logar (2009) found that the amount of solid waste was three times higher in August 2005 than in the February of the same year – the months with the highest and the lowest number of tourist overnight stays, respectively. The analysis also revealed that tourists produce more waste than the local population[2]. The findings of research in the Bafra region (North Cyprus) conducted by Altinay and Hussain (2005) have indicated that the environmental impact of tourism was related to waste disposal and the resulting pollution. Totáro and Simeone (2001) stress the fact that today's culture of

1 As a result of the concept of 'sustainable development', used for the first time in a 1987 World Commission on Environment and Development report entitled Our Common Future (also known as the Brundtland Report), defining sustainable development as development, which meets the needs of the present without compromising the ability of future generations to meet their own needs.

2 Research has been conducted in Crikvenica, one of the top Croatian tourist destinations.

tourism relies on a renovated and more sensitive environmental awareness aimed at a reflection of the behaviour of the tourists who have to be more respectful of nature and the cultural heritage.

Planned and executed in the right way, tourism has the potential to create beneficial effects on the environment by contributing to environmental protection and conservation. Its development planning requires the careful coordination and cooperation of all decision-makers, in both the public and private sector, in order to carry out a development that will remain sustainable over time (Font/Ahjem 1999). The problem though, with following a short-term profit-driven approach, is that once the product has in some way damaged the environment then people will no longer pay to consume. On the other hand, a product that works in harmony with the environment is likely to remain successful for much longer, generating income for both the public and private sectors (Eccles 1995).

Tourism in emerging countries

A number of countries in transition located in Central and Eastern Europe have emerged from centralized planning and moved towards models closer to Western European ones over the last 30 years (Hughes/Allen 2005). This 'opening effect' has had various influences on most industry sectors of the post-communist countries. One of the strongest impacts of economy liberalization was seen on tourism as the economy sector with one of the most elastic demands. As a complex, fragmented industry, the elements of which constitute what is commonly referred to as the travel and tourism industry (Davies/Cahill 2000), it has tremendous capacity for generating economic growth in destination areas (Saarinen 2006). By opening largely pre-undifferentiated destinations, host governments managed to target and exploit the benefits by attracting tourists from Western countries. Tourism has been perceived as one of the main generators of foreign exchange, foreign direct investments and positive national image as well as the job creator (Sasidharan et al. 2003), improving the inhabitants' welfare.

Countries in transition are following the world's increasing trend of trips abroad benefiting from the fact that tourism transforms locally non-traded goods and services into exports (Beladi et al. 2009). On the other hand, although world tourism is growing rapidly, it remains the privilege of the few coming mostly from developed Western countries. The WTO forecasts that only 7 per cent of the world population will have travelled abroad by 2020 (George/Henthorne 2007). It is more than obvious that such a practice leads to the confrontation of different cultures and behaviours between foreign tourists and local customs. While it is mostly emphasized in developing countries, to some extent it is the case with emerging countries as well due to the lower level of economic development versus developed economies. Their tourism entities are subjected to intense cost and development pressures by their more developed business (country) partners (Hindley/Smith 1994).

The increased number of foreign visitors and their demands generate changes within the community so that the *status quo* from a social perspective is not viable (Wheeler 1995). So, contrary to positive impacts deriving from a mainly economic point of view, tourism development implies certain negative effects. It is especially immanent in less developed as well as in the countries in transition having little or no former experience of managing tourism as the competitive industry sector.

Environmental challenges of tourism in Croatia

Introduction

Croatia, as an emerging country, strives to achieve economic prosperity through the development of tourism Croatia has an obvious potential to do that, as its advantages as a tourist destination include: (1) unspoiled natural beauty, (2) cultural and historical heritage, (3) mild Mediterranean climate, (4) Central European location; and (5) long tourist tradition (Meler/Cerovic 2003). Accordingly, Fox (2000) stresses the importance of tourism in Croatia that goes well beyond its economic role due to its social importance. As classical and traditional Mediterranean destinations with growing global competition of various other destinations, Croatia has managed to differentiate itself from other sun and sea destinations by emphasizing its shift towards a product that offers both beach and culture (Hughes/Allen 2005).

Its long-term tourism development plan aims to reposition Croatia amongst the near-the top European tourism countries of Austria, the Czech Republic, Germany and Russia (Vukonic 1999). As Font and Ahjem (1999) point out, if tourism is to be considered as a source of regional development, planning of local resources and infrastructure is required. The adoption of a sustainable tourism strategy requires changes on the macro-level – in particular, improvements to the transport infrastructure and wider acceptance of privatization and reorganization (Bunja 2003). Although hotel facilities in Croatia are not adapted to the needs of tourists coming from developed countries, the Croatian government has built new motorways in the last decade making its coast more accessible than ever, making possible further tourism development. It was needed in order to build better linkage with tourists from targeted neighbourhood countries. However, the protection of the environment seems to have been rather neglected during the past.

Packaging waste and recycling in Croatia – an overview

Recycling in Croatia, in a limited form, existed during the socialism era (i.e. before the 1990s) with a partially-organized collection of metals, paper and glass (Buljan 1986). It was a result of initiatives started up by several state-owned companies reprocessing scrap metal, paper or glass. These initiatives were occasionally introduced within the educational system (e.g. elementary schools), but cannot be considered as a recycling system. By the late 1980s, first recycling containers for the collection of used glass appeared but all the activities were stopped in the early 1990s due to the war.

The activities resumed in the mid-1990s with the introduction of new environmental laws. One of the first legal acts that referred to packaging waste was the Regulations on Packaging Waste Treatment (1996) that government introduced with the aim to reduce packaging waste. Unfortunately, it was mostly ignored by the industry and was even mistreated by the government itself, so it failed to achieve its goals. Because of legislative issues and non-existence of the national recycling system, the separate collection of packaging waste in Croatia was mostly organized by the local municipal companies on a voluntarily basis in the second half of the 1990s. Beside traditionally present glass and paper recycling facilities, the collection of PET (polyethylene terephthalate), which began in the late 1990s, initiated the development of rudimental PET recycling activities and also resulted in exporting significant amount of non-processed PET waste to China (Pavicic/Draskovic/Gnjidic 2007). Since nationwide recycling initiative had not yet been introduced, except for the basic educational programs in elementary schools, recycling rates were and still are far below EU requirements. According to packaging industry sources, the recycling rates in 2005 were at 19 per cent for glass and approximately at 5 per cent for PET while the recycling of multilayer (carton) packaging did not exist.

The new deposit system

As part of a harmonization of the legal system with the EU, Croatia introduced a number of environmental laws based on European Community (EC) Directive 94/62/EC and its Amendments 2004/12/EC and 2005/20/EC. After the initial failure in the 1990s, the situation dramatically changed with the introduction of the new Regulations on Packaging and Packaging Waste (2005), which presented a new packaging recycling and recovery deposit system managed by a government agency. In the dawn of the introduction of the new Regulations, industry formed an association called EKO-OZRA with the intention to stop or further delay the introduction of the Regulations with the implementation of a new industry-managed recycling and recovery system based on some positive foreign experiences (Draskovic/Pavicic/Vlasic 2007). However, this initiative came much too late and it was not realistic that the government would advocate a system proposed by the industry at the point when the new Regulations passed all the formal procedures.

Figure 2 The structure of fees and the deposit

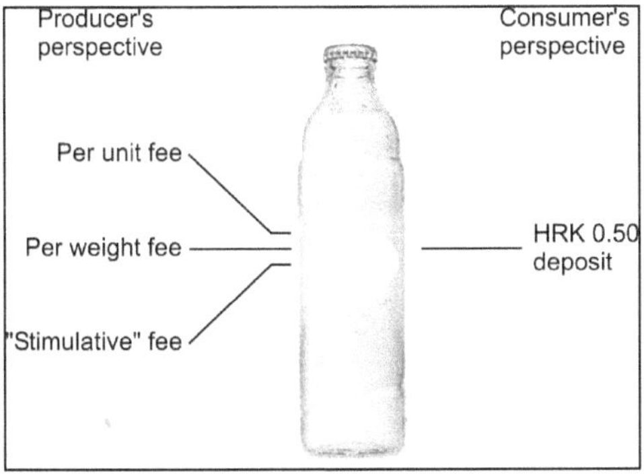

In a nutshell, the new deposit system introduced a system consisting of various environmental fees and a deposit, which is received when the waste package is returned to the collecting point (Figure 1). The system stimulates the usage of returnable packaging through a set of specific returnable packaging quotas for different product categories (Regulations on Packaging and Packaging Waste, 2005). The system of environmental fees is rather complicated and is related to the packaging material, container capacity and the achievement of the national returnable packaging quota. The new system solely deals with beverage and dairy packaging with a capacity above 20 cl while other product categories are not an element of specified regulation at the moment. The Regulations make a slight difference in taxation among different packaging materials (e.g. glass, PET, other plastic materials, metal). The new recycling system introduced a return deposit that is set at HRK 0.50 (approx. EUR 0.07) per piece of packaging. From the consumers' point of view, this is the deposit that will be returned to them at the moment they bring the package back to the retail outlet or to another licensed collector. This deposit is mandatory for almost all packaging materials used for beverages and dairy products. However, it should be noted that for some undefined reason carton packaging has been omitted at this point, creating a situation of discrimination between different packaging materials.

The new deposit system has achieved a certain short-term success. The recycling rate for glass reached almost 60 per cent, while the PET bottles recycling rate reached about 90 per cent (Runjic-Sokele/Sercer/Pilipovic 2008).

Foreign tourists and the Croatian packaging waste deposit system

The Croatian deposit system, which was established in order solve the issues with packaging waste, is rather unique and has no significant similarities with the recycling systems implemented in the neighbouring countries and EU. Consequently, foreign tourists visiting Croatia have limited or no knowledge about the deposit system, neither they have any experience with the system. Only a minority of foreign tourists, who originate from the neighbouring countries (e.g. Slovenia, Bosnia, Serbia) and live in the areas near the border with Croatia, have a certain experience with the system. Therefore, it could be concluded that a majority of foreign tourists visiting Croatia are not familiar with the system, nor they are aware of its existence.

The primary research conducted in this study consists of authors' observations of selected Croatian touristic sites on the coastline and in-depth interviews with waste management professionals in Croatia. Findings from both primary research activities are presented in the following sections.

Recycling infrastructure and tourism

Since the implementation of the deposit system, packaging waste collection is implemented through two separate systems – the deposit system, which is established through the retail sector, and the voluntary system, which includes recycling bins distributed in public places and 'eco-islands'. Since the deposit system does not cover all types of packaging, the existence of a parallel system is still a necessity. However, it seems that the number of recycling bins has decreased in the last few years. According to the waste management professionals, this happened mainly due to the fact that the majority of packaging waste is collected through the deposit system, which is well-financed by the government, while the voluntary disposal of waste packaging in recycling bins is considered as an additional expense for the local communities. It seems that the government simply neglected this means of separated packaging waste collection, by favouring the deposit system.

In recent years some progress has been noted on the motorways. Croatian Motorways Ltd implemented recycling bins for the separate collection of packaging waste on most of the rest areas and petrol stations. This has becomes a solid solution for the collection of packaging waste generated by incoming and outgoing tourists.

Recycling infrastructure in the touristic areas and on the touristic sites is still mostly undeveloped, with some exceptions. There are some positive trends in the northern parts of the Croatian coastline (i.e. the Istrian peninsula). It seems that certain local communities have recognized the need for separate packaging waste collection among tourists who are not familiar with the deposit system. Furthermore, these communities seem to dedicate certain funds for the protection of the environment. Unfortunately, the majority of municipalities and cities on the Croatian coastline still have undeveloped systems for the separated collection of packaging waste. All the waste generated by tourists is in most cases collected through the utilisation of trash bins and containers. After a limited compression process, the waste is taken to the local landfills. Unfortunately, those landfills are neither built nor maintained properly due to a lack of legislation in the past, insufficient funds and rocky terrain. Consequently, during the hot summer months uncontrolled fires on sites are no exception. The government has plans for regional waste collection sites, which should replace all today's improper waste dumps managed by the local municipal companies.

In order to improve the waste collection activities managed by municipalities and cities, the Croatian National Tourist Board[3] is commencing regular educational activities. The communication is usually executed through the mass media every year before the start of the summer touristic season. The Croatian National Tourist Board, through its regional branches, also assists municipalities and cities with various printed promotional materials and by organizing waste collection activities through volunteers.

Tourists' (green) behaviour

During the touristic season, due to the increased number of inhabitants in touristic centres, the generation of waste increases dramatically. Local municipal companies are usually prepared for that and their common response is to increase the number of trash bins in all touristic areas (e.g. beaches, streets around touristic sites, etc.). Furthermore, they also increase the frequency of street cleaning to remove the litter, which is left by tourists. Since tourists, in most cases, are not familiar with the deposit system, they would commonly dispose of empty packages in trash bins.

The majority of foreign tourists in Croatia originate from EU countries with a long tradition of recycling and separate waste collection. Therefore, it could be expected that they would continue with the 'green' behaviour as tourists visiting a foreign country. However, all interviewees reported certain concerns about that. It seems that foreign tourists, despite their 'green' behaviour in their home countries, relax a bit and adjust their behaviour in a negative direction (e.g. no separate disposal of waste even when the infrastructure is available in a reasonable distance, littering on the beaches). As some of the interviewees tried to explain, it seems that the lack of repression mechanisms (e.g. fines for littering) gives tourists a boost for such 'non-green' behaviour.

Local municipal companies are usually aware of tourists' misbehaviour and the problem with the littering. Therefore, they communicate various recycling

[3] See [http://www.croatia.hr/English/Home/Naslovna.aspx].

related messages to tourists via outdoor media. Due to the language barrier, these messages are usually in the form of recognizable pictorials.

Conclusion

As an emerging country, Croatia still needs further refinement of the environmental laws in order to improve the current practice. As the primary research revealed, the new deposit system cannot solve the packaging waste generated by tourists. Due to the lack of knowledge about the deposit system and insufficient communication from the municipalities and cities, tourists need an alternative way for the separate disposal/collection of the packaging waste. Therefore, both the government and the responsible ministry should improve the voluntary system in order to provide tourists with a fully working alternative to the deposit system. Furthermore, municipalities and cities should also consider ways to communicate basic information on the deposit system to tourists.

The primary research also revealed an interesting remark about possible changes in tourists' 'green' behaviour when they are at the touristic destination. There are certain indications that tourists alter their recycling-related behaviour. However, in order to fully validate and describe the possible attitude-behaviour gap or a simple misbehaviour, some further research would be needed.

References

Aloj Totáro, E./A. Simeone (2001), 'Environmental and cultural tourism as a model of an economic sustainable activity: Sensibility and participation of Sannio University students', *International Journal of Sustainability in Higher Education*, Vol. 2 No. 3, pp. 238-249

Altinay, M./K. Hussain (2005), 'Sustainable tourism development: a case study of North Cyprus', *International Journal of Contemporary Hospitality Management*, Vol. 17 No. 3, pp. 272-280

Beladi, Hamid/ Chi-Chur Chao/ Bharat R. Hazari/ Jean-Pierre Laffargue (2009), 'Tourism and the environment', *Resource and Energy Economics*, Vol. 31, pp. 39-49

Buljan, Radimir (1986), *Marketing i recikaza*, Samobor, Zagreb

Bunja, Dani (2003), 'Modernizing the Croatian tourism industry', *International Journal of Contemporary Hospitality Management*, Vol. 15 No. 2, pp.126-128

Croatian Ministry of Tourism (2010), 'Statistics', [http://www.mint.hr/default.aspx?ID=5778] retrieved on 10.01.2010

Davies, Terry/Sarah Cahill (2000), *Environmental Implications of the Tourism Industry (Discussion Paper 00-14)*, Resources for the Future, Washington

Eccles, Gavin (1995), 'Marketing, sustainable development and international tourism', *International Journal of Contemporary Hospitality Management*, Vol. 7 No. 7, pp. 20-26

European Parliament and Council Directive (EC) No. 2005/20 of 9 March 2005 on packaging and packaging waste, final version

European Parliament and Council Directive (EC) No. 2004/12 of 11 February 2004 on packaging and packaging waste, final version

European Parliament and Council Directive (EC) No. 94/62 of 20 December 1994 on packaging and packaging waste, final version

Font, Xavier/Tor E. Ahjem (1999), 'Searching for a balance in tourism development strategies', *International Journal of Contemporary Hospitality Management*, Vol. 11 No. 2/3, pp. 73-77

Fox, John (2000), 'Approaching managerial ethical standards in Croatia's hotel industry', *International Journal of Contemporary Hospitality Management*, Vol. 12 No. 1, pp. 70-74

George, Babu. P./Tony L. Henthorne (2007), 'Tourism and the general agreement on trade in services: Sustainability and other developmental concerns', *International Journal of Social Economics*, Vol. 34 No. 3, pp. 136-146

Hindley, Brian/Alisdar Smith (1994), 'Comparative advantage and trade in services', *The World Economy*, Vol. 7, pp. 369-390

Horobin, Helen/Jonathan Long (1996), 'Sustainable tourism: the role of the small firm', *International Journal of Contemporary Hospitality Management*, Vol. 8 No. 5, pp. 15-19

Hughes, Horward/Danielle Allen (2005), 'Cultural tourism in Central and Eastern Europe: the views of "induced image formation agents"', *Tourism Management*, Vol. 26, pp. 173-183

Liu, Juanita C./Pauline J. Sheldon/Turgut Var (1987), 'Resident perceptions of the environmental impacts of tourism', *Annals of Tourism Research*, Vol. 14, pp. 17-37

Logar, Ivana (2009), 'Sustainable tourism management in Crikvenica, Croatia: An assessment of policy instruments', *Tourism Management*, Vol. xxx, pp. 1-11

Meler, Marcel/Zdenko Cerovic (2003), 'Food marketing in the function of tourist product development', *British Food Journal*, Vol. 105 No.3, pp. 175-192

Mihalic, Tanja (1999), 'Equity in outgoing tourism through tourist Certificates', *International Journal of Contemporary Hospitality Management*, Vol. 11 No. 2/3, pp. 128-131

Palmer, Teresa/Antoni Riera (2003), 'Tourism and environmental taxes. With special reference to the Balearic ecotax', *Tourism Management*, Vol. 24, pp. 665-674

Pavicic, Jurica/Nikola Draskovic/Vladimir Gnjidic (2007), 'Environmental Laws in Croatia: Strategical Implications for the Beer Industry', in Reic, Zlatan/Fredotovic, Maja (eds.), *Enterprise in Transition*, pp. 92-95

Regulations on packaging and packaging waste (2005), *Official Gazette of Republic of Croatia*, No. 97/05

Regulations on packaging and packaging waste treatment (1996), *Official Gazette of Republic of Croatia*, No. 53/96

Runjic-Sokele, Maja/Mladen Sercer/Ana Pilipovic (2008), 'PET bottles recycling waste – utilization and properties', *Archives of Materials Science*, Vol. 29 No. 1-2, pp. 68-72

Saarinen, Jarkko (2006), 'Traditions of Sustainability in Tourism Studies', *Annals of Tourism Research*, Vol. 33 No. 4, pp. 1121-1140

Sasidharan, Vinod/Ercan Sirakaya/Deborah Kerstetter (2002), 'Developing countries and tourism ecolabels', *Tourism Management*, Vol. 23, pp. 161-174

Sawkar, Kalidas/Ligia Noronha/Antonio Mascarenhas/O.S. Chauhan/Simad Saeed (eds.) (1998), *Tourism and the Environment: Case Studies on Goa, India, and the Maldives*, The Economic Development Institute of the World Bank, Washington

The European Opinion Research Group (EORG) for Directorate General Environment (2002), 'Eurobarometer 58.0: The attitudes of Europeans towards the environment', [http://ec.europa.eu/public_opinion/archives/ebs/ebs_180_en.pdf] retrieved 15.01.2010

Vukonic, Boris (1999), *UT*, Vol. 47 No. 1, pp. 4-7, quoted in Fox, John (2000), 'Approaching managerial ethical standards in Croatia's hotel industry', *International Journal of Contemporary Hospitality Management*, Vol. 12 No. 1, pp. 70-74

Wheeler, Marion (1995), 'Tourism marketing ethics: an introduction', *International Marketing Review*, Vol. 12 No. 4, pp. 38-49

World Summit on Sustainable Development (2002), Tourism and the Earth Summit, World Summit on Sustainable Development, August 26-September 6, quoted in Altinay, M./Hussain, K. (2005), 'Sustainable tourism development: a case study of North Cyprus', *International Journal of Contemporary Hospitality Management*, Vol. 17 No. 3, pp. 272-280

World Travel and Tourism Council (2008), *Progression and Priorities 2008/09*, World Travel and Tourism Council, London, p. 6

Ivan Bakula

Changing Attitudes Regarding the Cultural Needs of Students

Introduction

Numerous factors influence the activities and contents, which occupy the free time of students, namely their cultural heritage, degree of general education and culture as well as current trends and numerous cultural and entertainment events at hand.

Comparisons and analyses of studies on the needs of students with regard to cultural and entertainment activities, conducted in 1995, during the War of Independence in Croatia and again in 2008, at the time of Croatia's integration into the EU, draw attention to numerous changes that influence, or can significantly influence the current market supply of cultural and entertainment activities for young people, especially students, which is the thesis of this paper. Culture is defined as the integrated pattern of material and spiritual heritage created by man in the course of his socio-historical existence, a system of values that give form to a level of human life superior to animals. The term culture mostly appears as a mark for mentality, a standard form of behaviour and type of routine human relations, also marking the achieved level of competences, abilities and skills of an individual or community as a whole, and is also taken as a characteristic of those individuals possessing these fundamental elements. A particular feature of culture is its sociability, shaped in the human community. (JLZ 1978).

In his study "Völkerpsychologie" (Ethnopsychology), the German psychologist and founder of Psychology, Wilhelm Wundt, translates the term culture from Latin as "regard for enrichment and refinement of life" (Kukić 1995).

Overview of previously conducted studies

Assuming that cultural activities of students are inseparable from their overall activities, the author presents the results of some previously conducted studies on the same theme.

Free time in industrial societies has continuously gained in value ever since the end of the 19th century (Duda 2005) During the second half of the 20th century (after 1970), leisure time activities and their influence on man have increasingly roused interest for scientific research (Brdar/Lončarić 2004). As a result, today we have a significant amount of scientific proof on different aspects of leisure time, which also explain different aspects of free time of the youth.

Authors mostly agree on the fact that leisure time should offer the opportunity to fulfil a variety of needs through individual or team activities. Young people expect the opportunity to entertain themselves during their leisure time, to enjoy the company of friends, to acquire new skills and a chance to actively participate in the everyday activities of their local community. Authors (Jeđud/Novak 2006) write that activities and leisure time are recognized as an important agent to invigorate young people as well as an area where every an individual or a group can fulfil their interests.

Activities undertaken during leisure time generate positive emotions. They safeguard, distract from stress and alleviate the consequences of negative incidences. The way we spend our leisure time can generally be regarded as a way of confronting stress (Anić/Brdar 2007). Different activities undertaken during leisure time produce numerous positive effects on the biological-psychosocial status of young people (Sabourin/Irwin 2008), and most young people wish to be more active during their leisure time (Hiu-Lun Tsai 2005).

Authors (Karam et al. 2000; Mustaine/Tewksbury 2004) point out that students are exposed to different behaviour during their leisure time, stressing the use of psychoactive substances, insufficient physical activity (Reed/Phillips 2005) as well as insufficient representation of structured activities (Gilman 2001).

Research conducted by Mustaine and Tewksbury (2004) showed that 1,218 students in the USA confirmed how an orientation toward frequent attendance at parties, visits to night clubs and rock concerts are a significant precondition or a predictor of marihuana or even heavy drugs use.

Research conducted in Croatia shows a trend toward an increasing number of drug abusers among the student population in relation to the overall youth population (Bouillet 2007), which is evident from the late eighties onward (Ilišin 2002).

Current research in Croatia shows that there are relatively settled patterns of leisure time activities among the young, where spending time with friends, going out and the media take up most of their free time, i.e. activities oriented toward entertainment and amusement, while education-oriented activities and those oriented toward personality development are secondary (Ilišin 2007).

Studies conducted during 1987 and 1988 among the Zagreb University student population show that over half of all student respondents regularly or very frequently spend their free time with friends, listening to the radio, reading books and newspapers, cinemas, watching TV, while visits to sports events and public lectures, participation in games of chance or listening to folk music are part of leisure time of a very small percentage of students (Ilišin 1991).

A comparison of the leisure time activities of youths in Croatia during 1986 and 1999, (Ilišin 2002, p. 281) shows that the youth of 1999 participated less in the following activities than the youth fifteen years ago: cinemas, picnics and outings, listening to folk music, visiting various exhibitions, sports events, public gatherings or theatre performances. At the same time, the youth more frequently go to parties or coffee bars.

Authors (Brdar/Lončarić 2004) point out that the balance between significantly positive and negative effects of leisure time activities probably partly depends on how much time young people spend watching TV or with their peers, i.e. do they spend at least a part of their leisure time in structured leisure activities.

Authors (Spajić-Vrkaš/Ilišin 2005) stress that the most pronounced means of spending leisure time among the youth is spending time with friends (58.1%), followed by sports activities, visits to disco clubs and watching TV. Other studies show that female students spend more time watching TV (Andrijašević et al. 2005).

Studies on the Croatian adolescent population conducted so far show that a significant number spends their free time watching TV and listening to music, even in an ideal leisure time construct (Ilišin 2006; Ilišin 2007).

Changes can be detected in the period recently past, especially with regard to a higher level of interest in participating in games of chance, visits to sports events, active participation in sports and listening to folk music (Bouillet et al. 2008).

Although the abstention from additional educational activities as a result of a heavy university curriculum is somewhat understandable, the low level of interest in cultural activities (mentioned by less than 2% of respondents) as a form of ideal leisure time of the intellectual youth elite presents a problem. It would therefore be very indicative to investigate into the real reasons of such abstinence. (Bouillet 2008).

A common factor of students' leisure time activities is that they are all voluntary, with mostly intrinsic motives, requiring a higher degree of initiative, organizational and educational efforts than activities determined by others (Brdar/Lončarić 2004). Since a person independently chooses his leisure time activities, they offer him a sense of freedom and personal control to a far greater extent than some other activities such as school or work, therefore enabling an orientation toward self-determination. Leisure time should consequently be a highlight of pleasure and happiness, and as such a compulsory part of the code of values of modern man. The development of civil society and intensive production process has seriously threatened leisure time and the rhetorical refrain "I have no time" is becoming a specific personal identification card or even a code of value of the man of modern times (Babić 2003).

Research

Research goals

The objective of this study is to compare and determine the change in attitudes toward the cultural needs of students, defined in the study conducted in 1995 during the War of Independence in Croatia with the study results from 2008, during the period of Croatian integration into the EU, especially the following:

- Socio-demographic and economic characteristics and
- Behaviour, habits and affinities of students with regard to cultural activities.

Research hypothesis

Considering the assumptions and the goal of the study, a hypothesis has been established, which will, through its confirmation or rejection, help test the conclusions reached during the theoretical part of the study.

H0: In the period between the two studies cultural needs of students have changed due to their changed lifestyle, strong developments in information technology and the globalization trend.

Methodology

Primary data was gathered through the survey method, applying a form of structured questionnaire with closed type questions, whose clarity and intelligibility were checked separately for each question. The survey instrument was a questionnaire consisting of 100 questions. The questions were multiple choice questions, with only a small number of open type questions. Contents of the 2008 questionnaire were for the most part identical to the one used in 1995.

Students from different Zagreb Faculties were questioned during March and April of 2008, mostly in faculty restaurants and coffee shops. The gathered data was analysed in the form of descriptive statistics. Most significant results and differences between the results of these two studies are given in the analysis of survey results.

Analysis of research results

The study on the cultural needs of students conducted in 2008, during the period Croatia's integration to the EU, marks significant changes in attitudes, habits, affinities and interests of students in Zagreb, as opposed to the results of the study conducted in 1995, during the Croatian War of Independence. Students today, on average, show greater tendency for traditional forms of living and faith, a marked drop of interest in culture, lesser interest toward urban entertainment concepts, a change in attitude toward the public media and an increase in interest toward formal education.

Socio-demographic characteristics

The gender of respondents is given in Table 1. During the study conducted in 1995, 45 per cent were female students and 55 per cent were male students, while in 2008, 64.96 per cent were female students and 35.04 per cent male students.

Table 1 Students' gender

	1995.		2008.	
Category	Frequency	Percentage	Frequency	Percentage
Female	252	45.00	178	64.96
Male	308	55.00	96	35.04
Total	560	100.00	274	100,00

The characteristics of students according to the number of family members is given in Table 2. The 1995 study results show that students come from families with 4.06 members on average, while the 2008 study gives an average of 4.76 members per family. The results thus show that the number of family members has increased by 17 per cent in 2008 in relation to the 1995 study.

Table 2 Characteristics of students according to number of family members

Average number of family members		
1995	2008	2008/1995
4.06	4.76	+17.24%

The students' structure according to their place of origin, i.e. whether they come from a rural or urban milieu, is given in Table 3. According to the 1995 study results, 13.04 per cent of students come from a rural milieu and 86.96 per cent from an urban milieu. As opposed to this, the 2008 study shows that 36.86 per cent of students come from a rural milieu and 63.14 per cent from an urban milieu. These results show a marked increase in the number of students coming from rural areas, as opposed to the number originating from urban areas, and this significantly influences the 2008 study results. Namely, such a change in the socio-demographic picture of students imposes the conclusion that the number of students with yet undeveloped urban living habits is increasing, with the consequence that their need for quality urban cultural amenities is also not highly developed.

Table 3 Students' place of residence

	1995		2008	
Category	Frequency	Percentage	Frequency	Percentage
Rural	73	13.04	101	36.86
Urban	487	86.96	173	63.14
Total	560	100.00	274	100.00

The total monthly income of students' families is given in Table 4. The study conducted in 1995 shows that the total monthly income of students' families is 4,346 kn on average, while the 2008 study shows an increase of this average monthly income to 7,648 kn. The results show that students could allocate more funds to cultural amenities in 2008 than in 1995.

Table 4 Overall monthly income of students' families

1995

Average	4,346 kn
Median	3,000 kn
Range	45,000 kn
Minimum	0.00 kn
Maximum	45,000 kn

2008

Category	Frequency	Percentage	Average
up to 3,000 kn	17	6.20	7,648 kn
3,000 - 5,000 kn	38	13.87	
5,000 - 7,000 kn	72	26.28	
over 7,000 kn	143	52.19	

Table 5 shows the average monthly financial assets of students. Data from the 2008 study show that the average amount, which students have at their disposal per month is 1,624 kn, which is 21.23 per cent of the average monthly family income of 7,648 kn, and represents a significant portion of the overall family income. The 1995 study questionnaire did not contain this question, therefore a comparison is not possible.

Table 5 Financial assets of students (monthly)

Category	Frequency	Percentage	Average
Up to 500 kn	23	8.39	1,624 kn
From 500 to 1,000 kn	78	28.47	
From 1,000 to 2,000 kn	129	47.08	
From 2,000 to 5,000 kn	35	12.77	
Over 5,000 kn	5	1.82	

Table 6 shows the average sum that students spend on their cultural needs per month. The study conducted in 2008 shows that the average amount of money, which students spend on their cultural needs per month is 158 kn, i.e. 9.77 per cent out of the overall sum of money at their disposal per month. The percentage of money spent on cultural needs is not negligible but the basic amount is very low. Therefore, if we analyse the average price of tickets for various concerts, exhibitions and other cultural events, it is not difficult to conclude that students are very limited when it comes to visiting cultural events.

The 1995 study questionnaire did not contain this question, therefore a comparison is not possible.

Table 6 Students' cultural expenditure in 2008

Category	Frequency	Percentage	Average
Up to 100 kn	163	59.40	158 kn
From 100 to 200 kn	60	21.89	
From 200 to 500 kn	39	14.23	
Over 500 kn	8	2,92	

Students' perception on their own standard of living is given in Table 7.

Results of the 1995 study show that 61.43 per cent of students consider their living standard to be average, the standard of most, 20.54 per cent considers that their standard is somewhat to considerably higher than most and 15.54 per cent considers their living standard to be somewhat or considerably lower than most. Contrary to this, the 2008 study shows that 64.20 per cent students considers their standard of living to be average, i.e. standard of most, 24.50 per cent students considers their standard to be somewhat to considerably higher that most and 13.30 per cent considers their standard to be somewhat to considerably lower than most.

Two thirds of students in both studied periods considers their living standard to be similar to the standard of most. Yet, 1/5 of students sees their standard as somewhat higher than the standard of most Croatian citizens. This perception is surely supported by the fact that expenditures on food and accommodation of undergraduate, full-time students are relatively low because a significant percentage is subsidized by the State.

Table 7 Students' perception of their personal standard of living

	1995		2008	
Category	Frequency	Percentage	Frequency	Percentage
Considerably lower than most	29	5.18	6	2.20
Somewhat lower than most	58	10.36	25	9.10
Like most	344	61.43	176	64.20
Somewhat higher than most	107	19.11	59	21.50
Considerably higher than most	8	1.43	8	3.00
Did not answer	14	2.50	0	0.00
Total	560	100.00	274	100.00

Students' interests

Major changes are marked in their increased interest in family life, marriage and children. The 1995 study results show that 29.64 per cent of students express a high interest in family life, marriage and children, while 54.01 per cent expressed the same interest in the 2008 study. A growing interest in religion and participation in political life has also been marked. The 1995 study shows that 23.21 per cent of students have a high interest in religion and participation in political life, while the 2008 study showed that this percentage has increased to 39.42 per cent. Interest in education and training also marks a positive change. The 1995 study shows that 32.14 per cent of students expressed high interest in education and training while this percentage increased to 77.74 per cent in the 2008 study.

As opposed to this, among the general entertainment and amusement topics, a considerable drop in interest is noted for arts and culture. This is confirmed by the 1995 study results when only 4.64 per cent of students expressed a low interest in arts and culture, while at the same time 51.07 per cent showed a high interest. On the other hand a low interest in arts and culture in the 2008 study increased to 22.63 per cent, at the same time high interest dropped to 20.80 per cent.

Furthermore, a drop in the mean value of interest in science and scientific achievements is shown by the 1995 study when the mean value of this interest was 38.04 per cent, while in 2008 this respective value reached 21.53 per cent.

Also, interest in politics and political matters is dropping, as well as for the army and military matters. Thus, in the 1995 study 26.79 per cent of students expressed a high interest in politics while in 2008 study this interest dropped to

17.52 per cent. The mean value of interest in the army and military matters in the 1995 study was 39.29 per cent and in 2008 this value dropped to 18.61 per cent.

Table 8 shows the mean values of specific topics of interest to students, as well as the mean values and statistical importance of changes occurring in the period between 1995 and 2008.

Table 8 Mean values, discrepancies and statistical significance of differences in answers in 2008/1995

	Statements	Mean value in 2008	Mean value in 1995	Difference 2008/1995	Statistical significance 2008/1995
1.	Interest in family life, marriage, children	2.42	2.05	0.37	0.00
2.	Interest in religion and political life	2.17	1.93	0.24	0.00
3.	Interest in friendships and friends	2.85	2.76	0.09	0.00
4.	Interest in travel	2.68	2.81	-0.13	0.00
5.	Interest in national history and the fate of the nation	2.02	2.16	-0.14	0.00
6.	Interest in love and sex	2.67	2.73	-0.06	0.10
7.	Interest in education and training	2.75	2.64	0.11	0.00
8.	Interest in technology and technical achievements	2.03	2.02	0.01	0.70
9.	Interest in science and scientific achievements	2.02	2.30	-0.28	0.00
10.	Interest in work and job	2.50	2.45	0.05	0.17
11.	Interest in entertainment and amusement	2.74	2.73	0.01	0.77
12.	Interest in arts and culture	1.98	2.46	-0.48	0.00
13.	Interest in sports and sports achievements	2.24	2.23	0.01	0.69
14.	Interest in politics and political matters	1.76	1.98	-0.22	0.00
15.	Interest in the army and military matters	1.34	1.65	-0.31	0.00

Statements 1, 2, 3 and 7 showed and an increased interest of students in 2008 in relation to 1995, the difference also being statistically significant.

A smaller interest regarding questions no. 4, 5, 9, 12, 14 and 15 is marked in 2008 in relation to 1995. A statistically important difference in the mean values of study periods was determined using the t-test.

With question no. 6, the mean value difference in 2008 as opposed to 1995 is smaller but not statistically important. In questions no. 8, 10, 11 and 13 the difference in mean values in 2008 is greater than in 1995, but likewise, not statistically important.

Students' behaviour

The behaviour of students reveals the way they pursue their interests in everyday life. The greatest increase is marked in church attendance. Comparison between the 1995 and 2008 Studies shows a drop in the number of students occasionally attending church from 29.82 per cent in 1995 to 10.95 per cent in 2008, while church attendance on a regular basis increased from 18.75 per cent in 1995 to 39.42 per cent in 2008.

An important increase is also visible in all urban forms of collective entertainment and youth amusement.

Thus, the 1995 study shows that 7.14 per cent of students regularly attended parties, and in 2008 this percentage increased to 16.06 per cent. The percentage of students regularly attending disco clubs and other "dance" clubs has also significantly increased: According to the 1995 study, 10.54 per cent of students regularly visited disco clubs and other dancing clubs, while in 2008, the percentage of students regularly attending this form of entertainment increased to 21.90 per cent.

An interesting and significant factor is the increase of participants in games of chance and fortune. The 1995 study shows that 73.04 per cent of students never participates in these forms of games while 23.75 per cent occasionally participate. Contrary to that, the 2008 study reveals that the percentage of students never participating in games of chance and fortune dropped to 51.82 per cent, and the percentage of occasional participants increased to 37.23 per cent.

However, other students' activities included in this study show a drop in their tendency to participate in different forms of entertainment just for the sake of spending time.

Major changes are noticed with students that listen to pop-rock and jazz music, as well as classical music. This is confirmed by the results of the 1995 study, when the number of students listening to pop-rock and jazz music amounted to 3.39 per cent, while this percentage increased in 2008 to 9.49 per cent. Simultaneously, the number of students never listening to classical music increased from 29.11 per cent in 1995 to 52,19 per cent in 2008.

Also, the number of students going to cinemas is decreasing, thus the number of attended movie shows dropped from 20.40 in 1995 to 10.78 in 2008.

Visits to the theatre are also decreasing in number. The average number of attended performances in 1995 was 4.70. This decreased by one half, to 2.41 in 2008.

Interest in art exhibitions in the form of "regular" attendances is practically non-existent. In 1995, 6.61 per cent of students went to art exhibitions on a regular basis, this percentage decreasing to 0.73 per cent in 2008. The number of visits to public lectures is also dropping. The number of students regularly attending public lectures in 1995 was 1.79 per cent, and in 2008, this percentage came down to 0.73 per cent.

Students also rarely attended concerts. The average number of attended concerts dropped from 7.40 in 1995 to 5.50 in 2008.

Table 9 shows the mean values of the analysed forms of students' behaviour and the statistical importance of the differences in answers between the two Studies. The difference in mean values is greater in 2008 for questions no. 1, 2, 3, 4, 5, 6, 7, 9 and 14 than in 1995. The difference in mean values is determined to be statistically important. However, questions no. 10, 11, 12, 13, 16 and 17 showed a drop in 2008 in relation to 1995. These changes in mean values also showed to be statistically important.

The difference in mean values of question no. 8 in the year 2008 is greater than in 1995, but the difference is not statistically important. However, regarding question no. 15, the mean value difference in 2008 is less than in 1995 m, but the determined difference is also not statistically important.

Table 9 Mean values, discrepancies and statistical importance of differences between the students' answers in 2008/1995

	Statements	Mean value in 2008	Mean value in 1995	Difference 2008/1995	Statistical importance 2008/1995
1.	Church attendance	2.85	2.24	0.61	0.00
2.	Attendance on parties	2.63	2.40	0.23	0.00
3.	Visits to disco clubs and other dancing clubs	2.72	2.39	0.33	0.00
4.	Visits to coffee shops	3.14	2.83	0.31	0.00
5.	Hanging out with friends	3.72	3.65	0.07	0.05
6.	Sleep and resting	2.75	2.58	0.17	0.00

Table 9 contd.

	Statements	Mean value in 2008	Mean value in 1995	Difference 2008/1995	Statistical importance 2008/1995
7.	Active sports	2.32	2.15	0.17	0.00
8.	Picnics and outings	2.50	2.38	0.12	0.10
9.	Participating in games of chance and fortune	1.64	1.32	0.32	0.00
10.	Cinemas	2.34	2.57	-0.23	0.00
11.	Theatre performances	1.75	1.97	-0.22	0.00
12.	Art exhibitions	1.57	1.92	-0.35	0.00
13.	Attendance to Public lectures	1.41	1.52	-0.11	0.00
14.	Visits to sports events	2.02	1.90	0.12	0.03
15.	Visits to concerts	2.16	2.18	-0.02	0.81
16.	Listening to pop-rock and jazz music	2.86	3.21	-0.35	0.00
17	Listening to classical music	1.54	1.94	-0.40	0.00

Students' tendency toward reading books and following the media

The types of media that students follow, and the information they offer, is a significant indication of the change in the interests of students that has occurred in the past period. This is especially notable with regard to their preference of optional, non-obligatory literature and reading. In the 1995 study, the percentage of students never reading optional literature was 2.50 per cent, while in 2008, this percentage increased to 17.88 per cent.

Following the public media, is steadily increasing. The number of students reading the daily and/or weekly papers has doubled, which only confirms the worldwide revival of printed media.

The 1995 study showed that 24.11 per cent of students read on a regular basis, while in 2008, this percentage went up to 43.80 per cent.

Electronic media, i.e. radio and television show a different tendency, which is actually in accordance with the increasingly dynamic lifestyle of youth. The percentage of radio listeners on a regular basis is decreasing, which is evident if we compare the results from the 1995 study, when 51.25 per cent of students listened to the radio on a regular basis, and the 2008 study results, when this percentage dropped to 24.45 per cent. On the other hand, in 1995, we had 15.54 per cent of occasional listeners, and in 2008 this number increased to 43.43 per cent.

The tendency to watch television is increasing. The number of students regularly watching television in 1995 was 22.50 per cent , and in 2008 the percentage of regular student viewers increased to 32.85 per cent. However, the number of occasional student TV viewers dropped from 41.25 per cent in 1995 to 31.02 per cent in 2008.

Table 10 shows the mean values and statistical importance factors for the changes in interest toward certain types of media, for the two studied periods.

Table 10 Mean values, discrepancies and Statistical importance of the differences in answers given by students in 2008/1995

	Statements	Mean value in 2008	Mean value in 1995	Difference 2008/1995	Statistical importance 2008/1995
1.	Reading books (optional literature)	2.12	2.71	-0.59	0.00
2.	Reading daily/weekly newspapers	3.19	2.83	0.36	0.00
3.	Listening to radio	2.68	3.33	-0.65	0.00
4.	Watching television	2.88	2.68	0.20	0.00

Questions no. 2 and 4 show a greater mean value difference in 2008 in relation to 1995, which is statistically important.

In questions no. 1 and 3, the mean value difference in 2008 is negative as compared to 1995. The difference is statistically important.

Students' preferences toward cinema, theatre and literary services

A very significant part of this study is the part dealing with students' preferences toward certain types of literary, theatre and movie genres and their popularity among students.

When analysing the movie genre, only comedies mark an increase in popularity. Results of the 1995 study show that 44.64 per cent of students have a "strong preference" toward comedies and that this preference has increased to 64.96 per cent in 2008.

Erotic and porno films mark the biggest drop of interest among students. Thus, the percentage of students "not inclined" to this genre changed from 29.46 per cent in 1995 to 49.82 per cent in 2008.

Table 11 shows the mean values and statistical importance factors of the change in interest for movie and theatre repertoires in the two analysed periods.

Table 11 Mean values, discrepancies and statistical importance of differences in answers given by students in 2008/1995

	Statements	Mean value in 2008	Mean value in 1995	Difference 2008/1995	Statistical importance 2008/1995
1.	Historical and war spectacles	2.74	2.66	0.08	0.20
2.	Comedies	3.58	3.29	0.29	0.00
3.	Horror movies	2.16	2.33	-0.17	0.00
4.	Erotic and porno films	1.81	2.19	-0.38	0.00
5.	Movies with religious themes	2.09	2.01	0.08	0.18

With question no. 2, the mean value is greater in 2008 in relation to 1995, making the statistical importance outstanding. Difference in mean values for questions no. 3 and 4, are negative in 2008 in relation to 1995, marking the statistical importance of the difference.

With questions no. 1 and 5, the difference in mean values in 2008 is greater when compared to 1995, with a conclusion that there is no statistical importance.

Conclusion

The goal of this study was to determine the changes in students' interests regarding cultural programs in the period between 1995, during the Croatian War of Independence, and 2008, during Croatia's integration into the EU. Research confirmed the set hypothesis: Cultural needs of students have changed in the period between the two conducted Studies due to changes in their lifestyle habits, strong information technology development and the globalization trend, but it has also accentuated some new trends.

The results show a drop of students' interest for the urban culture market. On one hand, this is expressed by a drop of interest for cultural and artistic programs and events as well as by a drop of interest for active participation in public lectures. On the other hand, there is an increased interest for the traditional way of life, family, friends and faith.

Interest in various forms of entertainment shows that students seek amusement not requiring any intellectual effort. It actually shows their need for entertainment, which offers momentary enthusiasm or thrill (comedies), or which directly appeals to emotions not requiring any cognitive engagement while at the same time not leaving any aesthetic tags.

One significant factor is that the number of students participating in the 2008 study, with less opportunities to fulfil their cultural needs, increased by 48 per cent (coming from rural environments), at the same time decreasingly regarding their education as a life-long process.

A positive change is perceived in increased sports activities and the need for frequent outings to the countryside, while a small percentage of students showed increased appreciation for national literature. However, a percentage of students answered that they spend more time sleeping and resting than their colleagues did before them, and increasingly participate in games of chance and fortune.

If we cross-reference these indicators with the ones from the 1995 study, we come to the conclusion that present-day students, on average express less initiative and effort, they have a lower general knowledge level, and mostly seek 'cheap and on the spot forms of entertainment'.

This is why additional studies must be conducted with the aim to discover opportunities and chances to upgrade the elementary needs and wishes of students for better quality culture-related programs, after which a repertoire of various “lighter” programs should be established, which would attract students to 'discover culture', and in time turn them into loyal consumers of those cultural programs and events, which are of interest to the student as the creator and communicator of general social values, the authors of these programs and society as a whole.

References

Andrijašević, M./J. Paušić/T. Bavčević/D. Ciliga (2005), ‘Participation in leisure activities and self-perception of health in the students of the University of Split’, *Kinesiology*, Vol. 37, No. 1, pp. 21-31

Anić, P./I. Brdar (2007), ‘I. Obrasci suočavanja s neuspjehom u školi, konzumacija lakih droga i aktivnosti u slobodnom vremenu srednjoškolaca’, *Psihologijske teme*, Vol. 16, No. 1, pp. 99-120

Babić, D. (2003), ‘Slobodno vrijeme mladih stanovnika otočnih lokalnih zajednica – primjer zadarskih otoka (Iž, Dugi Otok, Ugljan)’, *Migracijske i etničke teme*, Vol. 19, No. 4, pp. 391-411

Bakula, I. (1998), ‘Marketinška strategija kulturnih usluga Studentskog centra’, Magistarski rad, Ekonomski fakultet Sveučilišta u Zagrebu, pp. 48-106

Brdar, I./D. Lončarić (2004), ‘Suočavanje s akademskim stresom i aktivnosti u slobodnom vremenu učenika’, *Društvena istraživanja*, Vol. 13, No. 74, pp. 967-988

Bouillet, D. (2007), ‘Mladi i psiho aktivne supstance: eksperimentiranje ili put u ovisnost’, in V. Ilišin/F. Radin (eds.), *Mladi: problem ili resurs, Institut za društvena istraživanja u Zagrebu*, Zagreb, pp. 203-235

Bouillet, D./M. Čale-Mratović (2007), ‘Konzumiranje alkoholnih pića i doživljaj škole’, *Hrvatska revija za rehabilitacijska istraživanja*, Vol. 43, No. 2, pp. 1-16

Bouillet, D./V. Ilišin/D. Potočnik (2008), 'Continuity and Changes in Croatian University Students' Leisure Time Activities (1999–2004)', *Sociologija i prostor*, Vol. 46, No. 2, pp. 123-142

Bouillet, D. (2008), 'Slobodno vrijeme zagrebačkih studenata: prilika za hedonizam ili samo ostvarenje', *Sociologija i prostor*, Vol. 46, No. 3-4, pp. 341-367

Duda, I. (2005), 'Tehnika narodu: Trajna dobra, potrošnja i slobodno vrijeme u socijalističkoj Hrvatskoj', *Časopis za suvremenu povijest*, Vol. 37, No. 2, pp. 371-392

Gilman, R. (2001), 'The relationship between life satisfaction, social interest, and frequency of extracurricular activities among adolescent students', *Journal of Youth and Adolescence*, Vol.30, No. 6, pp. 749-767

Hiu-Lun Tsai, E. (2005), 'A Cross-Cultural Study of the Influence of Perceived Positive Outcomes on Participation in Regular Active Recreation: Hong Kong and Australian University Students', *Leisure Sciences*, Vol. 27, pp. 385-404

Ilišin, V. (1991), 'Interesi i slobodno vrijeme studenata', in I. Magdalenić (ed.), *Društveni profil zagrebačkih studenata krajem osamdesetih*, Institut za društvena istraživanja Sveučilišta u Zagrebu, Zagreb, pp. 91-124

Ilišin, V. (2002), 'Interesi i slobodno vrijeme mladih', in V. Ilišin/R. Furio (eds.), *Mladi uoči trećeg milenija, Institut za društvena istraživanja u Zagrebu i Državni zavod za zaštitu obitelji*, materinstva i mladeži, Zagreb, pp. 269-303

Ilišin, V. (2006), 'Slobodno vrijeme i kultura mladih', in V. Ilišin (ed.), *Mladi između želja i mogućnosti. Položaj, problemi i potrebe mladih Zagrebačke županije*, Institut za društvena istraživanja u Zagrebu/Zagrebačka županija, Zagreb, pp. 299-330

Ilišin, V. (2007), 'Slobodno vrijeme i interesi mladih', in V. Ilišin/F. Radin (eds.), *Mladi: problem ili resurs, Institut za društvena istraživanja u Zagrebu*, Zagreb, pp. 179-201

Ilišin, V. (2007), 'Društveni status, problemi i budućnost mladih', in V. Ilišin/F. Radin (eds.), *Mladi: problem ili resurs, Institut za društvena istraživanja*, Zagreb, pp. 39-83

Jeđud, I./T. Novak (2006), 'Provođenje slobodnog vremena djece i mladih s poremećajima u ponašanju – kvalitativna metoda', *Revija za sociologiju*, Vol. 37, No. 1-2, pp. 77-90

JLZ (1978), *Opća Enciklopedija*, Zagreb, pp. 677-678

Karam, E./N. Melhem/Ch. Mansour/W. Maalouf/S. Saliba/A. Chami (2000), 'Use and Abuse of Licit and Illicit Substances: Prevalence and Risk Factors among Students in Lebanon', *European Addiction Research*, Vol. 57, No. 6, pp. 189-197

Kukić, S. (1995), *Sociologija*, HKD Napredak, Mostar, pp. 236-237

Mustaine, E.E./R. Tewksbury (2004), 'Profiling the Druggie Lifestyle: Characteristics Related to Southern College Student's Use of Illicit Drugs', *Sociological Spectrum*, Vol. 24, pp. 157-189

Reed, J.A./D.A. Phillips (2005), 'Relationships between Physical Activity and the Proximity of Exercise Facilities and Home Exercise Equipment Used by Undergraduate University Students', *Journal of American College Health*, Vol. 53, No. 6, pp. 285-290

Sabourin, Sh./J. Irwin (2008), 'Prevalence of Sufficient Physical Activity among Parents Attending a University', *Journal of American College Health*, Vol. 56, No. 6, pp. 680-685

Spajić-Vrkaš, V./V. Ilišin (2005), *Youth in Croatia, Research and Training Centre for Human Rights and Democratic Citizenship*, Faculty of Humanities and Social Sciences, University of Zagreb, Zagreb

Studentski centar Zagreb (1993), *Kvalitativno istraživanje uvjeta života i rada studenata u Zagrebu 1992/1993*, Studentski centar Zagreb, Zagreb

Chapter II

Education

Barbara Hönig

Experiences and Perspectives of European Higher Education[1]

Recent students' protests in several European countries point to a raging public debate on interests and experiences, purposes and perspectives, objectives and social practices of actors within systems of higher education in Europe. More particularly, strategies of European higher education like the Bologna Reform Process as well as the normative guidelines of the Lisbon Agenda have remarkably affected educational systems all across Europe. Since students, teacher and researchers on a day-to-day basis experience the very effects of these institutional and cognitive processes, apparently there is an urgent need in critically reflecting the very phenomenon from a social scientific perspective. This is particularly true for institutions as universities specialized for generating and mediating innovative knowledge and developing forms of social organization in shifting frameworks of EU's higher education. But what about modes of thinking sociologically about these European-wide strategies of science and knowledge politics? How did they actually affect university departments at regional level, for instance, in teaching and studying sociology, and which particular notion of "sociology" is intended?

The fact that sociology as a scientific discipline has been shaped by the rise of the modern nation state, also influenced its traditional object as society mainly conceived within that very framework. However, as European societies underwent deep transformations within the last decades, the institutional and intellectual conditions of sociology itself are remarkably influenced by European integration and transcended its national frameworks of reference itself (Beck/Grande 2004; Habermas 1998). While some authors underline the notion of "Europeanization" of national societies (Bach 2000; Delanty/Rumford 2005), the regionalization of European issues can be conceived as the other side of the same coin.

Firstly, this is particular relevant when dealing with cross-national "Euroregions" (Langer 2007) and the societal and economic dimensions of knowledge from a regional perspective: "[...] it is the region with its urban and institutional conglomerations where the role of knowledge in society becomes the most visible" (Langer/Pavičić/Alfirević 2009, p. 12). A regional approach towards analysing knowledge politics and knowledge societies has the advantage to enable more detailed analyses of the institutional conditions of

---

1 Detailed results on the empirical investigation of the European higher education system in Slovenia and Austria can be found in a PhD thesis written under the supervision of Univ. Prof. Dr. Gerald Angermann-Mozetic at Graz University, Austria (Hönig 2009).

knowledge-based societies; it takes the peculiar local effects and regional manifestations of European-wide policies of higher education into account.

Secondly, in analysing these knowledge processes from a particularly sociological perspective, it is reasonable to orient oneself towards the heritage of the sociology of knowledge and the sociology of science to apply this conceptual perspective to the new constellation which we find within border regions in an integrated Europe. In the traditional sense, the sociology of knowledge concerns the suggested influence of institutions, circumstance of the production of knowledge on the content of types of knowledge itself (Meja/Stehr 1982; Stehr 2005). The sociology of knowledge is interested in the social foundations of knowledge and investigates the relationships between knowledge claims and social reality. Part of the sociology of knowledge is the sociology of science, the sociology of scientific knowledge or, so to call, the sociology of sociology. The sociology of science does investigate the social character of science in its institutional, cognitive and historical dimensions (Merton 1996; Zuckerman 1988; Knorr-Cetina 1981; Knorr-Cetina 1999)[2].

After having shortly indicated the approach from taking the regional dimension of knowledge in European higher education policy into account, there follows overview on main strategies of European higher education. Then there is introduced the empirical research design concerning the situation of Slovenia and southern Austria in the European framework. In particular there are given some empirical results of the implementation of European higher education strategies at regional level as it manifests itself in the change of study curricula at five university departments of sociology in the respective common border region Slovenia and southern Austria. Moreover, there are explicated some remarkable ambivalences and contradictions between strategies and practices of the actual implementation of the Bologna Reform Process. There are presented and critically discussed experiences and positions of university scholars from the social sciences who often emphasize the ambivalent impact of European strategies on social practices of higher education. Finally there are drawn some conclusions on European higher education in the respective region.

European strategies of Higher Education: Sorbonne, Bologna, Lisbon

While attempts of the European Union to "Europeanize" higher education can be traced back to the 1950s, as visible in the historical and political analysis of this policy-making process by Anne Corbett (2005), for our purposes here we will focus on the most recent developments concerning higher education and

---

2 The usefulness of the sociology of knowledge and sociology of science for an analysis of current developments of European higher education is also underlined by Olgiati (2009). A recent empirical description and analysis of research cultures in Europe, drawn from a constructionist perspective of the sociology of science, has been developed by Felt (2009).

learning. Regarding implemented strategies of European higher education, first there has to be mentioned the Sorbonne Declaration (1998). From a current standpoint, it seems astonishing that it defined the role and value of knowledge explicitly in contrast to that of "the economy". Particularly, it has been outlined that European steps ahead in the European process "should not make one forget that Europe is not only that of the Euro, of the banks and the economy: it must be a Europe of knowledge as well. We must strengthen and build upon the intellectual, cultural, social and technical dimension of our continent" (Sorbonne 1998). The general aim of higher education policy, due to the Sorbonne Declaration, is "to create an European area of higher education, where national identities and interests can interact and strengthen each other for the benefit of Europe of its students, and more generally of its citizens" (Sorbonne 1998). An "open European area for higher learning" (Sorbonne 1998) hall be created specifically through the use of credits and semesters, in order to allow for the validation of these acquired credits in different European universities and to achieve an international recognition of first cycle degree as an appropriate level of qualification. Furthermore, the Sorbonne Declaration emphasized the role of the universities in developing an Europe of knowledge outlined so far; besides, the Declaration underlined the possibility of "progressive harmonization" of study curricula by building upon already existing experiences, joint degrees, policy initiatives, and dialogue with all concerned actors (ibid.). From this we can provisionally conclude that the Sorbonne Declaration formulated first steps towards harmonization and standardization of higher education, taking also mobility of its students and teachers into account.

Relating more or less closely to the Sorbonne Declaration in 1998, there has been formulated the so-called Bologna Reform Process of European member states. What is usually regarded as the Bologna Reform Process (Bologna 1999) is the division of university studies into three parts of undergraduate, graduate, and postgraduate studies (Bachelor, Master, Doctoral degrees) an their valuation with ECTS (European Credit Transfer System) points. One major goals of the Bologna Declaration is enforcing the mobility of citizens, through creating an European Higher Education Area. As new objectives there were formulated their "employability" and international "competitiveness" of European higher education as well.

However, at the Bologna Declaration articulated one year after the Sorbonne Declaration, we notice several remarkable shifts. What is new in the Bologna Declaration is the term of "employability" which eminently contradicts traditional humanistic goals in academic education where knowledge and the ability of gaining and generating it is an intrinsic value in itself (Kellermann 2006). "The notion of an 'Europe of Knowledge' transformed itself into the instrumental conceptualization of a new politico-economic strategy, in which higher education and knowledge should aim on the one hand to become the means of strengthening economic competitiveness, and on the other had should be offered as goods on markets" (Kellermann 2006, p. 58, transl. added).

Similarly to Paul Kellermann's critique, the rector of Ljubljana University (Mencinger 2004) once has noticed a remarkable difference between the Magna Charta of 1998 (European Universities 1988) signed in Bologna on the one hand and the Bologna Declaration from 1999 on the other hand. He was questioning the compatibility of the two texts, since the Magna Charta underlines a humanist tradition, its autonomy and diversity, while the Bologna Declaration emphasizes employability and competitiveness (Mencinger 2004: 3). Indeed, it can be hold the view that these new concepts are formulated in the same manner as the Lisbon Agenda with its ambitiously stated objective that Europe, till 2010, should "become the most competitive and dynamic knowledge-based economy of the world". As suggested in interviews with sociologists, the Lisbon Agenda might even be depicted as the normative guideline of the European higher education system.

In March 2000 there was formulated a common strategy of European political leaders and decision-makers (European Council 2000), the Lisbon Agenda, aiming, at making the European Union "to become the most competitive and dynamic knowledge-based economy in the world capable of sustainable economic growth with more and better jobs and greater social cohesion" (ibid.). The aim articulated was to achieve full employment by 2010, a quite ambitious objective which rests on three pillars: an economic, a social, and an environmental one. Furthermore, it is led by the so-called "open method of co-ordination" (ibid.) as an instrument of the European Council of a strategic and effective monitoring of the entire process, referring to the subsidiarity principle in order to support participation of EU institutions, social partners, and national, regional, and local actors of the member states. The Lisbon Agenda should help to achieve an economic growth of three per cent per year, with the aim of overtaking the US economic leading position within one decade (ibid.). Furthermore, it explicitly aimed at creating an European Area of Research and Innovation, resulting then in a Commission's paper to increase expenditures for research and development to three per cent of the European-wide GDP (European Commission 2002).

After five years taking stock of the strategy, the former President of the Netherlands, Wim Kok, has concluded that EU has not reached its objectives, but rather has distanced itself from it (Kok 2004). The unemployment rate has increased to eight per cent, economic growth only reached about half of the intended three per cent, and expenditures for research and development in fact did not increase but with 1,9 per cent were even lower than in 2000 (Huffschmid 2006, p. 82). This recognizable failure has been explained by Kok and others not so much by a general critique of the strategy per se, but rather by criticizing that it has not been put into practice at all. This is, for instance, also visible in one article of former European Commissioner Anna Diamantopoulo (Diamantopoulo 2006). Fundamental critics of the Lisbon Agenda (Huffschmid 2006) therefore come to the following conclusions: "Somehow pointedly expressed: The Lisbon Programme has been too good, because it aimed at giving something to everybody and therefore at the end no one took part in. Neither Kok's report nor the European Commission got the idea that the failure of the strategy might rest on the fact that their basic approach oriented towards liberalization and deregulation possibly is false. Both insist that the way of overcoming unemployment and weak economic growth is reached by a further liberalization of markets" (Huffschmid 2006, p. 83, transl. added).

The impact of the Bologna Reform Process on study curricula

Well, having outlined the most important EU frameworks for teaching and studying, how has the standard sociology curriculum of the region's universities changed after the EU accessions? In particular, can these changes reasonably be conceived as a result of the Bologna Reform Process? Or which other tendencies of reshaping sociology in study curricula can be recognized? Particularly, we have investigated the implementation of the Bologna Process as part of European strategies of higher education in an empirical way, namely its implementation at five university departments from 2006 onwards: at Graz and Klagenfurt in Austria, and at Maribor and Ljubljana in Slovenia, the latter both at Faculty of Social Sciences and at Faculty of Arts. Documentary analyses of study curricula at those university departments were applied. Moreover, we participated in a trans-nationally organized focus group on the implementation of the Bologna Reform Process at the respective universities and conducted 21 focused interviews (Merton 1956) with sociologists working at departments of sociology at the respective universities in the region. While we have chosen university departments of sociology as a pragmatically useful unit of sociological analysis, a closer investigation offers striking regional differences and specifications, but also some similarities in the empirical changes of study curricula.

At *Graz University*, since the 1980s there exists the possibility of studying sociology as a curriculum in its own right. As part of a former country-wide orientation in Austria to either offer a specialization in a stream towards economics or towards related subjects in the humanities, it has been introduced as a study with a clear orientation towards the humanities. In 2003 there have been important changes of the sociological curriculum taken place, which again were adopted in 2007 (Studienkommission 2003; Senat 2007a; Senat 2007b). Main differences from the 2003 curriculum to the older one of 2001are three characteristics: First, the former curriculum has been replaced by a focus on the social sciences and economics. This has been argued to take into account that managerial and economic knowledge from scientific and professional perspective are regarded as important for graduates (Studienkommission 2003). As part of the qualification profile it has been mentioned the "acquisition of economic basic knowledge as a complement of sociological core competencies" (Studienkommission 2003, transl. added), especially in acquiring and running of research projects, as by self-employed sociological free-lancers. Second, diploma studies were substituted by Bachelor and Master curricula in a 3 + 2 system. Within the change undertaken in 2007 (Senat 2007a) there has been added not only economics but also law as obligatory subject for all Bachelor students. Furthermore, as part of the curriculum, the variety of central sociological concepts is not mentioned any longer (as "family, gender, generation", "body, space, environment", "social problem, deviance") but are subsumed under "social structures and processes", as well as the trilogy of "labour, economics, technology" has been simplified to "economics" (similar to the area of the then simplified "culture" and "politics") and it might be possible to talk therefore of a more simplified, standardized and homogenized curriculum than that before. Third, however, the "traditionally tight relationship of Graz' sociology to other faculties and disciplines" (ibid., transl. added) shall be maintained, so that students of other faculties might be able to begin a Master study in sociology and on the other hand sociological students get the opportunity to visit courses of other faculties as well. Since 2009 there is prepared a reform of current Bachelor and Master curricula at the department again.

At *Klagenfurt University*, it is not possible to study a full undergraduate or graduate curriculum in sociology, but it is regarded as a "service subject" for other faculties in teaching[3]: Since 2004 it was possible to study sociology of education, for Klagenfurt University since the early 1970s has a strong tradition in educational studies and pedagogy. Some other disciplines contain sociological subjects within their curricula as obligatory (in pedagogy) or optional (in business administration and law or in informatics) study subject. For students there is the opportunity to take optional subjects in sociological areas like labour and enterprise, education and culture, and global society. Since the adoption of the Bologna Process in 2006 specific courses in sociology can be optionally taken as part of other Bachelor or Master studies. Furthermore, by an interdisciplinary working group it is planned to think of the possibility of a Mater study programme in sociology in Klagenfurt[4]. However, there is the opportunity to undertake a PhD curriculum in sociology. Since the decision in 2001 PhD studies in Social Sciences and Economics at Klagenfurt University last four semesters and imply the participation in five courses or ten hours per week (Doktoratsstudienkommission 2001): In general, it aims at the develop-

3 [http://www.uni-klu.ac.at/sozio/inhalt/253.htm] retrieved on 09.01.2010
4 [http://www.uni-klu.ac.at/sozio/inhalt/35.htm] retrieved on 9.1.2010

ment of disciplinary and interdisciplinary competencies in theory, methods and research, developing a reflexive-critical distancing attitude within scientific work.

At *Ljubljana University, Faculty of Social Sciences (FDV Fakulteta za družbene vede)*, Sociology has been offered as an independent curriculum since 1976; the course of study is divided into three programmes: theoretical analysis, human resources management, and social informatics[5]. The "Theoretical analysis" programme aims at the sociological analysis and in-depth knowledge of theory and methodology, of social processes and institutions, human behaviour and in advisory and pedagogical work. The "Human resources management" programme reflects the need for more adequate knowledge regarding this, for every organization and for society in general. The programme "Social informatics" combines sociological competencies with other discipline's knowledge like informatics, computer science, and statistics; particularly it is emphasized the competency in studying problems for an information society form a sociological perspective and in designing, creating and controlling information systems. At FDV Faculty it is possible to study sociology in several Master curricula due to different subject programmes like the sociology of everyday life, European social policy analysis, criticism of sexism as contemporary tradition, and social work in the community. These diverse curricula, generally oriented towards a 4 + 1 system of the Bologna implementation, not only show a specialization of the FDV in the sociology of everyday life and in gender studies as well, but also the fruitful co-existence of programmes related to traditionally important fields for sociology, like social work, as well as new fields of concern manifest in the curriculum of European Social Policy Analysis. Further Mater curricula available at the faculty focus on education in non-profit organizations management and in human resources management and work relations.

At *Ljubljana University, Faculty of Arts (FF Filizofska fakulteta)*, the department of sociology is specialized in the field of sociology of culture and social anthropology. It is regarded as the more theoretically and philosophically oriented one, compared to the FDV faculty. Since the Bologna Process implementation in 2008, sociology is no longer obliged to be combined with an additional subject from the faculty: There is implemented a 3 + 2 system of Bachelor and Master studies in sociology of culture, and a PhD study in sociology of culture or in social anthropology, taking four years.[6] The Bachelor curriculum at FF shows a specialization in subjects of sociology of culture, social philosophy and social anthropology, and in a later stage of the curriculum also subjects in global culture and the sociology of nation and nationalism. It

---

5 [http://old.fdv.uni-lj.si/anglescina/about.htm] retrieved on 9.1.2010

6 [http://www.sociologija.si] retrieved on 9.1.2010

also reveals a rather high amount of competencies in the fields of sociology of media and communication, journalism and discourse analysis, popular culture, and sociology of arts with a focus on sociology of theatre and visual arts.

At *Maribor University*, the department of sociology is rather specialized in the education of sociologists who want to teach sociology and social sciences at public high schools – a professional option open for sociologists in Slovenia, but not in Austria. This specialization explains the rather high amount of didactics, when compared to otherwise relatively heterogeneous subject fields at the respective department. In 2008 there has been introduced the Bologna Reform curriculum of a Bachelor study taking three years, one offered in sociology and one in the field of sociology and interdisciplinary social sciences, the latter dedicated for persons who want to become teachers at secondary high schools. Furthermore, it is possible to choose optional subjects among a scope of forty (!) different subjects in the amount of about 20per cent of the entire curriculum.

Pointing to some ambivalences and contradictions

So what about general tendencies in the changes of study curricula at the five respective university departments? Roughly speaking, as documentary analyses have shown, at all departments of sociology we observed continuing trends towards an enforced *economization and standardization* of higher education, visible in the integration of economic subjects, and project management skills, and the enforcement of students' internships at possible employing institutions. Moreover, there is supported *internationalization* in the creation of European studies and the support and enforcement of international exchange programmes for the mobility of students, teachers, and administrative staff like ERASMUS. In addition, university courses in English are offered more frequently than before, however, still not on a more regular basis, at several university departments. Beside this, also the *inter- and trans-disciplinarity* of curricula is actively supported by most of the respective departments in relation to more or less neighbouring disciplines like pedagogy, philosophy, psychology, cultural studies, law, history, economics and informatics.

However, contrasting standardizing trends as an effect of the Bologna Reform Process, it has to be emphasized that the *regional specialization* of departments in topics and approaches still prevail in its importance. Then we might not only detect a subject complementarity due to a fruitful division of labour among then and within the respective departments as well. Graz University has not only to offer a significant focus on history and theory of sociology, but also a lively tradition in international comparative social research. Klagenfurt University for decades has developed the sociology of education, work, and economic sociology. Faculty of Social Sciences at Ljubljana University is very well known not only for its programmes in social informatics, but also for its focus on the sociology of everyday life and for sociological theoretical analysis. Faculty of Arts at Ljubljana University has a broad offer in the field of sociology of culture, anthropology, and sociology of arts and the media. Maribor University is particularly specialized in the fields of sociology of religion, but also in didactics of teaching sociology.

The change towards and economization and standardization of sociological curricula has perhaps been experienced as a strong re-evaluation of sociology as being accepted, at last, as one of the 'harder' disciplines among the social sciences and economics. Sociology as a teaching subject had to undergo several changes towards a more economic-oriented discipline, which was indicated by the integration of more obligatory subjects in economics into the curriculum. By sociologists themselves, on the one hand this might have been perceived as a necessary and useful process of adapting to current trends in the social sciences and in the situation of sociology and forthcoming professional sociologists in society at large as well. On the other hand, it might have also been perceived as a trend that sociology professionalized itself at the cost of 'getting rid of all that metaphysical or humanity stuff' that means, a more pragmatically and practical sociology without taking into account the legacy of the enlightenment and more universal sciences of the humanities and cultural studies.

Results have also shown remarkable divergences between strategies of European higher education and its actual implementation in Slovenia and Austria. On the one hand, this concerns different institutional and hierarchical levels of the educational system. It has been highly criticized by sociologists that at departmental and faculty level often the individual power of staff or groups of staff is decisive in implementing particular subjects into the curriculum, instead of the interest and choice of students themselves. Moreover, the Bologna Process is implemented in coincidence with recent university reforms at national level in both states, which sometimes even betray the very goals of the Bologna Process itself. At international level, there are mobility programmes like ERASMUS available, but it often became harder for students to study abroad because of shorter study terms in The Bologna curriculum than before. On the other hand, there are also ambivalences and contradictions between the actual practice and the normative legislation of the Bologna Process observable. In Slovenia, only after the implementation of the bologna Process there has been ratified a national law that allows students to switch from diploma to Master curricula for not losing study semesters in this process.

Judging and evaluation these issues of developments of European higher education can be encountered by different forms and streams of scholarly critique on an imaginable continuum of critique and appreciation of the Bologna Process: In a more modest view (Aigner 2002), the Sorbonne and the Bologna Declarations have been criticized for not containing enough criteria and specialized aims of re-structuring educational departments, divergent types of higher education or disciplines, and for lacking social, cultural, political and economic factors to be taken into account that do have an important impact on the system of higher education as such (Aigner 2002, p. 29). In the perspective of a rather radical sociological critique of the Bologna Declaration, what is new is that fact that the ideology of Bologna lies in the orientation of studies towards the labour market and its instrumental usability in the business sense (Kellermann 2006, p. 56; Kellermann et al. 2009).

Conclusions

Seen from these experiences, there is the urgent need for increasing forms of international co-operation as visible in recent efforts to establish joint study programmes and enforce student and teacher's mobility as offered by EU programmes like Erasmus. Moreover, the observed divergences should be taken into account for preventing unintended consequences of the Bologna Process: to support the integration of several relevant actors in the decision making process as students, university staff, the government and potential employers; but also to find consensual practices across different social systems like the government, potential employers, the university, teaching, research and administration; and the co-operation of regional, national, and international levels of implementation as well. In times of globalization where problems of higher education do not know any national borders, it is a task and challenge to increase efforts in order to encounter those in a transnational co-operation of European states in the field of higher education and learning.

References

Aigner, Edith (2002), *Der Bologna Prozess*, Universitätsverlag Rudolf Trauner, Linz

Bach, Maurizio (ed.) (2000), *Die Europäisierung nationaler Gesellschaften*, Westdeutscher Verlag, Opladen

Beck, Ulrich/Edgard Grande (2004), *Das kosmopolitische Europa*, Suhrkamp, Frankfurt a/M.

Bologna Declaration (1999), *Joint Declaration of the European Ministers of Education of 19th June 1999*, Bologna

Corbett, Anne (2005), *Universities and the Europe of Knowledge. Ideas, Institutions and Policy Entrepeneurship in European Union Higher Education Policy 1955-2005*, Palgrave Macmillan, New York

Delanty, Gerard/Chris Rumford (2005), *Rethinking Europe. Social Theory and the Implications of Europeanization*, Routledge, London/NewYork

Department of Sociology at Klagenfurt University, Austria: [http://www.uni-klu.ac.at/sozio/inhalt/253.htm] retrieved on 09.01.2010

Department of Sociology at Ljubljana University, Faculty of Arts, Slovenia: [http://www.sociologija.si] retrieved on 09.01.2010

Department of Sociology at Ljubljana University, Faculty of Social Sciences, Slovenia: [http://old.fdv.uni-lj.si/anglescina/about.htm] retrieved on 09.01.2010

Diamantopoulo, Anna (2006), 'Why the Lisbon Strategy Has neither Friends nor Enemies', in E. Busek (ed.), *Europa – Macht und Ohnmacht: Europäisches Forum Alpbach 2005*, Verlag Österreich, Wien, pp. 98-105

Doktoratsstudienkommission Universität Klagenfurt (2001), *Studienplan für das Doktoratsstudium der Sozial- und Wirtschaftswissenschaften an der Fakultät für Wirtschaftswissenschaften und Informatik der Universität Klagenfurt*, Klagenfurt

European Council (2000), *Lisbon European Council 23rd and 24th March 2000: Presidency Conclusions*, Lisbon

European Universities (1988), *The Magna Charta of European Universities*, September 18th 1988, Bologna

Felt, Ulrike (ed.) (2009), *Knowing and Living in Academic Research. Convergence and heterogeneity in research cultures in the European Context*, Institute of Sociology of the Academy of Sciences of the Czech Republic, Prague

Habermas, Jürgen (1998), *Die postnationale Konstellation*, Suhrkamp, Frankfurt a/M

Hönig, Barbara (2009), *Two Neighbours, One Vision? The Impact of the European Union`s Accession on the Development of Sociology in the Common Border Region Slovenia – Southern Austria*, PhD thesis, Graz University

Huffschmid, J. (2006), 'Mailand, Maastricht, Lissabon: Das Scheitern der neoliberalen Intergrationsstreategie', in Attac (eds.), *Das kritische EU-Buch: Warum wir ein anderes Europa brauchen*, Deuticke, Wien, pp. 72-92

Kellermann, Paul (2006), 'Von Sorbonne nach Bologna und darüber hinaus. Zur Ideologie derzeitiger europäischer Hochschulpolitik', *Soziologie*, Vol. 35, No.1, pp. 56-69

Kellermann, Paul/Manfred Boni/Elisabeth Meyer-Renschhausen (eds.) (2009), *Zur Kritik europäischer Hochschulpolitik. Forschung und Lehre unter Kuratel betriebswirtschaftlicher Denkmuster*, VS Verlag, Wiesbaden

Knorr-Cetina, Karin (1981), *The Manufacture of Knowledge: An Essay on the Constructivist and Contextual Nature of Science*, Pergamon Pres, Oxford

Knorr-Cetina, Karin (1999), *Epistemic Cultures: How The Science Makes Knowledge*, Harvard University Press, Cambridge & London

Kok, Wim (2004), *Facing the Challenge: The Lisbon Strategy for Growth and Employment. Report fom the High Level Group Chaired by Wim Kok*, Brussels

Langer, Josef/Jurica Pavičić/Nikša Alfirević (eds.) (2009), *Knowledge Region: Alps-Adriatic Challenges. Volume I – General Perspective*, Peter Lang Verlag, Frankfurt/M

Langer, Josef/Jurica Pavičić/Nikša Alfirević, (2009), 'Knowledge in an Era of Societal Transformation,' in J. Langer/ J. Pavičić/ N. Alfirević (eds.), *Knowledge Region: Alps-Adriatic Challenges. Volume I – General Perspective*, Peter Lang Verlag, Frankfurt/M, pp. 11-22

Langer, Josef (ed.) (2007), *Euroregions - The Alps-Adriatic Context*, Peter Lang Verlag, Frankfurt/M

Meja, Volker/Nico Stehr (eds.) (1982), *Der Streit um die Wissenssoziologie*, 2. Vol. Suhrkamp, Frankfurt/M

Mencinger, Jozef (2004), *Can University Survive the Bologna Process?* Invited plenary lecture at the symposium "Socio-economic Perspectives in the Life Sciences" on February 16th 2004 in Vienna, Vienna

Merton, Robert K./Fiske, Majorie/Kendall, Patricia L. (1956), *The Focused Interview: A Manual of Problems and Procedures*, The Free Press, New York

Merton, Robert K. (1996), *On Social Structure and Science*, University of Chicago Press, Chicago

Olgiati, Vittorio (2009), 'Potentials and Obstacles in the Promotion of Higher Knowledge in the European Area: The Post-National Question of European Intellectuals', in J. Langer/J. Pavičić/N. Alfirević (eds.), *Knowledge Region: Alps-Adriatic Challenges. Volume I – General Perspective*, Peter Lang Verlag, Frankfurt/M, pp. 35-60

Sorbonne Declaration (1998), *Joint Declaration on Harmonisation of the Architecture of the European Higher Education System*, Paris

Studienkommision Universität Graz (2003), *Studienplan für die sozial- und wirtschaftswissenschaftliche Studienrichtung Soziologie am Studienstandort Graz: Bakkalaureats- und Magistra-/Magisterstudium*, vom 20. März 2003, Graz

Senat Universität Graz (2007a), *Änderung des Curriculums für das Masterstudium Soziologie*, Graz

Senat Universität Graz (2007b), *Änderung des Curriculums für das Bachelorstudium Soziologie*, Graz

Stehr, Nico/Volker Meja (eds.) (2005), *Society and Knowledge: Contemporary perspectives in the Sociology of Knowledge and Science*, Transaction Publishers, New Brunswick/London

Zuckerman, Harriet (1988), 'The sociology of science', in N. Smelser (ed.), *Handbook of Sociology*, Sage, London, pp. 511-576

Ljiljana Zekanović Korona – Kristijan Fučko

Vision of Education

Introduction

More than a quarter of a millennium has passed since the first published information on the first evidence of education by correspondence, the eldest form of distance education. Caleb Philips announced the offer of education by correspondence in 1728 in the American city of Boston so new educational possibilities started to arise and soon they were used by a great number of people. This form of education emerged at the right time as an exceptional and unexpected chance for education, especially for adults (Holmerg 1979, p. 9). The development of distance education depended on available communication media. The first forms of distance education were based on the press that had conquered the world and on postal delivery as a pioneering and fast communication instrument. Although working hours are gradually being shortened, more often an employed person has less free time. The reason for this is working in shifts, commuting to work and other aspects of migration, as well as a sparse population in certain areas.

As far back as in 1883 in the USA, several incentives were started in order to gain a university education by studying via correspondence. At the beginning of the 20th century, attention shifted to the creation of new educational models for studying via correspondence and to the standards of quality for their implementation. With the rise of the new communication media , new opportunities were open to changes in the way of distance education and for a transfer of educational contents. One such change was the application of radio combined with correspondence and the work of educational groups of listeners of the programme, first in Great Britain and later on elsewhere. Soon after that film as a medium saw a wider usage, its utility was recognized as a potential innovation in the field of education. In the period after World War I, interest in the educational possibilities of radio increased, and in the mid-20th century the interest in using television in distance education increased as well. At the beginning, educational courses were transmitted on the radio and public television, and later on via cable and satellite television. Commercial educational technologies based on television also included the “pay-per-view” and “video-by-request” systems. After the rise and fall of the courses on gramophone records and of audiocassette-based courses, video recordings were used more than before in distance education. (Bubaš 2003/04)

With the development of computers and computer technologies, systems for computer-assisted learning (CAL) as well as computer-based instruction

(CBI) were used more often. In the field of distance education in the last decade, the use of multimedia technology, i.e. CD-ROM, has become increasingly popular, and it has been used even for children of pre-school age. A specific technological and pedagogical revolution is still on-going in the use of the Internet and Web. Until the appearance of the Internet, studies by correspondence were the dominant mode of distance education in two-year and four-year university education courses, regardless of the possibilities of other electronic media. In the beginning, the postal service was used for maintaining contact with the participants in distance education, and later on telephone communication and two-way radio connections were used. Nowadays teleconference technology is used for contact with attendants of distance education. The Internet has provided for a different interaction with participants via electronic mail, distribution lists, discussion groups and forums. When high-speed Internet connections are used, there is a possibility for communication through computer video-conferences.

Communication technology plays a very important role in distance education. Advantages and limitations of communication technology have an impact on the manner of presenting information, the interaction with attendants and the verification of acquired knowledge. For a long time – because of its flexible organization, availability and the mode of educational communication – distance education has been the last and at the same time the only chance for people who cannot gain knowledge in other ways. Nowadays this kind of education is more often considered as very successful, efficient, feasible and economical way of further permanent education and further specialization of people who have already gained a certain educational level.

E-learning has been massively applied since the mid-1990s. E-learning, online learning or distance education, as it is generally called, is learning with the assistance of a computer and, very often, the Internet. This form of education is realized on more than one level – as a component part of classical education, but it also exists as fully independent form. The main characteristics of e-learning are time and geographic flexibility, and thanks to these characteristics e-learning introduces novelties into the process of education providing new possibilities for exchange of opinions, knowledge and experiences. Sometimes e-learning is present in the traditional education forms at schools and at universities so that computer and the Internet are used during lectures or while homework is being done. There are cases when educational programmes are partly performed online, i.e. they are assisted by the Internet or by materials distributed on CD-ROMs, and partly in a traditional way. This form of education is called "blended learning", "hybrid" or "mixed mode", and it is often applied in the implementation of professional seminars and other educational programmes for which it would be too expensive or impossible to gather participants for a longer time span. There are also educational programmes that are fully implemented online, which means that, from registration until diploma, all the communication between participants and a provider is performed via the Internet.

E-learning is no more complicated than traditional education. When one uses the Internet, sitting at home in front of one's own computer, one can meet professional experts from distant parts of the world, discuss themes of mutual interest, thus bonding people to their colleagues and gaining useful information. E-learning is applied in three fields of education: in schools and institutions of higher education, for training in the business world and training in the government sector. One should expect that progress in technology would encourage natural human instincts for learning that would be realized in connecting people, introducing personalization and encouraging cooperation.

Distance learning

In comparison to other countries of the post-communist region, the investments into technologies for the purpose of improving the teaching process are the largest in Croatia, especially in the realm of university education courses. There are advanced development plans in Croatia as well and CARNET is a generator of incentives aimed at the development of technology-supported teaching processes. However, the national-level documents barely mention distance learning and the technology-based teaching process improvement strategies either do not exist or have not yet been implemented; moreover, no state institution has been tasked with dealing with passing legislation to provide for the development of *e-learning* at the national level. The majority of countries in Europe as well as the Anglophone countries already passed legislation to support distance learning a few years ago. These countries also founded national agencies to support e-learning and the strategies of the development and financing of *e-learning* have become a part of the state strategies. The development of *e-learning* in Europe started indeed at the very moment when the national strategies were drafted and *e-learning* supporting legislation was passed.

Within the academic community, CARNet took first steps in Croatia and has been conducting experiments with *e-learning* for some years relying on Web CT. CARNet has also been running an *e-learning* academy since 2002. *E-learning* in the world is more present in the corporate environment, where "time is money". This process is very slow in Croatia. The very first commercial implementation was performed in LURA and it was based on a technological solution by the company Cognita[1]. What we have seen up to now is a series of

---

1 Cognita is a company concentrated on the e-learning specific features. There are specialists within Cognita who developed the very first Croatian LMS eLearner (a system for distance learning via the Internet).

decisions made within various segments of the state. Namely, these are EU action plans, the Republic of Croatia's strategy plan that incorporates ECDL (passed by the Croatian Parliament), the Directives by the National Council for Competitiveness, the Operative Plan of implementing the e-Croatia 2007 Programme and the strategy and the action plan for adult education, passed by the Ministry of Education. The EU Action Plans also incorporate recommendations for implementation and a continuous development of the *e-learning* technologies. These recommendations are particularly aimed at setting up a widely accessible and flexible infrastructure intended for contemporary distance learning modes for the purpose of a more intense integration of IT in training courses with a special emphasis on encouraging lifelong education.

The problem is how to implement the e-learning teaching process into primary and secondary schools in Croatia and how to encourage teachers to create e-learning contents, bearing in mind that such tasks are not officially included in their job tasks. As to the university education institutions, the teachers are to take additional courses and implement new modes of the teaching process; moreover, the Bologna Process encourages the use of *e-learner* contents. The Republic of Croatia's Agency for Education does support the e-learning activities that teachers implement but teachers get no additional financial stimulation for activities of this kind. CARNet started an E-learning Academy that trains *e-learning* experts. Since 2004, there have been 265 participants – from more than 60 cities in Croatia and the surrounding regions – that completed the course. The academy is about to train the 7th generation of participants. The course lasts for two terms and there are three educational programmes that train the participants to implement e-*learning* in educational institutions, how to implement quality *e-learning* in teaching in an online environment and how to design and apply education materials to conform to the online use. The programs were developed in cooperation with The University of British Columbia of Canada. The closing workshop is the last of the three live meetings of participants to take place during the one-year course that is otherwise performed via the Internet mostly. The course is presented in Croatian and it is a combination of an online teaching process and three live workshops. The course incorporates a high level of interaction among the participants themselves and among the participants and the trainer by means of online discussions, e-mails, various other online communication tools and live contacts. All the activities in the online environment as well as the teaching process itself are performed via a learning management system (LMS), whereas some segments of the teaching process as well uses other tools such as wiki, blogs, concept map editors etc. In the course of attending the academy course, the participants take part in a series of activities including taking part in discussions, writing papers, research, studying professional literature etc. A part of the contents is presented via case studies that include multimedia materials related to Croatian and the international *e-learning* projects. Pair work and group work are frequently used methods within activities that are expected from participants in the process of knowledge acquisition through independent work. The participants are to invest around 10 hours a week into the course, which amounts to around 320 hours of work at home in the course of 32 weeks of online learning plus 30 hours in the classroom; therefore, each programme lasts for a total of 350 hours.

For the purpose of improving the teaching process in Croatia and within the activities of a project, CARNet has developed the National Distance Learning Portal "Nikola Tesla". It is a system that provides for computer-assisted teaching and learning by means of the use of digital educational contents. In the portal, there are secondary school subjects-related contents (Mathematics, Physics, Biology and Chemistry), ECDL modules required for receiving basic IT literacy certificates, courses on applying and use of the Internet and tools for creating Internet contents. The contents related to Mathematics, Physics, Biology and Chemistry can be used for independent learning and/or knowledge revision.

The contents are divided into lessons in accordance with the national curriculum; the lessons are presented via multimedia with animated examples, audio-visual simulations of experiments and via interactive elements so that the understanding of the matter is made more interesting and easier. Picture 1 below shows an example of part of a Biology lesson. ECDL modules are intended for acquiring basic knowledge of the use of a computer and there are five modules covering the basic literature related to obtaining ECDL certificate, namely word processing, spread sheets, using databases, presentations and WEB browsing and communication.

Figure 1 Screenshot of a Biology lesson

The courses on applying and using the Internet comprise IT security basics, database searching and communication via the Internet. The courses on tools used for creating Internet contents comprise becoming familiar with picture, audio and video editing and rendering software, designing web pages and the use of web technologies.[2]

Even Microsoft Croatia – within its programme "Cooperative learning"– has developed a portal for distance learning by means of performing "webinars" broadcast through Live Meeting software. It is a somewhat simpler software that provides online communication and it is used within the Microsoft Corporation for internal communication and online meetings attended by several people. Live Meeting is simple to use and there are some ideas for it to be used within the LMS of some university education institutions in Croatia. The tools of this kind should be used experimentally as much as possible in order to assess their efficiency. There is a certain number of innovative primary, secondary and university education teachers included in this project implemented by Microsoft.

At schools where some sort of additional courses or educational workshops do exist and where teachers are financially stimulated for that, there is also an interest for creating e-learner contents. At universities in Croatia and especially at faculties offering study-as-you-work courses and even at PhD-receiving courses, LMS systems have been introduced to provide for distance learning. This method of the teaching process is, for the time being, a complement to the traditional teaching process. In Croatia, there is a trend of implementing online education into university education and there is also some resistance to it from older teachers who do not want to spend additional efforts on preparing educational contents. Creating online education contents is quite demanding work and a teacher is supposed to be creative and to invest some extra time. If e-learner as a mode of teaching process were used more, it would be easier to assess the efficacy and effects of this method of education.

When online learning is concerned, students are not limited by time, location or distance. When asynchronous learning is concerned, a (university) student or any online learning user can access the materials at any time; Synchronous online learning provides for a real-time interaction among students and a teacher. (University) students can use the Internet to access the newest teaching materials and the communication with skilled experts in the field researched is provided as well. Learning is facilitated because a person can take an online course in his/her room and the acquired knowledge can be applied in a context.

Online learning enables teachers to teach anywhere and at any time. Online materials can be updated and course participants can spot the changes instantly. When the teaching materials are accessible on the Internet a lecturer can easily

---

2 [http://lms.carnet.hr]

draw the attention of his /her students to the particular information in accordance with the students' needs. If an online learning system is designed properly, it can be used in assessing the needs of students-course participants and in assessing their current knowledge level. After assessing the knowledge level of students/university students and other participants, the materials needed for attaining the envisaged goals of learning can be addressed.

In accordance with Bank and Reynolds (1997), online learning should offer challenging activities that enables the participants to link the old information with the new information, to acquire meaningful knowledge and to use their metacognitive abilities; The activities thus encourage an advanced way of thinking in the Internet. (Ally 2004/05) The quality of learning is not influenced by a technology but by a teaching strategy. A medium does influence learning, but a computer itself is not the factor that motivates students to learn, but the design of real, lifelike models and simulations are the factor, as well as the interaction of (university) students with these models and simulations. A computer is but a means to make the transfer of information and performing the teaching process possible. In order for students to learn from simulations, the simulations should be developed by use of appropriate teaching process design principles. Online learning has many advantages but it requires dedication and means whereas materials – granted that an appropriate support has been provided – should be designed in a way that makes the materials centred on (university) students and learning.

Various terminologies are frequently used to address online learning. The most frequently used terms are: e-learning, learning via the Internet, distributed learning, network learning, tele-learning, virtual learning, computer-assisted learning, Internet-assisted learning and distance learning. What all the terms have in common is the distance between a (university) student and a trainer or lecturer. A student generally uses a computer as a technological means used to access teaching materials and to communicate with the trainer and other course participants. Online learning comprises more than the presentation itself and the delivery of materials via the Internet; what should be in the centre of online learning is a student and the learning process as well as the communication between a student and the teacher. This teaching method enables a student to acquire the learning content even at the time during which he/she is not present at regular classes.

Mobile-learning – M-learning and Nano-learning – N-learning

In Croatia, there have not been any m-learning and n-learning (as e-learning forms) cases recorded so far. These forms of learning and teaching are yet to be introduced.

M-learning[3] – in the context of e-learning – relates to the learning that is not performed in one place exclusively but takes place in different places in various time-spans and it is supported by portable devices such as PDAs (palmtops), mobile phones, smartphones, iPhone, portable audio and video devices and similar portable hybrid multimedia devices. Tablet PCs and laptops can also be included. M-learning is a form of both e-learning and d-learning (distance learning). This way of learning and teaching has a communicative and a collaborative characteristic with the possibility of a constant sharing and communication of contents, which in turn provides for a constant reception of feedback and instructions.

M-learning and the portable devices can be used creatively in numerous education situations. An extremely practical example is the use of a PDA when the teaching process is performed outdoors, in the countryside, with the use of multimedia files.

At the times of the post-information age, some compulsory changes in ways of learning and teaching have been made in order to avoid information overload and to gain general knowledge.

E-learning has contributed a lot to that purpose and m-learning emerges as a post product and results in turn with n-learning. N-learning is the future of education. N-learning relates to nano-deliveries of n-learning contents intended for n-teaching and n-learning. The academic expression *nano-learning*[4] was used for the first time by Albert Ip and Bob Corderoy in 2005.

N-learning is comprised of shorter time segments of educational units – 90 seconds, 120 seconds or 3 minutes – the smaller amount of time, the better. It also comprises the delivery of a small quantity of contents embedded in small portable devices. N-learning focuses on multiple use of content i.e. on a dynamic and adoptive sequencing of nano-contents in the multimode way of learning. Learning takes place in a short period of time, even within a minute. The new and innovative ways and theories have described the teaching and learning processes.

N-learning is characterised[5]: by key source information, delivery of timely information, practical quality, flexibility, adjustability, interaction, revision and monitoring of the acquired knowledge. So, what is typical of this mode of learning are features that provide for an ability of learning anywhere and any time, individual choice of the time of learning, displaying information at a minimal turnaround time, guaranteed acquisition and application of knowledge;

---

3 [http://www.amazon.com/Mobile-Learning-Handbook-Educators-Trainers/dp/0415357403] retrieved on 26.7.2010.

4 [http://elearningrandomwalk.blogspot.com/2005/11/nano-learning-n-learning-is-future.html] retrieved on 26.7.2010.

5 [http://www.intimelearning.com/nanoLearning.aspx] or [http://teachnet.edb.utexas.edu/~lynda_abbott/social.html] retrieved on 26.7.2010.

moreover, with one's own engagement at presenting the knowledge, it is even possible to have some fun; finally, it is possible for the real learning to be monitored and assessed.

When team learning is implied, the method of competition can be very well applied. The simple competition method creates a feasible environment for learning and revision of knowledge, the environment in which the absorption of knowledge is a real one. In a team, anyone can be both an instructor and a student. The powerful nano-learning technology accelerates the individual as well as the team performances through self-discovering and deep thinking.

Learning in this way allows our knowledge-acquiring strategies to crystallize and thus the belief in the personal limitations vanishes and new perspectives are set. It is therefore possible to learn some things in small educational blocks, an element or two of knowledge each day. One only has to concentrate on learning for a few moments and a new awareness of how something functions is acquired along with a new micro-skill. It is widely known that the majority of people acquire knowledge through smaller segments. Learning – based on this principle – in a society implies some behaviouristic and cognitive factors and leads us to the s-learning (social learning) theory.[6]

Research method

The research was conducted at the beginning of the 2009/2010 school year on a sample consisting of 51 students at the University of Zadar and 153 secondary school students at the Vocational School of Čakovec. The university students were aged 19-39 whereas the secondary school students were aged 15-19.

The research method was filling in an anonymous survey questionnaire consisting of 22 questions that had to be answered by means of circling the chosen answers. The gathered data was processed using Microsoft Excel.

Results and discussion

The purpose of this research was to assess to which extent university students and students use computers and for what purposes and whether there were some differences between the persons surveyed, depending on them being university students or students. The authors also wanted to learn about the attitudes of the university students and students with regard to education in the future and the level of their familiarity with the latest learning forms. The university students most frequently used computers at home (56 per cent), 20 per cent of them used computers both at home and at the university, whereas the remaining 24 per cent of them used computers somewhere else. At the University of Zadar, there is a specialized IT classroom that is accessible for students throughout the whole day, but the computers are over 5 years old. The self-imposing conclusion is that students do not use the computers at the faculty because they have got much better and faster machines at home. As the University of Zadar is generally very well equipped with computers, there is a newer IT classroom at the Hall of Residence and it is highly probable that students use these newer and faster computers more. The secondary school students gave somewhat different answers to this question. 11 per cent of them used computers only at home, 3 per cent only at school and 86 per cent of them used computers both at home and at school. This implies that almost each of the students has got a computer at home and that they are free to use one both at home and at school. All the surveyed students and university students use computers as follows: more than 50 per cent of the university students use computers for more than 10 hours per week whereas 63 per cent of the secondary school students use computers at the same rate (more than 10 hours per week) This data showed that younger generations used IT and computers increasingly and computers were more and more accessible for them both at home and at school. Those surveyed used computers and the Internet mostly for surfing, mail inbox checking, discussing in forums, electronic shopping and for fun and playing games. 50 per cent of the surveyed university students and 52 per cent of the students used online encyclopaedias. A high percentage of the university students used online educational contents (23%), whereas secondary school students used it less (12%). Both the students and the university students frequently used online knowledge assessment because in that way they could find out the level of their acquisition of knowledge and – depending on the results – start some additional learning accordingly. All the surveyed university students were acquainted with distance learning systems, whereas 20 per cent of secondary school students knew nothing about distance learning systems. 8 per cent of the university students and 36 per cent of secondary school students had heard of distance learning but did not use it. 82 per cent of the university students and 44 per cent of all the surveyed used some of the 4 distance learning systems.

37 per cent of the surveyed university students thought their education process would stop after they had completed their university courses. The secondary school students thought about continuing their education, which is understandable, so 51 per cent of them planned to update and supplement their knowledge over the course of their lives, whereas 48 per cent of them considered lifelong learning to be a good idea although they were not sure they would have motivation for it over the entire course of their life. The [http://www.net.hr] portal is the site that the surveyed visited the most. 18 per cent of the university students and 29 per cent of secondary school students had heard of mobile learning. An even smaller number of those surveyed had heard of social learning, namely 10 per cent of the university students and 12 per cent of the secondary school students). 75 per cent of the university students and 10

per cent of the secondary school students had heard of nano-learning. 75 per cent of the surveyed university students and 55 per cent of the secondary school students wanted to gain education by means of e-learning. The university students wanted to use distance education in their free time, namely in the fields of general knowledge, communication skills, managerial and executive skills; The secondary school students wanted just the same but they added IT education to the distance-learning wish list. The experience gathered by the users of online education is positive and arouses a wish of a repeated use of this mode of education. 50 per cent of university students had an opportunity to attend a video conference, whereas only 14 per cent of the secondary school students had an opportunity to attend a video conference. The result was expected as video conferences are used in the university education courses and for attending lectures given by renowned professors from abroad. All universities in the Republic of Croatia are fitted with video conference halls and the respective equipment, whereas only some secondary schools boast such equipment: Moreover, video conferences are not a standard teaching process tools. Video conferences have proved effective and thus both the university and secondary school students would like to participate in this mode of education. A Webinar as a form of a distance lecture is used for additional education of teachers mostly, so the feedback confirming that none of the surveyed participated in a Webinar was expected. However, a total of 6 students and university students had an opportunity to participate in a Webinar and they must have been invited by their teachers. Both the university and the secondary school students wanted to participate in distance learning courses but not at a strictly defined time as they preferred to participate in a course in their free time or at a time when they wanted to access some particular educational materials. The mode of education that does not impose a time limitation is more acceptable. Some of those surveyed did browse through some books in the Internet but these were only few. Chat as online fun and recreation activities were used the most.

Conclusion

After the conducted research, the evident conclusion is that those surveyed – both the university and secondary school students – do want to use distance learning. This mode of education is a trend worldwide and therefore in Croatia as well. Within the lifelong learning that is considered an imperative of the contemporary times, the use of the advanced information technology is a necessity.

The young persons surveyed are sufficiently acquainted with the newest education modes (m-learning, s-learning and n-learning. The educational system in our country should train teachers to use the new education modes. Teachers should be stimulated to use these teaching process forms because the teachers will pass on the possibilities of the kind of education to their students. For the time being, only enthusiastic teachers use the new modes of education but it is far from enough in terms of keeping pace with the European and the world trends in education. Thanks to the "Cooperative Learning" portal, enthusiastic teachers get together and exchange their experiences. The national distance learning portal "Nikola Tesla" deserves highlighting as well as this portal has been of great help to teachers and students alike. There are some incentives for the development of the new educational modes in Croatia, but additional stimulation of teachers through a system of rewards would lead to a quicker implementation of the new modes of education. The older generations of teachers are not inclined to change, but then the young generation of teachers should receive a high quality education. Young people should be stimulated to choose teaching as their vocation and be encouraged to keep pace with the European and the world trends in their use of educational technologies.

In our times of post information age, the digital era, there have been (r)evolutionary changes in learning and teaching thanks to the unstoppable advance of technologies that bring some new possibilities of communication, collaboration and education. Not much time was needed from the very beginnings of e-learning and its modes such as it is d (distance)-learning, before the existence of m-learning was recognized and m-learning has developed ever since and has brought n-learning in turn that is a part of the vision of the future as it has been adjusting to fit the new trends within the society.

The exclusively classic way of teaching turns classrooms into waiting rooms because students wait and think only of the moment when the bell will announce the end of a class and it is because they are bored/sleepy and do not think about the subject matter. It is the trend that makes everyone impatient – the old and the young alike – and everyone wants to get everything in no time, even to acquire knowledge in no time, especially nowadays with the lifelong learning principle being so popular. But it is precisely for those who have trouble concentrating and learning for whom the new perspectives have to be created. This also implies changes in the ways of learning, the learning methods, the techniques of acquiring new knowledge and keeping and updating what was previously acquired. Learning should turn into an adventure for a student/university student and a teacher/educator alike. The solution is in combining e/m/n-learning with the classroom hybrid/blended method, work in the field and motivated independent engagement. This combination is a part of the future s-learning (social learning) in an e-environment (an electronic environment).

References

Ally, M. (2004/5), Osnove obrazovne teorije online učenja, Časopis Edupoint br.1. godina.

Bubaš, G.: Metodika i komunikacija u obrazovanju na daljinu, Magazine Edupoint br.2. year 2003/04

Holmerg, B. (1979), Nastava na daljinu, Andragoška biblioteka Birotehnika, Zagreb, p. 9

Zoran Mihanović – Ana Bubalo – Mario Vučić

Marketing of Adult Education in Croatia

Introduction

Learning is one of the primeval human instincts. It is not only the key for sustainable competitive advantage but also for survival. The kind of learning, which results in a competitive advantage, is not limited by time, space or matter. A new approach to career development for individuals and corporations will be focussed at learning as an action-directed *lifelong* process where global partners work together on the production of a positive, prosperous future for all. (Fulmer/Gibbs 1998) Accordingly, the concept of *lifelong education* as a "transitional education" in modern society is suggested. It is seen as a link between the demands of market competitiveness on the one side and quality life on the other. Modern strategy of education is based on the principle of lifelong education. (Povjerenstvo za obrazovanje odraslih Vlade Republike Hrvatske 2004) *Education* is becoming continuous throughout life, from youth up to old age, and is used as an attempt to foresee the knowledge needed in the future. Croatia lacks scientific thought and empirical studies as well as clearly elaborate expert criteria and also a system of performing lifelong education and adult education activities. Therefore, it is considered important to theoretically analyse the marketing implementation in the field of lifelong education and adult education in Croatia, which the subject of this paper relates to.

Lifelong education in general

In order to better understand the following text, it is necessary to explain basic terms related to lifelong education: lifelong learning, adult education, formal, non-formal and informal education.

According to the definition by the Agency for Adult Education of the Republic of Croatia "*Lifelong learning* is every learning activity throughout life for the purpose of improving knowledge, skills and abilities, whether it is directed towards an individual's personal growth, employment and/or active participation in society and community with the objectives of permanent employability, active citizenship, the increase of economic competitiveness, the assurance of social inclusion of all groups and the individual's personal growth." (Puljiz 2007) Lifelong learning is often taken as a synonym of the phrase lifelong education, but these two terms differ in so much as lifelong education is a narrower term, which includes organised learning only.

Lifelong education is every organised form of learning from youth to old age. It is organised as formal, non-formal and informal and because it gives significance to non-formal and informal education, previous boundaries between formal education and non-formal and informal education are being erased. (Lavrnja 2002) As formal kind, it is implemented in primary, secondary and higher education, and as non-formal and informal kind, it is carried out through various programmes, seminars, courses etc. Unlike *formal education, non-formal education* is every form of education, which does not lead to acquiring new qualifications, diplomas or moving up on the qualification scale, but it indicates organised learning processes directed at enabling adults for work, different social activities and personal growth. (Agencija za obrazovanje odraslih 2009) Informal learning is a somewhat neglected area even though it is the natural, mostly unconscious learning from everyday experience, different sources and influence from the environment; contents and their organisation are freely chosen, and one of the tasks is creating social contacts and is therefore more appropriate to older people in their third age.

The term lifelong learning can be used in two different ways: one is as a synonym of *adult education*, and the other is as a system consisting of related elements (formal education – primary, secondary and higher education, and non-formal and formal education), which is based on the principle of the temporal prolonging of organised learning (from childhood and youth to the entire lifespan) and whose introduction provides distance from the dominant institutional approach to education because it is not connected to a particular life period, particular level of education or a specific purpose. (Bubalo 2008) This text will consider adult education as an important part of lifelong education. *Adult education is the education of persons older than 15 years, who are outside of the regular educational system in order to acquire and promote knowledge, skills and abilities.*[1]

State and prospects of lifelong education in the EU

Modern strategy of educational development is based on *the concept of lifelong learning and the society that learns*. These concepts were developed in the Seventies and Eighties by international organisations OECD, UNESCO, ILO, the Council of Europe and the European Commission; they considered international growth and the role of education in it and they referred them to their members as a basis for leading national teaching policy. (Ured za strategiju razvitka RH 2001) The goal of the European Union is for Europe to become the place of the most dynamic and competitive economy, which will be based on the knowledge of its citizens (Marinović 2004), and lifelong learning is crucial for the realisation of this goal. The concept of lifelong learning and adult education is becoming the essential policy for the 21st century and its main

---

1 Narodne novine (2007), "Zakon o obrazovanju odraslih" (online), Zagreb: Narodne novine d.d. Dostupno na: [http://www.nn.hr]. 17(07) (08.01.2008.)

objective is to increase the contribution of education to national growth and development by investing in necessary market-required knowledge and skills and thus achieving international competitiveness of national economies. (Delors 1996)

For education to contribute as much as possible to national growth, it needs to be qualitative, equally available to all citizens and economically worthwhile – hence the educational policy priorities, which are in common to all member countries of the EU arise – *educational quality, educational equality (social justice) and economic efficiency*. (Pastuović 2007) From many international action plans, declarations, documents and conferences[2], it is possible to extract guidelines for the further development of lifelong education:

1. The principal objective and priority of lifelong education development is ensuring *the possibility of basic education* for all people and *promoting basic skills*: reading, writing, mathematical and ICT skills. A focus on those skills, which enable the permanent ability of learning new concepts is necessary; (Radni materijal Europske komisije 2000)
2. *Promoting professional knowledge, skills and arts* – entrepreneurial and managerial knowledge; communication abilities, social skills and arts; abilities, skills and arts in creative expression; abilities, skills and arts for performing basic civil duties; abilities for solving various family problems; abilities for environmental preservation and protection; (Povjerenstvo za obrazovanje odraslih Vlade Republike Hrvatske 2004)
3. It is necessary to *recognise and evaluate non-formal and informal education* for it to gain the same status as formal education. That is why the European Union countries are working on the formation of "The European Qualifications Framework for Lifelong Learning (EQF)", which equalises levels of citizens' competence and qualifications. The Ministry of Science, Education and Sport has begun preparing the Croatian Qualifications Framework, which will ensure intelligibility and international recognition of secondary and higher education qualifications; (Primorac 2007)
4. *Financing* of formal, non-formal and informal *education* needs to be increased;
5. Extensive systems of *gathering* local, regional and national *statistical data* for adult education are needed. These data represent the basis for creating measurements, need estimates, planning, monitoring, reporting, evaluating and international comparison, and are also the basis for the successful implementation of a marketing concept in education.[3]

---

[2] Agencija za obrazovanje odraslih, [http://www. aoo.hr] retrieved on 6.2.2008.

[3] Konferencija o obrazovanju odraslih, Sofija (2002), "Cjeloživotno učenje u Europi: Ostvarivanje ciljeva EFA (Education for All –Obrazovanje za sve) i Agende CONFINTEA

6. Higher *mobility* for the purpose of education and employment throughout Europe;
7. The need for regular *Reports* on progress in realising set objectives has been noticed, for which measurements, indicators and rules of monitoring and reporting need to be developed;
8. *Governments* on all levels should ensure that *adult education* remains an explicit and integrated element within their policy and lifelong education practice;[4]
9. The main resource of developed countries, without which any future progress is inconceivable, is people – *human capital* – whose development is not possible without a quality educational system. For the quality of human capital to optimally develop on a national level, two strategic objectives need to be simultaneously realised by education: improving average quality of educational accomplishments of students and active population, and a higher average educational quality needs to be realised with less differences in the accomplishments of individuals belonging to various social groups; (Pastuović 2004, pp. 135-141)
10. Clearly *defined legal regulations*, regulated rights and financing obligations on the part of state, regional and local structures and funds;
11. Built *network of institutions*, associations and foundations that realise programmes and tasks of adult education/learning;
12. Development of *efficient* teaching and learning *methods*; (Radni materijal Europske komisije 2000)
13. Finally, *evaluation* of adult education/learning *effects*, on a scientific level in numerous research and development projects, as well as on an operational, practical level; (Bogdanović/Matković/Šojlev 2001)

In view of accomplishing mutual goals and the manner of their realisation in terms of the European Commission, intensive processes of coordinating national educational policies and forming a unique European educational policy are in progress. Each member state, with Croatia as well, is working to improve educational process according to basic and common principles, which are adjusted to the needs and traditions of its country. The European Union member countries have at their disposal international programmes, which deal with strengthening of lifelong education, mobility and social cohesion. Many organisations appear as a support to lifelong education and adult education (EAFA, UNESCO, OECD, ILO, The Council of Europe and The European Commission), which is important for the further development and expansion of lifelong education and adult education. The EU programme, which encourages

V." (online). Zagreb: Hrvatska zajednica pučkih otvorenih učilišta. Dostupno na: [http://www.hzpou.hr/stranice/3/16-100.pdf] retrieved on 9.1.2008.

4 Ibidem

education and professional training, was established in 2006, and it has continued on from the previous programmes *Socrates* and *Leonardo da Vinci*. These are: *Comenius* (programme for pre-school education, primary and secondary schools), *Erasmus* (programme for higher education, *Leonardo* (vocational education and training on all levels of education, except on the higher educational level with the aim of reducing unemployment and preparing young people for market needs), *Grundtvig* (promotes experience exchange within Europe in the area of adult education and wishes to encourage mobility, cooperation in adult education and to include socially endangered persons and persons without a completed primary school in the educational process), *Transversal* and *Jean Monnet*.

State and prospects of adult education in Croatia

Adult education in Croatia has a long history. It was founded by Albert Bazala in 1907. Subsequently, its development and the process of adjusting the educational system to tradition and to the political system, as well as the European teaching and educational standards, followed. (Erceg/Bolić 1995)

The strategy of educational development in the Republic of Croatia is based on the concept of lifelong learning, which was adopted at Confitea V in Hamburg in 1997. (Bogdanović/Matković/Šojlev 2001) By including lifelong learning in the strategic documents from the area of education, lifelong learning has become the basic principle of the development of the Croatian educational system.[5] Basic documents are: Croatia in the 21st century – education, White Paper on Croatian Education, the Government of the Republic of Croatia, Office for Development Strategy of the Republic of Croatia, 2001; Declaration on Knowledge, 2002; Croatia Based on Knowledge and Knowledge Application (HAZU), 2004; 55 Recommendations for Increasing Croatia's Competitiveness, The National Competitiveness Council (NVK), 2004; Strategy and Action Plan for Adult Education, Committee of the Government of the Republic of Croatia for Adult Education, 2004; Education System Development Plan 2005-2010, Ministry of Science, Education and Sports, 2005; Strategic Development Framework for 2006-2013, SDURF (Central State Office for Development Strategy and Coordination of EU funds), 2006; Decree on Establishing the Agency for Adult Education, 2006; Adult Education Act, 2007; Ordinances (Ordinance on Public Documents in Adult Education, Ordinance on the Content, Form and the Manner of Keeping Andragogical Documentation, Ordinance on Records of Adult Education Institutions; Ordinance on Standards and Norms), 2008.

At the end of 2004, the Government of the Republic of Croatia determined the adult education development with the documents *Strategy for Adult*

---

5 Agencija za obrazovanje odraslih, [http://www. aoo.hr] retrieved on 6.2.2008.

Education and *Action Plan for Implementation of Strategy for Adult Education*, and set the measures and activities needed to be realised for adult education to develop as an equal and no less important part of the educational system.[6]

The task of monitoring, evaluating and advancing adult education is performed by the Agency for Adult Education as a public institution established by the Decree of the Government of the Republic of Croatia in May 2006, using activities such as database management, information assurance, analytical and developmental work, professional supervision of the work of institutions, professional qualification and training of employees in the field of adult education, innovating, monitoring and evaluating implementation of programmes, cooperation and professional-counselling activity, defining criteria for systematic financing of adult education. (Puljiz 2007) Objectives of the Agency are (Ćavar/Čale 2007): replacing permanent employment with permanent employability, increasing adult involvement in lifelong learning, viability of literacy of the 21st century, coordinating the educational system with the labour market, promoting a learning culture. The role of the Agency is professional-counselling. It was established to look after the system – its coordination with laws and regulations, and its quality.

Table 1 Critical points and changes in the field of lifelong education in Croatia

Critical points	Changes
Programmes	• Universal test of programme check, various learning forms. • Flexible (educational qualifications) and open (available to all, motivating). • They need to provide elementary education, which helps acquire functional literacy necessary for development of other skills. • Universal skills – languages, informatic literacy, communication skills, team cooperation, problem solving skills • Entrepreneurial skills
Quality of human capital	• For a successful transition, the quality of human capital is of utmost importance. And, considering the educational structure and established value orientations and habits of population, it is behind the one in developed countries.
Institutions	• Better organisation, activity and business. • Colleges need to be included in the process of lifelong learning (initiate more postgraduate and scientific studies). • Networking.
Market needs	Connect with education, solve unemployment problem, strengthen the role of labour market institutions

6 Ministarstvo znanosti obrazovanja i športa RH (2005), *Plan razvoja sustava odgoja i obrazovanja 2005 – 2010*, Zagreb [http://www.public.mzos.hr].

Table 1 contd.

Support by the state	Needs to be strengthened
Legal regulation	Drafting of laws, regulations, acts
Statistical monitoring	Database creation
Financing	The support of state and local self-government
Promotion	Info desk, lifelong education week

Adapted from: Gruber, E. (2000) Modernizacija pomoću fleksibilnosti doškolavanja. in Gartenschlaeger, U., Hinzen, H. Perspektive i tendencije obrazovanja odraslih u Europi. Zagreb: HZPOU; Povjerenstvo za obrazovanje odraslih Vlade Republike Hrvatske (2004), *Strategija i akcijski plan za 2005. godinu obrazovanja odraslih*, Zagreb, Ministarstvo znanosti, obrazovanja i športa; Središnji državni ured za razvojnu strategiju i koordinaciju fondova EU (2006), *Strateški okvir za razvoj 2006.- 2013*, Vlada Republike Hrvatske, Zagreb; Pastuović, N. (2004), "Obrazovanje odraslih i nacionalni razvoj ljudskog kapitala", in Klapan, A. i Matijević, M., ur. *Zbornik radova 2. međunarodne konferencije "Obrazovanje odraslih – ključ za XXI. Stoljeće"* Šibenik, 27.- 29. svibnja 2004. godine. Zagreb: Hrvatsko andragoško društvo, pp. 135-141

Table 1 shows that *the support of state and local self-government* provided to adult education is poor, education expenses are covered by the individual himself or, when the acquisition of professional knowledge is in question, by the employer. According to the research of work force competitiveness, the level of investment by Croatian companies into the development of their employee competitiveness is far below global and European standards. (Pološki/Frajlić 2004) One of the main characteristics of the Croatian labour market is a relatively weak *link between education results and market needs.*[7] Schooling, training and advancing for market needs could solve the problem of unemployment. The condition of successful lifelong learning is a solid *basic education*, which acquires functional literacy necessary for the development of other skills and is the starting point for obtaining new competencies. (Pastuovič 2002, pp. 305-316) Lifelong education institutions, particularly adult education institutions, which are a part of the lifelong process, like public colleges, formal education institutions, cultural and educational centres, nongovernment associations etc., should be used to continually promote education. The promotion is directed at individuals, but also at the overall system in order to

[7] Središnji državni ured za razvojnu strategiju i koordinaciju fondova EU (2006), *Strateški okvir za razvoj 2006 - 2013*, Vlada Republike Hrvatske, Zagreb, [http://www.nhs.hr] retrieved on 6.2.2008.

develop and emphasise the story of significance and the need for education and training. The analysis of the current state should be performed for existing positions to be exposed. Adult education tendencies have to be evident and clear to everyone, and the evaluation of the adult education process, namely the quality and success of programmes, teacher quality and qualifications, student satisfaction and market needs, will show whether lifelong education objectives, which were established in the Strategy and Action Plan, are being realised.

In the context of lifelong learning, adult education practice has registered increasing interest. The Republic of Croatia cannot exist outside of these global processes and educational efforts because that would make it economically and politically marginalised. (Ured za strategiju razvitka RH 2001) The European Union has always avoided the unification of educational policies; instead of a uniform educational policy, the emphasis is on different systems and mutual goals.[8] Croatia will contribute to its national development if it improves the efficiency of educational system for it to be compatible with developed countries.

Marketing in adult education

According to Kotler and Fox, "marketing in education presents analysis, planning, implementation and control of carefully elaborate programmes, whose objective or purpose is to achieve voluntary exchange on specific markets and thus enable organisational objectives. In doing so, marketing relies on needs and wants of target groups, as well as on effective price formation, promotion and distribution in order to inform, motivate and serve the market." (Kotler/Fox 1995) Marketing concept attempts to convince companies to consider what they do and why they do it and motivate them to create a plan for achieving, executing and implementing their objectives. (McCarthy/Perreault 2006, p. 19) Although the marketing concept is just a theoretical one, many organisations do not understand it – they do not comprehend its meaning and implementation.[9] In recent years, marketing has been increasingly applied in adult education too, making it possible to conclude that market analysis and the implementation of marketing concept are inevitable in planning growth and development of adult education institutions. (Vančina 1998) With education institutions marketing, the benefit is twofold (Pavičić 2003): (1) systematic implementation of marketing precipitates functioning of the mentioned institutions and a higher quality realisation of their mission and objectives; (2) by improving the

---

8 Žiljak, T. (2005), *Politike cjeloživotnog učenja u EU i Hrvatskoj* (online). [http://politologija.hr/casopis.php?kateg=1&sub=1] retrieved on 10.6.2008.

9 Daubek, H. G. i Feldman, L. S. (1995), *Applying The Marketing Concept To The Marketing Of Higher Education* (online). Purdue University Calumet. [http://www.sbaer.uca.edu/research/sma/1995/pdf/toc.pdf] retrieved on 15.2.2008.

realisation of mission and objectives, marketing implementation in educational institutions has a positive effect on solving social problems, namely, it contributes to a better functioning of society as a whole.

In terms of marketing, education is an example of a service based on trust with the user who is usually not capable of assessing the product even after performed purchase because the user rarely possesses the required technical expertise. (Driscoll/Wicks 1998, p. 59) The implementation of a marketing concept in the field of education should contribute to the benefit of a wider segment of society and the labour market, raising the awareness of the significance of lifelong education. It is based on the study of needs and the interest for educational contents, the concept of educational content and the promotion on the occasion of its operationalisation. (Bubalo 2008) Specificities of the marketing mix of educational institutions can be summarised as the following elements[10]:

- *Product* in education is difficult to define and is therefore perceived as a process and/or knowledge incorporated into those who use it or as a combination of these. Education has its educational function, which implies a certain behaviour we want target audience to accept.
- *Price* represents the price, which society pays for an educational institution to be able to function without disturbances. Society has limited material capabilities to follow the demands of educational institutions for propulsive development. Thus, a part of the educational process' price is covered from the funds of those students who pay for their studies, the funds realised from various institution's projects, institution's additional activities (for example, lifelong education programmes) or possibly donations. Price cannot be perceived solely as an economic sacrifice, but also as a sacrifice associated with a psychological benefit (time spent, effort invested) of those who choose education and whom the education process affects.
- *Distribution* is presented by the spatial proximity of the educational institution in regards to potential users of the educational process, but also other congenial and divers "competitive" institutions. Since *the idea*, which educational institution offers is also a part of its overall product, it should be "socially available" – with support within the user's social sphere.
- *Promotion* includes marketing, publicity and public relations activities with the purpose of informing potential users, actual users and the public about the elements of the institution's educational process.

Marketing implementation in adult education in Croatia is limited and marketing principles and strategies are insufficiently applied – there is a strictly selling role related to enrolments, and long-term strategies are poorly

---

[10] Kotler, P., Fox, K.F.A.: op. cit., 1995; Meler, M. (1994), *Društveni marketing*, Ekonomski fakultet Sveučilišta u Osijeku, Osijek, pp. 293.

developed, but one should not forget that educational institutions are both institutions present on the market and those whose success may be reduced to a classical economic relationship of supply and demand. (Jurković-Majić/Trupeljak 2007, p. 65-69)

The aim is to enable students, i.e. the consumers of education, to think: to facilitate critical opinion and analysis, creative problem solving, adapting to changes and understanding the social dynamics of organisations they will work in. (Mihanović 2007) This kind of education would better prepare those who are about to graduate for the challenges they will encounter during their working life.[11] That is exactly where *lifelong education* reaches its full expression.

Organisation follows the marketing concept in so much as its structure, culture, systems and procedures are established and developed in a way, which ensures long-term relationships with consumers (both clients and employees) within limited resources and conditions of the organisation's long-term survival, (Siu Noel/Wilson 1998, p. 303) and it is proposed that marketing needs start from the organisation itself due to the service nature of education, and top management's understanding of and commitment to market orientation is of great importance.[12]

A strategic marketing framework should enable marketing experts who work for educational institutions to recognise unsatisfied needs and develop new products and services (new forms of providing education such as distance learning etc.) for the purpose of satisfying expected demands. It is evident that marketing experts in education will have to be educated in the field of strategic marketing and they will have to particularly develop a specialty in discovering unsatisfied needs. (Aaker 2003, p. 63-64) It is suggested[13] that limits in the implementation of a marketing concept in educational institutions be set and relevant stakeholders are asked to take into consideration dangers, which a too wide view of the consumer-seller analogy implies. It is believed that maximum regard to consumer needs may be harmful for education in the long run because "the need" for quality education is not obvious and clear to all students (or potential students) and, as such, consumer orientation cannot ensure high quality programmes.

One common source of educational institution problems is that they cannot establish a balance between diverse stakeholders and they often turn to resources more than to their original partner – the direct consumer of education. The mission of education is to satisfy expected future needs in the function of development and it is often mistakenly considered that education is directed at existing needs. (Hrvatska u 21. stoljeću 2002, p. 68-69) It is these needs that give marketing and the implementation of the marketing concept in education its

---

[11] Driscoll, C., Wicks, D.,: op. cit. p. 60.
[12] Ibidem, p. 314.
[13] Driscoll, C., Wicks, D.: op. cit., p. 60.

importance because marketing can play an important role in joining long-term needs of the entire society and satisfying consumer needs with a quality presentation of what he does not want in the short-term but which will affect his growth and society growth in the long-term, directing those needs in a socially acceptable manner, thus, eventually, fulfilling the institution's mission and aims. (Mihanović 2006)

Conclusions

Personal motivation for learning, acknowledgement of skills, previously acquired general and expert knowledge and diversity of education possibilities are a principle condition for the successful implementation of lifelong learning. The entire educational system has to be prepared for providing educational services, which have to satisfy the different needs and ages of their potential students. These tasks should be used for connecting with the local community and different social and other partners. It is crucial to increase the demand for education, as well as the offer, especially for those who have not had much benefit from the education and improvement so far. *It simply means that the system of education and improvement has to be adjusted to the needs of an individual, and not the opposite*[14].

Marketing may be of help here by way of studying needs and interest for such contents, but also by conceptualising such contents, in promotion as well as during their operationalisation. With the implementation of a marketing model, we have to keep in mind environment specificities of particular institutions, which preclude the imitation of a foreign model.

Considering accelerating social and economic changes, the flexibility of the educational system has to be improved along with its fluency. In that way individuals would have a greater opportunity for changing the education/training, according to the changing needs in the labour market and the concept of lifelong learning.[15] Thus a significant shift to consumer-directed educational systems is implied, with loose borders between various sectors. Experts would follow individuals on their way through life and continuous education *based on the research* of their needs and market demand, in order to facilitate their important decisions. *An efficient management* of the educational system demands collection of information along with supervision and prediction of changes considering providers of education and users of education along with their needs. It naturally requires an active approach from users. It is necessary to develop a *partnership* at all levels, in order to be involved in creation, monitoring and development of adult education. This refers to the organised

[14] Europska komisija: Memorandum o cjeloživotnom učenju, op. cit., pp. 8-9.

[15] Ministarstvo znanosti obrazovanja i športa RH (2005), *Plan razvoja sustava odgoja i obrazovanja 2005. – 2010.* op. cit., pp. 9.

involvement of universities, colleges and other education institutions in a programme of lifelong education.

Considering the specificities and demands of lifelong education, the repositioning of higher education sector from a slightly distant, elite and inflexible system to a system that is sensitive and responsible, available and adaptable to the changing needs of people and society in general is implied. (Candy 2000, p. 121) In the context of lifelong learning, adult education practice notes increasing interest for adult higher education, which is motivated by professional advancement, the wish or need for vocational change, and an individual's personal needs and wants. Higher education can offer a response to these needs through an open and flexible approach, which would accomplish a greater connection with the interests and needs of economic development. (Ministarstvo znanosti, obrazovanja i športa 2007, p. 15)

The need for education increases, and numerous stakeholders and complex relationships in the education process point to a need for marketing for the purpose of promoting education to all relevant subjects and thus bringing its programmes and their quality closer to all relevant subjects. (Mihanović 2006) For further education to expand and eventually pay off, participation in further education has to be increased, particularly in target groups, which are not sufficiently familiar with it, and, in addition to that, there is a current tendency to establish stronger marketing campaigns for further education (for example, learning entertainment, databases, educational servers, rewards for further education). (Gartenschlaeger/Hinzen 2004)

Marketing and education about marketing principles are important as a guide to the institutions. It also represents a tool, which enables institutions and the state to present the importance of adult education, which in the end creates high quality programmes and better motivation of the users for lifelong learning. The planning of the development of institutions involved in the adult education requires an analysis of the market and the implementation of a marketing concept. It is also important to continuously educate people about various possibilities of marketing application in different sectors. The association of adult education with changing market and work needs for specific knowledge (while satisfying social responsibility) is a goal that can never be thoroughly reached, but it is a direction that should be followed. An adapted frame of the marketing concept, directed to social interests, can significantly help with the efficient management of relations between adult education institutions and their stakeholders. Finally, this also helps to improve the performance of the aforementioned institutions in satisfying their basic mission and their goals, as well as the needs of various stakeholders, which they relate to.

References

Agencija za obrazovanje odraslih (2009), *Međunarodne organizacije o obrazovanju odraslih 1.dio*. Zagreb

Bogdanović, S./J. Matković/D. Šojlev (2001), *Razvojni model pučkog otvorenog učilišta*, Zagreb: Hrvatska zajednica pučkih otvorenih učilišta

Bubalo, A. (2008), *Primjena marketinške koncepcije u cjeloživotnom obrazovanju odraslih u Hrvatskoj*. Specijalistički poslijediplomski rad, Ekonomski fakultet, Zagreb

Candy, Philip C. (2000), 'Reaffirming a proud tradition: Universities and lifelong learning', *Active Learning in Higher Education*, Vol. 1

Ćavar, J./Z. Čale (2007), 'Agencija za obrazovanje odraslih kao faktor razvoja sustava obrazovanja odraslih' in M. Matijević (ed.), *Andragoški glasnik. Glasilo Hrvatskog andragoškog društva*. Zagreb: Hrvatsko andragoško društvo, Vol. 11,br. 2, pp. 107-121

Delors, J. (1996), *Učenje blago u nama: Izvješće Unesco-u međunarodnog povjerenstva za razvoj obrazovanja za 21. stoljeće*. Zagreb: Educa

Driscoll, C./D. Wicks (1998), 'The Customer-Driven Approach in Business Education: A Possible Danger?', *Journal of* Education *for Business*, Vol. 74, No. 1, pp. 59

Erceg, Z./J. Bolić (1995), *Mogućnosti obrazovanja i zapošljavanja odraslih u Republici Hrvatskoj*, Zagreb: Ministarstvo prosvjete i športa, Ministarstvo rada i socijalne skrbi – Zavod za zapošljavanje

Fulmer, M.R./A.P. Gibbs (1998), 'Lifelong learning at the corporate university', *Career Development International*, 3/5, pp. 177-184

Gartenschlaeger, U./H. Hinzen (2004), *Perspektive i tendencije obrazovanja odraslih u Europi: izbor tekstova*. Zagreb: Hrvatska zajednica pučkih otvorenih učilišta

Hrvatska u 21. stoljeću (2002), *ODGOJ I OBRAZOVANJE, Bijeli dokument o hrvatskom obrazovanju, Koncepcija promjena odgojno-obrazovnog sustava u Republici Hrvatskoj*, Ured za strategiju razvitka Republike Hrvatske

Jurković-Majić, O./S. Trupeljak (2007), 'Marketinško promišljanje koncepta cjeloživotnog obrazovanja' in A. Klapan/M. Matijević (eds.), *Zbornik radova 3. međunarodne konferencije "Obrazovanje odraslih za ekonomiju znanja"*. Šibenik, 3. i 4. lipnja 2007, Zagreb: Hrvatsko andragoško društvo

Kotler, P./K.F.A. Fox (1995), *Strategic marketing for educational institutions*. Englewood Cliffs: Prentice Hall

Lavrnja, I. (2002), 'Neka teorijsko-metodološka pitanja proučavanja obrazovanja odraslih u kontekstu cjeloživotnog učenja', in A. Klapan/M. Matijević (eds.), *Zbornik radova međunarodne konferencije Obrazovanje odraslih u republici Hrvatskoj u kontekstu cjeloživotnog učenja*, Lovran, 14.-16. veljače 2002. Zagreb: Hrvatsko andragoško društvo, pp. 237-244

Marinović, V. (2004) 'Europljani i cjeloživotno učenje', in A. Klapan/M. Matijević (eds.) *Zbornik radova 2. međunarodne konferencije 'Obrazovanje odraslih – ključ za XXI. Stoljeće'*. Šibenik, 27.- 29. svibnja 2004. godine. Zagreb: Hrvatsko andragoško društvo, pp. 103-110

McCarthy, E. J./W.D. Perreault (2006), *Essentials of marketing: a global-managerial approach*. 10th ed. McGraw-Hill Irwin

Meler, M. (1994), *Društveni marketing*, Ekonomski fakultet Sveučilišta u Osijeku, Osijek

Mihanović, Z. (2006), *Marketinška orijentacija i odnosi s ciljnim skupinama visokoškolskih institucija*, magistarski rad, Ekonomski fakultet, Zagreb

Mihanović, Z. (2007), 'Uloga korisnika u visokom obrazovanju: jesu li studenti aktivni dionici?' ('The role of customers in higher education are students active stakeholders?'). *Tržište*, Vol. 19, No. 1

Ministarstvo znanosti, obrazovanja i športa (2007), Strategija obrazovanja odraslih, Zagreb

Pastuović, N. (2007), 'Konceptualizacija standarda u obrazovanju odraslih u RH', in A. Klapan/M. Matijević, M. (eds.), *Zbornik radova 3. međunarodne konferencije Obrazovanje odraslih za ekonomiju znanja* Šibenik, 3. i 4. lipnja 2007. Zagreb: Hrvatsko andragoško društvo

Pastuović, N. (2004), 'Obrazovanje odraslih i nacionalni razvoj ljudskog kapitala', in A. Klapan/M. Matijević (eds.), *Zbornik radova 2. međunarodne konferencije "Obrazovanje odraslih – ključ za XXI. Stoljeće"*. Šibenik, 27.- 29. svibnja 2004. godine. Zagreb: Hrvatsko andragoško društvo

Pastuovič, N. (2002), 'Obrazovanje odraslih u kontekstu cjeloživotnog učenja – iskustvo i perspektive razvijenih zemalja', in A. Klapan/M. Matijević (eds.), *Zbornik radova međunarodne konferencije Obrazovanje odraslih u republici Hrvatskoj u kontekstu cjeloživotnog učenja,* Lovran, 14.-16. veljače 2002. Zagreb: Hrvatsko andragoško društvo

Pavičić, J. (2003), *Strategija marketinga neprofitnih organizacija*, Masmedia, Zagreb

Pološki, N./D. Frajlić (2004), 'Pokazatelji konkurentnosti hrvatske radne snage – rezultati empirijskog istraživanja' ('Croatian Labor Force Competitiveness Indicators: Results of Empirical Research'), in P. Bejaković/J. Lowther (eds.), *Konkurentnost hrvatske radne snage (Croatian Human Resrouce Competitiveness Study*). Zagreb: Institut za javne financije (Institute of Public Finance)

Povjerenstvo za obrazovanje odraslih Vlade Republike Hrvatske (2004), *Strategija i akcijski plan za 2005. godinu obrazovanja odraslih*, Ministarstvo znanosti, obrazovanja i športa, Zagreb

Primorac, D. et al. (eds.) (2007), *Pregled postignuća. Siječanj 2004 – travanj 2007*, Zagreb: Vlada RH. Ministarstvo znanosti, obrazovanja i športa

Puljiz, I. (2007), 'Obrazovanje odraslih: obrazovna politika i institucionalni okvir', Uvodno predstavljanje projekta Cards 2004 Obrazovanje odraslih. Hotel Dubrovnik Zagreb, 18.12.2007.

Radni materijal Europske komisije (2000), *Memorandum o cjeloživotnom učenju, Bruxelles SEC(2000), 1832* (online). Zagreb: Hrvatska zajednica pučkih otvorenih učilišta

Siu Noel, Y.M./R.M.S. Wilson (1998), 'Modelling Market Orientation: An Application in the Education Sector', *Journal of* Marketing *Management*, Vol. 14 No. 4/5

Središnji državni ured za razvojnu strategiju i koordinaciju fondova EU (2006), *Strateški okvir za razvoj 2006- 2013*, Vlada Republike Hrvatske. Zagreb, [http://www.nhs.hr]

Trim, P.R.J. (2003), 'Strategic marketing of further and higher educational institutions: partnership arrangements and centres of entrepreneurship', *International Journal of Educational Management*, Vol. 17, No. 2

Ured za strategiju razvitka RH (2001), *Bijeli dokument o hrvatskom obrazovanju. Projekt strategija razvitka Republike Hrvatske: Republika Hrvatska u 21. stoljeću.* Zagreb: Vlada Republike Hrvatske

Vančina, I. (1998), *Marketing u obrazovanju odraslih.* Magistarski rad. Ekonomski fakultet Zagreb

Agencija za obrazovanje odraslih [http://www.aoo.hr]

Chapter III

Communication

Tena Perišin

Media Trends in Croatia: Television News or News on the Internet

Introduction

Croatia is a country with more than 3,000 registered journalists, four national terrestrial television channels, 23 local and regional TV stations, 150 radio stations, more than 950 print media and with a population of 4.5 million. Croatian citizens have no problem in accessing the media. More and more of them are using the Internet and the latest information cites some 47 per cent of the population using it.

Croatian citizens still receive most of their information via the television, which means that television is the most widely spread media in Croatia. The national TV stations – the public HRT television and commercial television stations Nova TV and RTL – are equipped with the latest technology and have digitalised their program production and are preparing to completely switch over to digital broadcasting by January 1, 2011. The trends that dominate world editorial boards like cross-media production of content have also entered Croatian ones. Content is distributed and spread via different media platforms and in different media forms. Those producing content constantly face new technological challenges that enable them to transfer their content. At the same time, media houses are facing different types of pressure – among them, those of a political nature seem to be less forceful than those linked to commercial interests: the survival on the market and the race for profit and the pressures of the owners and the corporations that take out ads in their publications (Malovic 2007).

Media market development

Technology advancements have enabled the participation of readers, listeners and viewers in creating content. Croatian media have readily accepted this possibility. RTL's main news shows have a regular section titled "Your News" where footage and information sent in by citizens is broadcast. The editorial board of the 24 sata daily paper has taken this format to a higher level. Within its Internet portal it regularly publishes footage recorded by readers. The publishers of the 24 sata daily tabloid that also own the company that publishes the daily with the traditionally highest circulation, Vecernji list, have also launched their own Internet television. They produce news each day, broadcast and constantly repeated on the TV sets of viewers who watch their TV program via IPTV services, which enable the receiving of digital television, as well as digital video renting, HD reception, taping etc.

This has practically meant that 24 sata had launched, as its representatives like to describe it, the first TV news channel and in reality, Internet television, and had overtaken public television in this niche, despite the latter announcing the launch of specialised channels, a current affairs and a sports channel. Namely, HRT had announced, some three years ago, the launching of specialised terrestrial channels, but this had been hindered by appeals put forth by commercial television stations RTL and Nova TV, which believed this to be standing in the way of competitiveness. Although the Law on HRT stipulates that HRT has the right to launch specialised channels, the unclear and not precise enough legal stipulations had allowed for different interpretations of the two key laws: The Law on Electronic Media and the Law on HRT. The case has still not been resolved and public television HRT is now trailing behind smaller, but more flexible producers of media content, which had launched 24-hour channels either using cable or via IPTV.

In view of the living standard, the prices of domestic and foreign newspapers in Croatia are too high.

Newspaper publishers are hiding the figures relating to copies sold, but there are indications that the circulation of the most popular newspapers in Croatia, (Vecernji list and Jutarnji list) has been the lowest so far. This trend has been recorded in a report that the European Journalism Centre published back in 2006. The revenue from advertising is also shrinking. The prices of domestic and foreign newspapers in Croatia are relatively high. Newspapers are recording a drop in the number of readers also due to an increase in the use of the Internet.

Newspaper publishers are investing in multimedia, attempting to put out their news using different platforms (Perišin/Škaljac 2009). They cite three reasons for this:

1. To lower costs
2. To make use of the cross-media production and cut the number of staff
3. To use the convergence to secure more content and increase the usability of the content (journalists and staff).

Which of these reasons is put first depends on strategic decisions. However, it is possible that all three intertwine. It is a fact that the media houses in Croatia have also found themselves in a punishing race for profit. There is less and less journalistic content, which is the product of research, analysis and the wish for new and unbiased information. Foreign corporations have brought along modern technologies, but have not brought along the media that still exists in the developed countries. In Croatia, most of the print media is in the ownership of two foreign corporations: WAZ and Styria, which claim not to be meddling in the editorial policies of their newspapers while they are returning a profit. The result of the need for quick profit is a market with an increasing number of tabloids, while the leading dailies like Jutarnji list and Vecernji list are increasingly dealing with scandals and sensationalist topics. Many established journalists have left those papers as they were not getting enough space to write analytical articles and have moved to Internet portals' pages. Blogs, forums and particularly Facebook have become places of civil action and initiative, but also of 'dissemination' of newspaper articles, which are unable to make it into high-circulation newspapers.

Digital broadcasting: analogue switch-off 2011

In the period from 2010 to 2011 Croatia experienced a transition to digital television, which further impacted the Croatian media picture.

The way the project has been implemented is described in the Strategy of the transition from the analogue to digital broadcasting of television programs, which was adopted by the Croatian government on July 31, 2008.[1] The goals of this strategy are as follows:

1. As of January 1, 2011 complete digital terrestrial broadcasts of television programs will begin throughout the territory of the Republic of Croatia,
2. Create the conditions for the retention of free, universal and public services of broadcasting television programs of the public television, as well as the services of other television providers at the national, regional and local level,
3. Secure the technical and technological conditions for the managing of the relevant segment of the radio frequency spectre through the optimal use of transfer capacities in a way that to the highest measure meets the public interest,
4. Create the conditions for access of independent producers of content to the digital terrestrial television network and develop pluralism of content on the open market of services,
5. Based on the favourable conditions offered by the digital system of terrestrial broadcasts of television programming, open up as wide a space as possible for the diversified expression of the cultural identity of the Republic of Croatia and for the new media, which represent an integral part of the impact and development of democracy through the comprehensive services, which enable all citizens the ability to freely access, free-of-charge program content at the national, regional and local levels.

---

1 [http://www.hakom.hr/UserDocsImages/dokumenti/Strategija%20prelaska%20s%20analognog%20na%20digitalno%20emitiranje%20televizijskih%20programa%20u%20RH.pdf] retrieved on 1.12.2011.

In order for this strategy to be implemented, Croatia has been divided into nine regions, each of them made up of one or more counties. The first region that has been switched over to digital broadcasting is Istria, Hrvatsko primorje and Gorski kotar.

The digitalisation project in Croatia is being implemented by the government of the Republic of Croatia, i.e. the Central State Office for e-Croatia, whose video clip is shown as part of the television program.

The campaign aimed at preparing the people for the digitalisation of the television broadcasts has been accompanied by a series of advertisements and TV ads titled 'Climb Down from the Roofs'. The content calling on people to 'climb down from the roofs' had missed the target making the people think that they no longer needed a TV antenna. The damage done by that campaign is now being rectified with a new promotional campaign, which emphasizes the fact that antennas are still indispensable.

In order for all television viewers to be able to transfer to receiving digital broadcasts, they needed to acquire a digital receiver – a piece of equipment, which "translates" the digital signal to the existing TV set. In line with the mentioned strategy, to all those who regularly pay their TV license fee, the government of the Republic of Croatia issued special coupons for the cheaper purchase of such equipment. The coupons were distributed gradually, in different areas of Croatia, as the digital signal was introduced, so that by 2011, the whole of Croatia has been covered.

The financial support for the purchase of the equipment is sent to citizens in the form of coupons that are brought to their address by the Croatian Postal Service. This coupon reduces the price of the digital receiver to the end consumer. Each vendor should accept such a coupon and verify it. The vendor then returns the coupon to Croatian Television.

New digital channels

Simultaneously with the campaign promoting the transition to digital broadcasting, the possibility of viewing new channels that are broadcast via the terrestrial digital transmitters is being announced.

HRT public television has been announcing the launch of two new terrestrial digital channels since 2007. The channels were to have been launched back in 2008. Croatian Radio Television believes that by launching additional programs it will help citizens to more quickly transfer to the digital network. Namely, without a wide offer of channels on the digital terrestrial network, citizens will not be motivated to use digital receivers. The base for such a belief is the Law on HRT. Article 3, paragraph 2 of the Law on Croatian Radio Television, which reads:

The actions in paragraph 1 of this article HRT can perform through the production and broadcasting of three radio programs in three radio networks at the state level and radio networks at the county or regional level, as well as TV programs at two TV networks at the state level, the work of music production, choir performances, organising of events and concerts, especially of national music heritage and contemporary works of Croatian composers and artists' renditions. HRT can produce [...]'

HRT has been announcing the transformation of its HRTplus program to HRT 3, which should have become a sports and leisure channel and HRT 4 (news and current affairs channel), which should have become a 24-hour news channel. The new channel was to have been broadcast on the digital terrestrial network.

However, the competition voiced its disapproval of the HRT intention to launch specialised channels. Namely, back in 2008, RTL lodged an appeal with the Croatian Competition Agency and the Culture Ministry. The aim of the RTL appeal was, according to its claims, to stop the illegal broadcasting of satellite and cable channel HRT Plus and the digital broadcasting of two other channels HRT 3 and HRT 4. RTL was joined in this by the second commercial television, Nova TV. They demanded that the launch of the digital channels by HRT be prevented, citing as their key argument the lack of transparency of such a procedure. They believe that the money from TV license fees should not be used for the launching of new channels and that HRT should provide proof that it would not use those channels in a commercial manner.

All of this has puzzled the general public and this has also been helped by a legislation that lacks precision and allows both sides to cite it. While one side is speaking of the Law on the Electronic media as lacking precision, HRT is citing the Law on HRT, which explicitly says that it can launch specialised channels, the sports and news channels would fit this description and that this is the very role of public television.

In this case, HRT, RTL and Nova TV have interpreted differently the existing laws – the Law on Croatian Radio Television and the Law on Electronic Media, which points to the fact that they are flawed when referring to the rights and obligations of national television stations. RTL claims that HRT has the right to broadcast TV programmes of a general nature, but on two networks on the state level at the most and that it should seek a concession for additional channels based on a public tender for topical TV programs in line with the Law on Electronic Media. RTL has also noted in its statement (hina.hr) that the launching of new channels represents a breach of the agreement between Croatia and the EU and the Law on State Subsidies.

The HRT arguments, on the other hand, lie in the fact that all public television stations in Europe have been given a chance to launch specialised channels. Namely, article 3, paragraph 2 of the Law on HRT is a legal document for the production and broadcasting of HRT programming. Based on a similar law – the founding act, most radio television services, including specialised programming, members of the EBU are operating. The production and broadcasting of specialised programs mentioned in article 3 or paragraph 2 of the Law at the same time represent the HRT task according to the strategy of transferring from analogue to digital broadcasting of TV programs in the Republic of Croatia, which had been adopted by the Croatian government in 2008.

Since by the year 2011 the transition to broadcasting on digital terrestrial network had been completed, the national television station believes that the additional two channels (HRT 3 and HRT 4) will help to motivate people to transfer more quickly to the digital network. The better the offer of digital programs, the sooner the viewers will acquire a digital receiver. HRT has actually acted in a way that many other public televisions in Europe acted before. By offering more channels it is attempting to attract TV license fee payers to more easily transfer to digital television. The argument as far as HRT is concerned lies in the Law on HRT. The discussion on the new channels has sparked interest among Internet forum visitors.[2] They have taken sides, so that one group believes that HRT should launch specialised channels and the other believes that HRT is unduly privileged due to receiving all the money from the TV license fees.

Some order in that realm should come out of the decision of the Croatian Post and Electronic Communications Agency (HAKOM), which – at its session held on April 24, 2009 – passed a decision to issue a license to the Odasiljaci i veze (OIV) company to administer digital TV networks (MUX A and MUX B). This happened after a tender had been put out.

Cross-media content production

Cross-media production is being more and more encouraged in Croatian editorial offices. It envisages the integration of the production of content and at the same time the distribution and spreading through different platforms in different media forms (Quinn/Filak 2005). Content producers are facing numerous challenges, while the ways of distribution and the possibilities via different platforms (TV, Internet, mobile telephony, IPTV) are growing. The vast offer enables them to reach their viewers whenever and wherever[3]. That the cross-media content production in Croatia is not negligible is proved by two main news publishers that are aware of the need for change. Speaking about trends in the development of publications in relation to the digital media, it is obvious that the classic division will soon disappear. Communication with the users will be done through all the available platforms that a certain media outlet is operating on. Basically, the borders that are currently set up by the classic

2 [http://www.forum.hr/archive/index.php/t-292132.html]
3 [http://www.idmmusic.com/press/Weekend-media-festival-2008-2.pdf]

binary division of print and electronic media will no longer exist. The battles of the future will be waged for taking over the hearts and the minds of the users under new rules. This means that it is necessary to also intensify the development of other channels of communication. Through the usage of several channels of communication and with their total personalisation, a much larger synergic effect is accomplished than in the case of using just a single medium. This enables interactivity and in this provides the accomplishment of better results. Nowadays the leading media houses are mobilising all their available resources and content is being processed through Internet portals, video news, magazines and reports, mobile phones' projects etc. (Krajina/Perišin 2009). Such a convergent approach enables them to address all the target groups, depending on the media.

The new possibilities allowing users to access information and news, irrespective of where they are or what platform they are using to access the news, are changing the habits in the receiving of information. This also envisages fundamental changes in the 'content packaging' within the legal provisions and habits of the users for each of the communication platforms – mediums.

The example of the Jutarnji list daily is interesting in this respect, as the paper had launched a high-profile campaign over its Internet pages with video content and dubbed it Jutarnji TV. It, actually, represents a video edition of Jutarnji list, a newspaper that is published within the EuropaPress Holding (EPH) media concern and is available across Croatia.

The Jutarnji list portal has a link to Jutarnji TV where it is possible to watch video news produced by Jutarnji list journalists. Publishing is becoming more complex and more demanding in preparation and the challenges and the potential become enormous. Those pages include reports, pictures that were covered by the newsreader in the 'off', in the form of a TV report meant for a TV show. The editorial staff of this segment of Jutarnji list content production did not completely grasp the 'philosophy' of the Internet public, which approaches information differently from the viewers of TV shows. Namely, it has been proven that users have a different way of 'reading' and 'watching' Internet pages to the way this is done by classic TV or newspaper consumers. The video clips in question need to complement the text that is being published on the same page (Eyetracking the News, Poynter Institute, 2007).

Jutarnji TV began its work by using principles of a genuine small TV crew made up of journalists, camera journalists and editors shooting important events and publishing them on the Internet pages. The quality of their footage was for the most part much lower than when it is shot by professional TV camera people, but practice has shown on several occasions that this was not the most important thing.

On September 28, 2008 the small cameras of Jutarnji followed a police operation and captured the arrest of university teachers suspected of corruption in the Index scandal. This date, in itself, would not have been important, had the footage not been used in the main public television HTV news show Dnevnik. The showing of the footage was also accompanied by a 'footage Jutarnji TV' inscription. The fact that footage produced by a newspaper was used to illustrate the key report in the HTV central news program Dnevnik speaks volumes about the changes that are happening on the media market. The footage had literally shown the arrests of university teachers in front of their flats. They were in their gowns, wearing pyjamas and nighties. Despite the ethically questionable and extremely sensationalist content, the public television, which is in possession of numerous cameras and teams, used the material produced by the competition assessing that the footage would lure viewers. Regardless of the content, the very fact that the main TV news show of the public television began its broadcast with footage obtained from a newspaper daily clearly denotes that the borders between the classic media have become blurred.

Internet television in Croatia

Internet television or Internet TV is television distributed via the Internet. Viewers can pick the program they wish to view from a number of programs on offer. At the beginning it was believed that Internet TV was the same thing as 'streaming' TV, i.e. the live broadcast of programs from the Internet. When talking about Internet television some refer to the Internet location where the video clips are stored. These two ways of direct flow (streaming) TV and video clips on web pages differ from IPTV (Internet Protocol Television).

Internet television , as well as the upsurge in Internet portals was enabled by the expansion of broadband Internet, mostly through ADSL connection. Internet television or eTV has developed more intensively since 2004, while users were enabled to freely watch videos via the Internet with the introduction of MAX ADSL which represented the first broadband infrastructure in Croatia. Currently, IPTV services in Croatia are offered by other operators as well (MAXtv, Bnet, Iskon, Optima). The existing operators are offering different combinations of services. For example, Iskon TV offers a combination of Internet and telephone or just the Internet. It is also possible to search the Internet on the TV screen and watch several channels simultaneously, as well as tape shows on demand.

The number of Internet pages that offer some type of Internet television is quite large for a country as small as Croatia. When speaking about 'forms' of Internet television, we are referring to different forms of presentation of the television on the Internet, which differs from one portal to another. At some portals the term 'Internet television' is used referring to 'live streaming'. The user is able to follow live the television programming of a certain TV channel.

This method is mostly used by TV companies and portals, which don't have a large number of staff or by those who are unable to offer more than that. More developed portals, apart from 'live streaming', offer another type of Internet television and that is 'video on demand', where the user chooses a certain show or report.

Internet television can be used for bridging administrative issues. Each radio and TV station is limited to the area where it can broadcast by the frequency license. The importance of the web pages is the strengthening of the own media and this was quickly picked up by some editors. By transferring the programming onto the Internet, an owner of a local television station can instead of having a limited scope, have an unlimited one and an audience from across the world.

In the case of Croatian national and local television, Internet television mostly has to do with playing shows on demand. Under the title 'video on demand' or 'show on demand' the television house portals offer mostly their own production programs. This option has some of the functions of a VCR, which means that it is possible to stop the show and rewind it or fast forward it. In view of the fact that users can only watch the station's own programs, the service is free of charge.

Television stations are not the only ones to have developed Internet television. This was also done by some Croatian dailies (for example: Jutarnji list, Vecernji list, 24 sata), as well as different portals (for example: Index.hr, Javno.hr, etc.).

Of all the media houses, only the 24sata daily owned by the Austrian Styria publisher has used the Internet in order to launch what they described as 'the first news channel' in Croatia. The Kanal 24 stata channel broadcasts news from Croatia and the world 24 hours a day. The 10-minte news reports are mostly repeated, containing news from all areas of domestic and foreign politics, economy, sports etc. Obviously, due to the editorial policy of the paper the crime stories, entertainment and showbiz are mostly represented. Thanks to the Reuters television news agency they include world news, so that they air the latest Hollywood news as well, including what new films are being shot and what the celebrities are up to. This channel is characterised by non-stop news that changes very little throughout the day.

Citizen journalism

The RTL commercial television is one of the rate media and the only of the three national television stations, which has launched and is maintaining the project of 'citizen journalism'. The term "citizen or public journalism" derives from the USA of the 1980s, with the idea of citizens being made into 'active participants of a public discussion' (Grbesa 2005, p. 184-196). Although this model has been readily accepted with a lot of enthusiasm in many editorial rooms of local American papers it has also sparked a lot of criticism, as suspicions have been expressed about whether this idea is ethical, as written by Grbeša Marijana (2005). This form of content is also sometimes known as User Generated Content (UGC) and also as 'consumer-generated media' CGM (Krajina/Perišin 2009).

Media using this form regularly call on citizens to send in their video news and broadcast it in their Vijesti (news) show. When the topics are interesting they also follow up the story and send their reporters and own crews to the scene.

The news received by citizens and published is titled 'Your News' on RTL. This is also the name of the segment they broadcast regularly and where they call on citizens to participate.

At the RTL Internet page titled Look, UGC is the format where users by a simple click of the mouse upload their footage in categories like sport, fun, look, music, humour, animals etc. I have not found anywhere the heading 'Your News', but it can as such be found at the end of their news and current affairs broadcast.

When we speak of citizen journalism or journalism on the Internet, the obvious issue is that of bloggers and blogs. They do not even sign the articles with their full names and bloggers cannot be equated to journalists. There, of course, exist views that this also represents a form of journalism, as it should not be important what media it is expressed through. And in truth, if blogs are read with a little more care, it has to be said that some of them harbour genuine quality works of 'journalistic' calibre.

How is the information published on blogs checked, whether the information is genuinely impartial and well-presented and how this can be checked and who should be responsible for this? Despite the inability to answer these questions there has been an upsurge in the trust in blogs and the usage of information published on them.

According to Brautovic anyone can be a publisher on the Internet today (blogs, personal pages, YouTube, etc.), however not everything that is published on the Internet is journalism (Brautovic 2005). A journalist, according to Brautovic, is a person who publishes something that is in line with the basic ethics postulates of journalism which are: truthfulness, accuracy, balanced reporting and impartiality (Brautovic 2006).

Recently, reporters unhappy with the level of freedom of speech in the 'classic' media have started writing blogs or have launched their own Internet portals. Former Jutarnji list journalist Hrvoje Appelt has launched the [http://www.napadi-na-novinare.com] (attacks-on-journalists.com) page.

Conclusion

Although the government of the Republic of Croatia has adopted strategic documents under the joint title Program for e-Croatia, at lower levels that program is not developing as effectively as it was announced.

Despite huge progress in the realm of media legislation over the past few years it is clear that the Law on Electronic Media has not defined clearly enough the area of the new media and the production of content in the multi-platform sphere. At the moment, the new Law on Electronic Media and a new Law on HRT are being worked on.

Although Croatia had ambitiously set the date of the full transfer to digital television broadcasting as December 1, 2011, which is a year earlier than the European Commission had ordered, the implementation itself faced a number of problems. Citizens were not well informed and were also not motivated to purchase digital receivers. This was happening, among other things, because they did not understand whether they were being offered anything new. Public television has not managed to launch the two specialised digital channels, which should have prompted citizens to move more quickly from analogue to digital broadcasts. Also, there has not been enough public discussion, which would include reporters, media researchers, sociologists and not just engineers and technicians.

This is why in Croatia work is being done on improving media legislation, which should precisely define the guidelines for the development of technology and information structure and their role in the distribution of the content on different channels and different platforms. Also, the relationship between public and commercial television should be defined, as well as rules regarding the introduction of new content producers, which are taking up their space on the Internet. Apart from this, it is necessary to stimulate public discussion, research and monitor the media, which are following the level of information and technological structure and the impact of pluralism and the democratisation of the media on the development of the independent media.

References

Brautović, Mato (2005), 'Brze promjene uzrokuju zastarijevanje. Pregled literature iz Internetskog novinarstva' ('Swift Changes Cause Outdating. An Overview of Internet journalism literature'), *Medianali*, no. 3, pp. 167-178

Brautović, Mato (2006), 'Karakteristike novih medija u funkciji online novinarstva' ('Characteristics of the New Media in Online Journalism'), unpublished doctoral thesis, report in *Naše more* (2006), no. 53 (3-4), pp. 175-176

Grbeša, Marijana (2005), 'Kriza javnog komuniciranja i ideja građanskog novinarstva' ('The Crisis of Public Communication and the Idea of Citizens' Journalism'), *Političko obrazovanje*, Vol. 1, no. 3, pp. 184-196

Krajina, Zlatan/Tena Perišin (2009), 'Digitalne vijesti: Mediji, tehnologija i društvo' ('Digital News: Media, Technology and Society'), *Društveno istraživanje*, Vol.18, no.6, pp. 925-956

Malović, Stjepan (2007), 'Senzacionalizam; potreba tržišta, nemoć novinara ili imperative profita?' ('Sensationalism: A media necessity, the powerlessness of journalists or an imperative of profit?'), 21/11/2007 [http://www.media.ba/mcsonline/bs/tekst]

Quinn, Stephen/Vinecent Filak (2006), *Convergent Journalism An Introduction*, Focal Press

Perišin, Tena/Gordana Škaljac (2009), 'Uloga deska u organizaciji informativnog programa' ('The Role of Newsdesk in the Organisation of News and Current Affairs Programme'), *MediaAnali,* no. 5, pp. 203-228

Prijedlog Zakona o elektroničkim medijima, lipanj (2009), Proposed Bill on Electronic Media, June 2009

Strategija prelaska s analognog na digitalno emitiranje televizijskih programa na [http://www.hakom.hr/] Strategy of Transition from Analogue to Digital Broadcasts of TV Programmes [http://www.hakom.hr]

Zakon o izmjenama i dopunama Zakona o elektroničkim medijima, NN 32/08/Law on Changes and Amendments to Law on Electronic Media, Narodne Novine gazette 32/8

Zakon o izmjenama i dopunama Zakona o elektroničkim medijima, NN 79/07 Law on Changes and Amendments to Law on Electronic Media, Narodne Novine gazette

Zakon o elektroničkim medijima, NN 122/03 /Law on Electronic Media, Narodne Novine gazette 79/07

Zakon o izmjenama i dopunama Zakona o telekomunikacijama NN 70/05/ Law on Changes and Amendments to Law on Electronic Media, Narodne Novine gazette 70/05

Zakon o izmjenama i dopunama Zakona o telekomunikacijama, NN 60/03/ Law on Changes and Amendments to the Law on Telecommunications Narodne Novine gazette 60/03

Zakon o izmjenama i dopunama Zakona o telekomunikacijama NN 158/03 Law on Changes and Amendments to the Law on Telecommunications Narodne Novine gazette 158/03

Zakon o telekomunikacijama, 122/03/Law on Telecommunications 122/03

Zakon o HRT, NN 25/03/ Law on HRT, Narodne Novine gazette 25/03

[http://www.gfk.hr]

[http://www.hakom.hr]

[http://www.hurin.hr]

[http://www.weekendmediafestival.com]

Nada Zgrabljić-Rotar – Silvio Šop

Creating the Profile of a New Radio: The Case of Croatian Radio

> *"The world we are living in is not one I would have created on my own drawing board, but it's the one in which I must live, and in which the students I teach must live". (Marshall McLuhan[1])*

The draft Audiovisual Media Services (AVMS) Directive, ready for adoption in 2007, says: "The Resolution concerning public service broadcasting reaffirmed that the fulfilment of the public service broadcasting's mission must continue to benefit from technological progress. The co-existence of private and public audiovisual media service providers is a future which distinguishes the European audiovisual media market". The Council of Europe, Committee of Ministers (2007) The recommendation states that "public service media should use 'new interactive technologies' and should be 'present on significant platforms', and 'in view of changing user habits, public service media should be able to offer both generalist and specialised contents and services, as well as personalised and on-demand services'". It seems that "PSM is still needed in the digital world", (Jakubowicz 2007), but there is a lot of work ahead for public radio in order to survive in this new environment and to keep its listeners in view of the recent trend of fragmentation and disappearance of audience.[2]

Old versus new: analogue versus digital

It was all straightforward until the beginning of the 1990s: analogue equipment, linear broadcasting, one platform. But then came digitization, the Internet followed, and things will never be the same for radio ever again. Digitization came quietly, with CDs replacing records. This change was widely accepted very enthusiastically: The new media was a lot easy to operate and store than the records, sound was superior too and there were far fewer possibilities to damage the CD than the record.

The real transition from analogue to digital equipment came in the early 1990s, with the development of PCs, now able to handle audio. Large quantities of songs, opening titles, jingles and all other radio material was converted to digital (usually to MPEG 1 layer 2 format, also known as MP 2), and the radio programme was automatized for the first time in history.

---

1 From "The Playboy Interview: Marshall McLuhan", Playboy Magazine (March 1969).
2 More on the subject of audience and the cultural aspects of digitalization in Marshall (2004).

Then came the Internet. Radio as a secondary media was well prepared – instead of depending on the power of the terrestrial transmitter, programmes broadcasted over the Internet can be heard anywhere in the world, wherever an Internet connection is available. With the development of special algorithms, AAC, AAC+ (now known as HE-AAC, High Efficiency Audio Advanced Coding) the quality of sound was equal or sometimes better than the quality of sound over terrestrial FM transmitter. The transition from FM-only broadcast to broadcast over the Internet, which is a completely new platform, and in AAC(+) format, which is a completely different format, can be seen as the first media convergence in radio, concerning both format and platform change, or, better to say, extension.

Looking at modern radio broadcasting, to be able to say that a station is multimedia/convergence adapted, three conditions must be fulfilled:

1) Multiplatform – beside broadcasting over terrestrial transmitters, the station must be on air through the second platform. This is usually an Internet stream, playing the same programme that is also on terrestrial FM transmitters. This is essential, but stations that are more multimedia orientated usually provide many different kinds of content on their web pages: podcasts, audio on demand, special Internet-only programmes.

2) Multiformat – analogue programmes broadcasted over terrestrial transmitters must be available in other formats. Most commonly these are streamed over the Internet, usually in Windows Media, Real or AAC+ format. Many stations' own produced material usually can be downloaded from the Internet, in MP3 as the most common format.

3) Non-linear broadcast – the main difference between analogue and digital: while programs broadcasted analogue over terrestrial transmitters must be listened to at exactly the same time, non-linear audio can be obtained and listen-to whenever is the most convenient time for the listeners. With the introduction of radio to the Internet, many consumers are able to listen to audio content when, where and on whichever device they like, and some predictions say that the number of non-linear consumers will rise rapidly in the next 20 years, surpassing the number of linear listeners.

Case studies – EBU Public Service Broadcasters

As an illustration of public service broadcasters undertaking organizational changes, expanding content distribution and marketing strategies to adjust to the evolving Internet climate, case studies of four PSBs were undertaken: Danish Radio and Television (DR), Swedish radio (SR), the BBC and the Dutch NPO. In the following the authors present the brief highlights of the above-mentioned PBS on their role in multimedia convergence surroundings.

1) Danish Radio and Television

- The newly implemented DR organization maintains a strict distinction between commissioned and in-house media production, with production units making programming content across the boundaries of radio, TV and Internet
- dr.dk is the most popular media site in Denmark, with a weekly reach of 18 per cent and a monthly reach of 40 per cent. The site is the one of the largest Internet news providers in the country
- new distribution techniques like P2P have already been tested for live streaming of special events
- to encourage user participation and promote democratic values, interactive blogging, debates and political as well as local initiatives will be launched or extended
- according to DR, market fragmentation is one of the major trends that will influence their business most in the future. Audiences moving towards more individualized viewing means that website content needs to offer more personalized services.
The DR budget for new media online content is about 10 million Euros, excluding technical costs, such as hardware and software.

2) Swedish Radio (SR)
- SR New Media's main focus is to establish a strong position on the Internet and to bring programmes to users through new distribution platforms. They want to become market leaders for web and mobile radio and to give users freedom in terms of time and space
- content is distributed through multiple channels and the on-demand service contains all FM, DAB and Internet-only programmes. SR reaches about 8 per cent of the Swedes through their web-radio on a weekly basis
- as a part of its public service mission online news is delivered in 16 languages and one of the most popular national channels has developed a community aimed especially at younger people
- SR sees relevant content and on-demand as key for the future of public service
The Swedish Radio Internet budget is approximately one million Euros.

3) British Broadcasting Corporation (BBC)
- the BBC's vision is to be the most creative broadcasting organization in the world and their future plans rely heavily on new technologies and creative partnerships
- bbc.co.uk has over 15 million unique visitors in the UK each week and is one of Britain's most popular websites
- the BBC launched the iPlayer, an interactive catch-up service on the Internet, allowing UK license fee payers to download programmes from all the BBC's network TV channels

- to get a wider content distribution the BBC has partnered with sites like YouTube, Flickr and Yahoo!
- several initiatives have been launched to drive audience participation and create a direct link with consumers. Most recently the BBC opened a special division for Social Networks
- the BBC is continuously looking for external media partners to create new audience services

The BBC's on-line budget is unknown.

4) Nederlandse Omroep Stiching (NPO)
- two new departments, Internet and New Media, have been incorporated into the organizational structure of NPO as a reflection of the developments of on-line media distribution
- unlike the BBC, NPO carries advertising on the Internet websites and the on-demand video material to digital TV operators is the main source of Internet revenue
- like many other public broadcasters NPO has chosen to cooperate with YouTube as a way to maximize audience reach
- NPO sees on-demand distribution becoming more popular and believes that on-demand might be the second biggest opportunity for the future next to linear TV and radio broadcasting

The NPO Internet and New Media budget is unknown.

Croatia moving towards a digital Europe – new media law

Croatian authorities are preparing a new media law, which can meet the requirements both of the European Union and of the new technologies that were not mentioned in the previous law.[3] In the Introduction section authors emphasize that the new law on electronic media is necessary, because the new Directive on audiovisual media services, which was adopted by EU Parliament and Council on 11th December 2007, besides television or radio programmes, as linear services, also regulates audiovisual services on-demand as non-linear services. The new Directive also regulates audiovisual commercial communications, product placement, audiovisual programmes and the Program Director's responsibilities. TV broadcast includes analogue and digital broadcasting as different categories, live coverage and Internet broadcasting, and video-on-demand as a special audiovisual media service. In the existing Croatian Media Law there is no regulations for the new audiovisual services, which are the result of fast development in technology and digitization. The new law, for the first time, will regulate conditions for audio and audiovisual on-demand services, which providers must meet. Audiovisual on-demand service,

3 More about media policy for the digital age in Croatia in Peruško/Popović (2008).

by proposed definition, is a service, which providers provide when a user chooses a certain audiovisual content from the provider's catalogue. Audio media service on-demand is a radio service, which providers provide when a user chooses a certain audio content from the provider's catalogue. Also, for the first time the term "specialized channel" is introduced, regulating channels, which must include a scheme, which specifies the type of program, of which over 70 per cent must be equivalent programs. Services that are protected by the media of television and radio services provided for a fee and on conditioned access, or providing access to the previously mentioned conditioned media services such services itself. They are coded services, toll TV and similar. The adoption of the proposed law performing the activities of audio and/or audiovisual media service providers shall be harmonized with the Directive on audiovisual media services (Directive 2007/65/EZ which amended Directive 89/552/EEZ Television without Frontiers) Directive 98/84 / EC on the legal protection of services based on conditioned access and services that provide access to and conditioned part of the terms and 206/114/EZ Directive on misleading and comparative advertising, each with its views of governing the area of audiovisual media services. It will also regulate for the providers of media services, media services with existing television and radio, to edit, and ability to provide new services such as audiovisual media services at the request and utilization of all available distribution platforms (terrestrial, satellite, cable and internet) on the basis of obtaining a concession or approval.

Croatian PBS – Croatian Radio and Television

Croatian Radio and Television is the Croatian Public Broadcasting Service. Croatian Radio Television has three organizational units, three sister companies – Croatian Radio *(Hrvatski radio)*, Croatian Television *(Hrvatska televizija)* and Music Production *(Glazbena proizvodnja)*. [4]The HRT is mainly financed by viewer/listener license fees (currently 79 Croatian Kuna per month) and advertising (currently a maximum of 9 minutes per hour). Croatian Radio *(Hrvatski radio)*, which is the main subject of this paper, features thirteen channels:

- National radio channels
  - HR 1, which mostly does serious mosaic programmes, with regular news every full hour.
  - HR 2, which mostly airs entertainment mosaic programmes, with news usually every hour at the half-hour mark.
  - HR 3, which is mostly for classical music and similar programmes.

---

[4] More about the broadcast concept and program of Croatian Radio in Zgrabljić Rotar (2007).

- Local radio channels
    - HR Sljeme, Local station for Zagreb
    - HR Rijeka, Local station for Rijeka
    - HR Pula, Local station for Pula
    - HR Osijek, Local station for Osijek
    - HR Split, Local station for Split
    - HR Zadar, Local station for Zadar
    - HR Knin, Local station for Knin
- International station for Croatian Immigrants
    - Glas Hrvatske (Voice of Croatia)
- Internet radio channels
    - HR Stream 1 – Croatian music
    - HR Stream 2 – International music
    - HR Stream 3 – best of Science-Educational-Children-Cultural and Drama programme

History

Croatia was among the first countries in Central and Eastern Europe to establish a radio station – to be more precise – on 15 May 1926. Croatian television made its appearance on the same date thirty years later and, at the time, it was perceived as quite a phenomenon. At 8:30 p.m. on 15 May 1926, beginning with the sounds of the Croatian National Anthem and an announcement read by Božena Begović, followed by a speech by Dr. Stern, Radio Zagreb was heard for the first time on the frequency MW 350 m. That night, the listeners were able to hear the radio station's official bulletin, music by L.v. Beethoven, J. Haydn, F. Chopin, J. Ph. Rameau, and C. Saint-Saens, concluding with a 15-minute news program. The first on-site broadcasts began in the autumn, while the first live coverage took place at the unveiling of J.J. Strossmeyer's monument in November. Later that month, two more live broadcasts of the operas, "The Sea" and "The Rusalka" were aired from the Croatian National Theatre. It continued with broadcasts of the masses from St. Mark's and other churches. By December, Radio Zagreb was among the first radio stations in Europe to invite public participation in the creation of original manuscripts for radio plays. In 1934 the radio transmitter from the Upper Town of Zagreb was relocated to the shores of the river Sava, where Radio Zagreb had already erected a new system of antennae and a new building. In 1940 the Government nationalized the property of the shareholder's company – Radio Zagreb, and a new Managing Board led by Vladimir Kovačević took over the radio station. The Government authorities of what was then the Banovina of Croatia, made it possible for the radio station to acquire new equipment and to move into new, considerably larger premises at the beginning of November of that year. In 1942 the transmitter in Zagreb was upgraded to 10 kW. Local radio stations in Dubrovnik, Sarajevo, and Banja Luka also began broadcasting. In 1943 a local radio station in Osijek started broadcasting. In 1945 Radio Split began broadcasting in April, while Radio Rijeka went on air in September. In 1953 Radio Sljeme began broadcasting in the Zagreb region. In 1961 Radio Pula began broadcasting on New Year's Day. From 1964 to 1965 Radio Zagreb underwent programming and organizational restructuring, which created three separate radio channels: Radio Zagreb 1, Radio Zagreb 2, and Radio Zagreb 3. Each channel had separate editorial boards. In 1968 Radio Zadar began broadcasting. On the 50th anniversary of Radio Zagreb, 1976 Radio Zagreb 1 began broadcasting around the clock. Radio Zagreb programs, along with those of local radio stations were now being broadcast by 39MW transmitters with a total power output of 626 kW and 22 VHF transmitters and translators with a total power output of 158 kW. In June 1990, the Croatian Parliament adopted an act to rename Radio-Television Zagreb to Croatian Radio-Television (Hrvatska radiotelevizija: HRT). The period from July 1991 to February 1992 was marked by a brutally aggressive war waged against Croatia. During the war, 80 per cent of Croatia's transmitters and more than 30 TV translators were either occupied or damaged – some were totally destroyed. As one of the successors to the former Yugoslav Radio-Television (JRT) umbrella organization, the HRT in 1993 gained full "active" membership in the European Broadcasting Union (EBU). In October 1994, Croatian Radio News was aired from the HRT Broadcasting Centre at Prisavlje. In February 1995, the main control room at Šubićeva Street was relocated to the new main control room at Prisavlje. This meant that all three channels of Croatian Radio, alongside Radio Sljeme, were aired from the new HRT Broadcasting Centre. The same year HRT established an Internet page at [http://www.hrt.hr]. The following year audio streaming of national channels started in Real and Windows Media format. In January 1997, Radio Sljeme began broadcasting around the clock; in October Channel 2 of Croatian Radio followed, and in December Channel 3 of Croatian Radio. In September, Croatian Radio began test broadcasts of all three of its programs using digital technology simultaneously via a T-DAB 800 W transmitter installed on Sljeme. In May 2003, "Voice of Croatia", a radio program for Croatians abroad in Croatian, English and Spanish, began airing around the clock. The program began airing in 2001, but in a more condensed form. Apart from fully equipping its new recording studio and obtaining two modern (multi-track) digital OB vans, Croatian Radio in 2004 also built an integrated system for the acquisition, production and broadcasting of 5 channels – something that included the digitalization and unification of the existing sound and archive libraries. [5]

---

5 McLuhan contends that all media – in and of themselves and regardless of the messages

Croatian radio – digitization

As mentioned before, Croatian Radio in 2004 built an integrated system for the acquisition, production and broadcasting of 5 channels – something that included the digitalization and unification of the existing sound and archive libraries. It was the beginning of a tremendous effort, because the musical archives of the Croatian Radio are the richest in Southeast Europe. Digitizing affected 40 thousand stereo tapes containing pop music, 22 thousand mono pop music recordings, 15 thousand recordings of classical music and 12 thousand recordings of folk music.

The whole project actually started 2 years before, in 2002, with the establishment of Newsroom network, as an ancestor to Tehnet production and on-air network, established in 2003. It is a network of computers with a central server, designed to meet all Croatian Radio needs for storing, producing, editing and playing all kinds of audio material. It is based on two computer programs: AVID iNews, system for obtaining, editing and producing text news and NETIA Radio Assist, system for recording, importing, exporting, editing and playing audio sound bites. The play-out system is also product of NETIA, on-air module AIR DDO. In the next few years all Croatian Radio departments will be networked in the Netia system, as well as regional centres (radio stations). Centres are connected with Zagreb by permanent flow connections 20, 10 or a minimum of 6 Mb/s. In 2006 MEDIARC was purchased – a system of digital archives to catalogue records and a system for digitizing music from tape, records and CDs. The actual digitization of recordings started in 2007, with the digitization of the pop music catalogue. All CDs are digitized in uncompressed .wav 16 bit 44.1 kHz format, while all recordings on tapes and records are digitized in .wav 48 kHz 24 bit format, to be able to digitally clean more noises and hums. So far, about 100 thousand recordings of popular music have been digitized, and another 200 thousand recordings await digitization. Archive capacity scheduled for the first phase of digitization is 10 TB, of which 8 have already been filled. The assumed need for the whole digitization of the current archive is 75 TB, with an annual increase of 3 to 5 TB. It is estimated that the time period for digitizing the entire archive will be between 5 and 10 years.

---

they communicate – exert a compelling influence on man and society. According to McLuhan, there have been three basic technological innovations: the invention of the phonetic alphabet, which jolted tribal man out of his sensory balance and gave dominance to the eye; the introduction of movable type in the 16th century, which accelerated this process; and the invention of the telegraph in 1844, which heralded an electronics revolution that will ultimately retribalize man by restoring his sensory balance.

Croatian radio – audio streams project

In December 2008 came an idea about launching Internet-only programs for Croatian Radio. As the primary reasons we can give the optimal number of high-speed Internet connections that will allow listening without interruption, as well as the growing convergence of radio content to another platform – the web. The initial idea was to include 4 programs: Stream 1 – Croatian music, Stream 2 – international music, Stream 3 – talk program (HR talk) and Stream 4 – classical music. A trial broadcast took place in January last year in two sound qualities: 48 kbit/s and 96 kbit/s, HE-AAC format (formerly known as AAC +). The idea was that even listeners with old analogue modems can enjoy smooth and uninterrupted listening stream quality 48 kbit/s. In the course of the international public tender for an Internet broadcast service provider Croatian Radio selected the Canadian company Streamtheworld, which in the past 12 months, which is how long the Internet broadcast of Croatian Radio programmes has been in progress, has never failed, not even for one single minute! The company also provided Flash player for Internet broadcast. Each broadcast via the Internet consists of four stages, or links in the chain: play out systems, processing, encoding and distribution. In our case, the broadcasting program is NETIA, which requires a sound card, Digigram, so it had to be included in the mandatory equipment. Its function, in the case of any other playout programs (programs for the radio automation like Jazzler or Zara radio), is taken by the Orban card, which also processes the sound to match the dynamics and quality of listening to the radio via terrestrial or satellite transmitters. Encoding audio is performed by the Streamtheworld company via their encoder, and as a result audio appears in two formats: HE-AAC (High Efficiency AAC, also known as AAC+) and MP3. The specificity of broadcasting over the Streamtheworld company is also a system known as "MP3 fall back" – if the end user does not have a computer version of the Flash program that is required to listen to streams, the server automatically sends the MP3 format, noting that the player is needs to upgrade Flash for listening in high quality. The first two streams that were introduced in January 2009 attracted great attention of the audience, and during the first month over 35 thousand connections were recorded. Also encouraging was the time spent listening to stream – more than one hour on average. At the end of July 2009 all terrestrial Croatian Radio programs (with the exception of Radio Knin, which is currently in progress to ensure an audio route to Zagreb) were also transferred to the HE-AAC broadcasting format, in a quality of 64 kbit/s. There were many reasons to transfer, just to name a few: 1) the sound quality was notably worse in previous streaming via Windows Media and Real formats 2) higher bit rate format and worse sound 3) frequent broken links and buffering 4) statistics on the number of listeners were difficult to come by and hard to interpret, regions and listening time. Switch proved to be a big hit – the number of listeners of radio programs via the Internet grew from 43,788 in July to

89,149 in August, more than 100 per cent! We have also been swamped with e-mail messages from enthusiastic listeners who pointed out that Croatian Radio has finally adopted 21st century technology and they can finally enjoy a continuous program in top-quality sound. We were more than satisfied – predictions on the number of listeners of all HR programs online had been exceeded by far!

According to the definition of public media, there are three basic functions to be met: to inform, educate and entertain. Croatian radio, the only non-commercial radio provider in Croatia, is the only producer of children's programmes, educational programmes, drama programmes and cultural programmes. Expanding its role to the other media platforms – the Internet – Croatian Radio launched Stream 3 – HR Talk, an Internet voice program. It consists of a selection of children's shows, educational, cultural and scientific and drama programmes from Croatian Radio. The broadcast scheme is a daily 6 hour premiere programmes and 18 hours of re-run programmes, so the audience can listen to some shows when it best suits them – morning, afternoon, evening or night. Broadcast Stream 3 – HR talk began on 19th October 2009. According to statistics, about 1500 listeners tune in every month.

Croatian radio – future plans

The creation of a custom player for the Croatian radio programs that are broadcast via the Internet (customized player) is in progress. It will be possible on a single programming interface to select which program you want to listen to and through the same interface you will be able to follow the latest news headlines from the HRT website (with the possibility of opening the news by single click), there will be an EPG (electronic program guide) with information about the content of the selected program, a weather window, and a multifunctional window that can be used for advertising space for static or dynamic advertising (jpeg or flash), or as space for a variety of information. We believe that with an appealing interface we will attract more Internet listeners, who will be better informed and will have more reason to stay on the stream for longer. Stream 4, classical music, is scheduled for later this year. The reason for this delay is the small number of digitized records in the system so far.

References

Cavell, Richard (2002), *McLuhan in Space: A Cultural Geography*. Toronto: University of Toronto Press

Crowley, David/Paul Heyer (1991), *Communication in History. Technology, Culture, S ociety*, New York, London, Longman

Berger, Richard (2004), 'Digital Media Futures', in D. Gauntlett/R. Horsley (eds.), *Web.Studies*, London, Arnold, pp. 274-285

Ferguson, R. (2004), *The Media in Question,* London, Arnold

Jakubowitz, K. (2007), 'Public Service Broadcasting in the 21st Century. What Chance for a New Beginning?', in G. Ferrell Love/J. Bardoel (eds.), *From Public Service Broadcasting to Public Service Media,* Goteborg, Nordicom, pp. 29-51

Krug, Gary (2006), *Communication, Technology and Cutural Change,* London, SAGE

Marshall, P.D. (2004), *New Media Culture,* London, New York, Cambridge University Press

Peruško, Z./H. Popović (2008), 'From Transmission to the Public Good: Media Policy for the Digital Age in Croatia', in M. Sukosd/A. Isanovic (eds.), *Public Service Television in the Digital Age: Strategies and Opportunities in Five South-East European Countries,* Mediacentar Sarajevo

Shulzycki, Alexander (ed.) (2007), 'Broadcasters and the Internet – EBU Members' Internet Presence', European Broadcast Union, Geneva

Zgrabljić Rotar, Nada (2007), *Radio - mit i informacija, dijalog i demokracija,* Zagreb, Golden Marketing i tehnička knjiga

[http://www.mcluhan.utoronto.ca/tsc_mcluhan_basic_innovations.htm]

[http://www.mcluhanmedia.com/mmclpb01.html] 'The Playboy Interview: Marshall McLuhan', Playboy Magazine, March 1969 [http://www.playboy.com/]

Stjepan Malović

The Double Standards of the EU Media Companies

Introduction

The Croatian media are in deep crisis. The Parliamentary Media Committee concluded in March 2010 that the media situation has never been worse. In its annual report for 2009 the Reporters Sans Frontiers organization passed very deflating remarks about media freedom in Croatia. According to their evaluation, Croatia was downgraded from 33rd to 69th place in their list. Such a negative score shocked the Croatian public.

What is happening to the Croatian media? Why now, after 20 years of democracy and transition, are the media worse than ever? Is it a result of the negative role of local politicians? Or, is it a result of the low professional level of journalists and editors? What is the role of the publishers and media owners? What are the reasons for such a negative evaluation?

The Croatian media has managed, supported by international media institutions, to achieve a relatively high level of media freedom. It is no longer possible for an eminent politician to directly calls the editor of the prime time TV news and command what should be published and what is not allowed. Such behaviour belongs to history.

Most media analysts, scientists and journalists from developed European countries write or speak very critically about changes that have happened in the last ten years in their states: from trivialized media content, total commercialization and tyranny of strong media owners to the formal change of format of broadsheet toward tabloid papers. One very important fact is that in these states, the audience still has the chance to read genuinely serious newspapers. In comparison, in the SEE region mostly, readers, listeners and viewers do not have such an opportunity. We are completely submerged by bad media products owned by West European media tycoons.

The level of the professional standard of Croatian journalists is better than before, thanks to the various state and private studies of journalism, communications science and public relations.

One of the possible answers lies in the media itself. The key players in the media are publishers and owners. They make the decisions about media content. They tell journalists how to report. They develop relationships to the advertisers and sign contracts for media financing under undisclosed conditions. They are involved with companies in other realms of business not related to media and communication. And, they sell and buy media outlets on the market, deciding which media will survive, and which will become bankrupt.

The Croatian media market is owned by global media corporations: German WAZ and Austrian Styria own almost 90 per cent of the daily newspaper market. The two national commercial TV stations (*Nova TV* and *RTL*) are also foreign-owned. Adria Media Holding controls the market for magazines and revues in Croatia, Slovenia and Serbia, owning the majority of weekly and monthly newspapers.

The first impression is that the Croatian media respect and act according to EU media standards and that the days of the Soviet media model are far behind us. Unfortunately, this is not true. Global corporations are implementing the worst elements of EU media standards and relicts of the Soviet media model are still present.

Result: public and media experts were never so disappointed by media content!

What a disappointment to all of Croatian citizens who were dreaming about a time when the Croatian media would be integrated into EU media standards, offering the same products as in the democratic Western countries.

What happened? Why are Croatian media not implementing the good professional standards typical for the Western media? Especially when the owners of the Croatian media are well known Western media companies!

The same story is happening in the other South East European countries in transition. Is the global corporative journalism negative in general or are local SEE media not capable of producing quality products?

Why do global corporations not respect the EU media standards in the same way as they do in their home countries? Why do they not produce high-quality media or promote serious journalism?

Profit is the answer to all these questions. All corporations want, is to earn as much profit as fast as possible. Everything else is irrelevant to them. Even the great words of freedom and independence of the media what the international promoters of media freedom and democracy were pronounced to SEE media.

Profit is best achieved by releasing the ads. If the corporation owns a large number of media in the region, it can distribute promotional messages on a larger market. The media have become the platform for the ads. The same ad, only in another language, can be seen in Croatia, Serbia, Slovenia, Montenegro, but also in Hungary, Romania, etc. Advertisers do not want a serious and high quality media for their ads. They prefer those, which are distributed on the broader market. Serious and quality media are not popular enough and corporations cannot place ads in quality media. It is much better to use the best-selling media and to cover the bigger market. Thus the circle is closed and the media scene is irreversibly vulgarized.

Transitional problems of the Croatian media

Croatian media roots stem from the former, Communist Yugoslavian system. Basically, it is the Soviet Media Model, but just as the Yugoslav version of Communism was softer than the original version, the same happened to media also. The media of former Yugoslavia served the ruling Communist Party, but it was allowed to practice some good journalistic standards.

Nevertheless, we have to acknowledge the influence of the Soviet Media Model on the Yugoslavian press, including the Croatian media. Wilbur Schramm, author of the Soviet Media Model theory defined it as a system where media and journalists report mainly about the ruling party, neglecting real news values.

The Yugoslav media model was softer: journalists never criticized President Tito, Communism or JNA (Yugoslav National Army), but were allowed to criticize low ranking officials and publish news from the Western world.

The strong roots of Communism can be better understood if we consider that almost every working Croatian citizen was born in this system! The generation from 1945 is going to retire this year. This means that they were all educated during the period of Communism. They bring with them the social values, morals and the understanding of life based on the Communist ideology! Only the younger generation, born in 1990 and later, is without direct Communist influence, but they have not had a chance to change anything. At least one more generation will have to pass before the Communist roots will vanish.

The Communist way of life, morals, and the understanding of social relations are having a great impact on the media role in society. There is no longer any direct influence of Communism, but political parties still maintain the same understanding of the role of media. Politicians, like Franjo Tuđman, the first president of the new, independent Croatia, wanted to control the media. And he did this very successfully.

"In this view appears overly pessimistic, you must set your 'history channel' back to the period between the two 'Ts' – Tito and Tuđman. Those were the critical years in which the present relationship among the press, the people and the political system in Croatia took form. The three elements were mutually depressing and progressively destructive to the fabric of society. Political leaders restrained the press and the people, the press became a promotional extension of the government. The people, cowed by the government and ignored by the press, demanded little from either institution. It was negative synergy, a cycle of complacency, compliance and control." (Malović/Selnowary 2001, pp. 3-4)

The decade of Tuđman's rule was also characterised by a cruel war and aggression by Serbian forces, including the JNA and paramilitary Serbian units lead by Milošević, hundreds of thousands of refugees and displaced persons, heavy damages, leaving cities and industry destroyed. All of this influenced the role of the media. The media were under the control of Tuđman's party. Only a few independent media, such as *Feral Tribune*, criticized the government. Slavko Goldstein, an independent intellectual, described it like this: "Media are either pro government or contra. There is nothing in between".

One of the best-known cases of broadcast control was the governments' repression of *Radio 101*, an independent radio in Zagreb. "With an ownership and editorial board that was not afraid to criticize the party, the station found itself in hot water in November 1996. The Telecommunications Council had already rejected the station's application for a long-term operating license. Bruising stories in the world press led to an unprecedented demonstration by 100.000 people in Zagreb's main square. Finally, in the face of intense public pressure *Radio 101* was allowed to broadcast."[1]

The public were aware of the importance of free media and under such pressure journalists were granted more freedom, which resulted in the electoral victory of the opposition parties in January 2000.

The long period of control was over. Media freedom had been achieved. The Croatian media market was open to international influences. It was a clear sign for global media corporations to enter into the Croatian market.

International monitoring and evaluation

During the decade of Tuđman's media control, the international community did not remain passive. A great number of international media monitoring organizations were present in the country, carefully evaluating what was happening, and trying to implement Western democratic media values.
Numerous media organizations such as Press Now from the Netherlands, BBC, Deutsche Welle, The Guardian, The Thompson Foundation, IREX, IPI and others were present in the country working on developing various activities, mostly training and dissemination of media freedom and independent journalism.

International organizations such as OSCE, Helsinki Committee, Open Society Institute, Unidea, German foundations like Konrad Adenauer Stiftung, Friedrich Ebert Stiftung and others developed different activities.

Under such influences two media organizations were founded by the journalists and local media centres. The first one was SEENPM: South East European Network for Professionalization of Media (Sarajevo 2000) and SEEMO: South East European Media Organizations (Zagreb 2002), affiliated to the International Press Institute (IPI) based in Vienna.

---

[1] Ibid, p. 8.

All these institutions were very active during the Nineties. The funds earmarked for media activities in Croatia were significant. Some donors supported independent media, such as *Feral Tribune,* or founded new media, such as *Tjednik*.

International donors assisted in the education of journalists, including the organization of study trips to the major media companies in the world. Many eminent journalists from all over the world were engaged to train their Croatian colleagues.

It was a significant help, which resulted in a better understanding of free media and independent journalism.

Stojan Obradovic, media expert from the STINA news agency and eminent journalist, stated:

"The Croatian media has succeeded to a great extent in freeing itself from the steel hold of the authorities, but the media situation in Croatia is still unregulated and in many aspects below European democratic standards. Transformation of Croatian Radio-Television (HRT), the most powerful medium in the country, from a partisan and state television into a public service, started a couple of years ago, has still not been fully completed. HRT is still not fully shaped either legally or in terms of programming. Frequent changes of laws which each government urges raise a lot of doubts as to whether their aim is real transformation of television into a public service or establishing some new form of political control."[2]

A typical example of the misuse of media coverage is provided by the elections. The international community was monitoring the presidential elections in 1997. Some monitors presented shocking data on media coverage.

"The Press Now (Netherlands) reports that, in the days leading up to the (1997) presidential election, the main daily news programme gave President Tuđman eight to twelve times more coverage than the other two candidates combined."[3]

Malovic and Selnow report: "Faced with dirty tricks of this calibre, the OSCE final report declared the election "free, but not fair". In Croatia, independent news shows never mentioned this report. HRTV news (Croatian public television) quoted OSCE as saying that the elections were "free". Somehow, they could not squeeze in the words "not fair". (Malović/Selnow 2001, p. 9)

Training of journalist became very important, especially because the existing education of journalists in Croatia was based on theory mostly, less on practical skills. Therefore, the Croatian Journalists' Association founded the

---

2 [http://www.mediaonline.ba/en/?ID=209]

3 *Press Now* citing 1997 OSCE report.

International Centre for Education of Journalists (ICEJ), the main task of which was to train young journalists in basic journalism.

During the annual meeting in Zaton in October 1997, Croatian journalists concluded that they needed to pay more attention to the education and training of journalists, especially the young, who sometimes join newsrooms without any previous knowledge, literally off the street. The Croatian Journalists' Association (CJA) has opened its doors to numerous local and international organizations dedicated to educating journalists but it wasn't satisfied with existing forms of training. The majority of international organizations concentrated on general issues such as media freedom, producing no significant influence on the majority of journalists. That was why CJA initiated the idea of providing permanent education for young journalists, which would be organized and carried out by CJA with the financial and expert support of international organizations whose field of activity is the advancement of media freedom. That was the beginning of the Journalistic Workshop that started in February 1997 and enabled the training of more than a hundred young journalists coming from all parts of Croatia by the end of 1998. (Malović/Vilović 1999, p. 8)

Another educational program, based on the qualities of the Western press, was Advanced European Media Training (AEMT), sponsored by UNIDEA and realized in ICEJ in cooperation with the Jacques Maritaine Institute from Trieste.

All these training activities were for the promotion of good journalism and EU standards of reporting. Hundreds of young journalists received proper knowledge about independent journalism. They were always disappointed that it did not seem possible to implement such standards in the Croatian media, looking to the future and waiting for the kind of media ownership that would fulfil their desires.

Tuđman's party lost the elections in 2000, simultaneously with a general donors' fatigue related to the former Yugoslavian crisis. Donors had no more funds. The new crisis areas, like in Afghanistan, Iraqi and Iran, became more important than the former YU region and most of the programs were shifted or reduced.

At the same time global media corporations started to show an interest in buying local media companies or investing in new media projects, such as commercial TV channels.

The Croatian media were left alone, journalists lost the international support and the doors to the new media relationship were opened.

In his column published in the daily newspaper *Jutarnji list* (23.03.2010, p. 22) Miljenko Jergović, a Croatian writer, wrote: "At that time there were Soros and his Open Society Fund. Freedom of speech and journalists' right in Croatia and in the region are closely monitored by State Department and the hundreds of

European delegations, missions and commissions, and today is all around us somehow deaf and lonely."

Corporations are arriving

The first Croatian experiences with global media corporations happened in 1990, when the late British media mogul Robert Maxwell wanted to buy the biggest publishing company, *Vjesnik*. This buyout failed, but for the first time Croatian journalists experienced the possibility that their company could be sold, which was a completely shocking experience, unknown in the former Yugoslavian socialist country.

Whether it is a good thing or not, for the next ten years international media corporations were not present on the Croatian media market, until the new opposition Government was elected in 2000, no doors were opened to the international media companies.

Then, corporations came to the new market, which was relatively small, but promising as an entrance to the greater market of similar languages in the Western Balkans.

Today, the Croatian media market is largely owned by global media corporations. Austria's *Styria* owns the dailies *24 hours, Poslovni dnevnik* and *Večernji list*. Together, *Styria* and the German *WAZ* own almost 90 per cent of the daily newspaper market. Even revues and magazines are mostly owned by foreign corporations. At one time, when Communism disappeared, and when democracy was knocking at the door of Croatia, we were all waiting for the media standards that apply in the West. But, very soon the corporations had bought every media that had any value. Not only in Croatia, but also in all the neighbouring countries in transition.

What a disappointment! Corporations not only vulgarized professional standards, but also adopted the worst type of journalism based on sensationalism, gossip, and resulted in the tabloids. Suddenly we are facing "yellow journalism" of the worst kind.

The European norm has been reached, but as Mehmed Halilovic, media ombudsman from Bosnia and Hercegovina says: "Journalists have not profited too much."

The consequences are serious: corporative journalism brought sensationalism, tabloidization and infotainment. In Croatia quality newspapers no longer exist, the public broadcasting service produces commercial media content, journalists – especially well-educated ones – have lost their jobs, and the advertising industry is imposing its interests.

WAZ Empire is a typical example: as a result of the corporative form of journalism the correspondent offices of the daily newspapers *Jutarnji list* and *Slobodna Dalmacija* were combined, the newly founded EPEHA news agency now reports for all WAZ media. *Slobodna Dalmacija*, once the best edited daily newspaper was turned into a tabloid, journalists are fired if they do not implement sensationalism in their reporting ... Journalists are afraid to talk about such pressure for fear of losing their jobs.

A similar situation exists in the other global media corporations. The Styria products *Večernji list* and *24 sata* have received international awards from WAN-IFRA and IPI, eminent international media organizations. The awards were bestowed for the most innovative daily newspaper and the best web site. It is a great success on the international media market, showing how the world media leaders are evaluating the role of the newspapers. Styria managers proudly announce how they are developing a content company, whatever that means. It is possible only if the newsrooms turn into an integrated newsroom and if they apply converged journalism. In practice, it means that a reporter sends short news bulletins for the SMS Breaking News service during the parliamentary sessions. Immediately after that the reporter sends news for the web site, simultaneously taking photos and making a video report. After the end of the parliamentary session, the reporter sends the new version of the news. Later, he writes a new version for the print edition. In short, the reporter is serving several different media, without having time to check the information, look for other sources, and investigate the background of the information. The result of such reporting is that the public knows only the basic facts and has no possibility to be better informed about a crucial decision made by Parliament or any other institution.

The result of such content and this corporate reporting style is that journalists are ready to take strike action. But, corporations are able to solve such expressions of dissatisfaction by the workers without major difficulties. The year 2009 ended with the media-owning corporations sending dozens of journalist into early retirement. The same recipe is applied in other media companies. Journalists are protesting, publically demonstrating their difficult position, but only on the verbal level, as they have no strength for more drastic measures.

The crucial question is this: Does the media consumer really want such a type of media? Are the readers, listeners and viewers happy with such a style of journalism?

The answer is coming from numerous expert organizations. Associations of psychiatrists, professors of the Croatian language, philosophers, eminent NGOs have stated at their annual conferences how dissatisfied they are. Even the Conference of Croatian Bishops expressed a very negative opinion of Croatian media and journalism. Finally, some polling indicated how the public would like to consume different type of media.

Publishers, on the other hand, have a simple explanation: we publish what the audience is interested in. They are asking for blood, sex, sensation, gossip and crime. We are fulfilling the audience interest only.

Serious research should be carried out to solve this dilemma, but waiting for the real answers one can state: Croatian media are at the very bottom.

References

Malović, Stjepan (2005), 'The Real Game Has Only Started', *The Stumbling of the Media in Times of Transition*, MediaPlan Institute, Sarajevo

Malović, Stjepan/Gary W. Selnow (2001), *The People, Press and Politics of Croatia*, Praeger, Westport

Malović, Stjepan (2005), 'Gli effetti della globalizzazione', *Mass media e nuova Europa*, Bruno Mondadori, Milano

Malović, Stjepan/Vilović (1999), *Training for Better Media*, Izvori, Zagreb

Medijski pristupi promociji EU integracija, ur. Obradović, Stojan, Institut STINE, Split, 2009

Siebert, Fred S./Theodore Peterson/Wilbur Schramm (1956), *Four Theories of the Press*, USA

[http://www.mediaonline.ba/en/?ID=209] retrieved on 25.3.2010.

Morana Fudurić – Andreina Mandelli

(How) has Social Media Changed the Way we Measure Brand Equity? A Literature Review

Introduction

The marketing literature provides substantial discussion on the concept of brand equity. For the most part, researchers have been focusing on traditional ways of measuring brand equity in the offline markets, namely the marketing and financial approaches (Aaker 1991; Keller 1993; Farquhar 1989; Simon/Sullivan 1993; Pappu/Quester/Cooksey 2005). The advances in digital technology, however, brought forth new ways of communicating within the market, which in turn, influenced the way companies do business and the way brands and brand equity are being built and measured. These changes resulted in a new body of research that has focused on the relationship between brands, brand equity and the online environment (McEnally/de Chernatony 1999; Christodoulides et al. 2006; Kollmann/Suckhow 2007; Horppu et al. 2008; Rios/Riquelme 2008; Na/Marshall 2005).

Moreover, with the emergence of Social Media, (i.e. blogs, podcasting, social networks, wikis etc.) organizations have gained the opportunity to reach their target market directly, reducing and changing the role of advertising, professional media and PR agencies (Meerman Scott 2007). Unlike the traditional and the new Internet-specific measures of brand equity that have been extensively researched, the impact of Social Media on brands and brand equity still remains a relatively under-researched area. This paper reviews the literature that addresses both the principles of brand equity applied to offline and online markets, and the change brand managers face dealing with new metrics for branding in Social Media.

Traditional versus online brand equity measures

For decades numerous marketers and scholars discussed and studied the importance of brands, their definition, function and value (Calderon/Cervera/Mollo 1997; Aaker 1991; Keller 1993; Farquhar 1989). A somewhat broad definition of what brand equity stands for was given in the late 1980s by Farquhar (1989) who presented it as added value endowed by the brand to the product. Consequently, other researchers built upon his definition, narrowing it down and placing it in one of two distinct categories – some authors relied on the consumer perspective when defining brand equity (Keller 1993; Aaker 1991), while others were more inclined to view the financial perspective, stressing the value of the brand to the company (Simon/Sullivan 1993; Mahajan et al. 1990).

Essentially, almost all definitions of brand equity today agree that the phenomenon involves value added to a product by consumers' associations and perceptions of a particular brand name, which, in turn, results in greater value for the brand name from the company's perspective (Winters 1991; Chaudhuri 1995; Keller 1993). Aaker (1991) provided one of the most comprehensive and frequently cited definitions of brand equity defining the former as "a set of brand assets and liabilities linked to a brand, its name and symbol, that add to or subtract from the value provided by a product or service to a firm and/or to that firm's customers proposing brand awareness, brand loyalty, brand associations, perceived quality and other proprietary assets as the five key assets of brand equity."

With that being said, it is only natural that brands and brand equity are regarded as very important resources, allowing companies to gain a competitive advantage (Lassar/Banwari/Sharma 1995). The competitive advantage which the authors refer to is not only linked to the ability to create added value and form long-term relationships (Calderon/Cervera/Mollo 1997) or introduce brand extensions (Keller/Aaker 1992), but also to the fact that, in the increasingly competitive environment in which companies operate, brands represent the strongest, most stable values companies can count on (Aaker 1996). The reasoning behind this great interest in brand equity also lies in the financial benefits, in terms of brand value estimation for accounting purposes on the one hand and in the strategy-based motivation to improve marketing productivity (Keller 1993). Additionally, we can observe a positive correlation between brand equity, market share and stock value of a firm (Aaker 1991), which only adds to the importance of the concept. By the mid-1990s, however, the concept had been challenged by the theory of "double jeopardy" (Ehrenberg et al. 1990; Donthu 1994) that questioned the very existence of brand equity, since factors such as repeated buying and consumer attitudes were *directly* related to market share. The theory suggests that there is a *direct and positive* correlation between the previously mentioned factors and market share as a brand equity outcome, completely bypassing brand loyalty and the brand equity process. Specifically, the "double jeopardy" theory claims that brands with small market shares are at a disadvantage in comparison to large market share brands, due to the fact they have fewer buyers that purchase less frequently than large market share brands' buyers (Ehrenberg et al. 1990; Chaudhury 1995). Furthermore, a study by Chaudhury (1995) confirmed the "double jeopardy" theory through an observed direct and positive link between repetitive buying and market share. However, it also provided evidence to support the "brand equity" theory, confirming the existence of an *indirect* link (namely, the brand equity process) that relates the previously mentioned factors (i.e. repetitive buying and consumer attitudes) to brand equity outcomes (i.e. market share).

Monitoring brand equity is considered to be an essential step in effective brand management (Pappu/Quester/Cooksey 2006). It is therefore becoming increasingly important to quantify these intangible assets. This dual significance (strategic and financial) of brand equity brought forth two different methods of measuring brand equity, these being (1) the marketing (or consumer) perspective and (2) the financial (or company) perspective:

(1) Brand equity from the consumer's perspective is based on the analysis of the assets that constitute brand value, their inner relations and derived aspects such as brand extensions (Pappu/Quester/Cooksey 2006; Keller 2003; Keller/Aaker 1992).

(2) Brand equity from the company's perspective is based on the analysis of cash flows and short-term profits (Simon/Sullivan 1993; Farquhad 1989). Specifically, in 1993, Simon and Sullivan define brand equity from a financial point of view as the incremental cash flows that accrue to branded products over and above the cash flows that would result from the sale of unbranded products.

Farquhar, Han and Ijiri (1992) presented three general methods for assessing a brand's value – (1) cost based methods (brands are valued either on actual or replacement costs), (2) market-based methods (brand value is determined from the selling prices of similar brands recently traded or the royalty payments for licensing similar brands) and (3) economic-based methods (relate current earnings or cash flows of the brand to future profitability of the brand based on continuing its existing uses or expanding them). Still, many researchers (Keller 1993; Aaker 1996; Cobb-Walgren et al. 1995; Pappu et al. 2005) have argued in favour of a consumer-based measurement of brand equity. Several brand equity measurement methods have been suggested based on the marketing or consumer perspective, both by researchers (Aaker 1996; Keller 1993; Pappu et al. 2006) and marketing practitioners or consulting firms (Winters 1991). Many of these measurement approaches, however, showed some limitations since brand equity was not broken down into components that could have been related to factors such as favourable customer perceptions (Pappu et al. 2006). In order to overcome this problem, some researchers (Park/Srinivasan 1994) divided brand equity into attributes-based and non-attributes-based components (i.e. components based on distortions caused by the brand to consumer perceptions of product attributes, and components that are not based on those attributes), while others (Aaker 1991; Cobb-Walgren et al. 1995; Yoo/Donthu 2002) suggested a brand equity measurement method that was based on dividing brand equity into different dimensions (brand awareness, brand associations, perceived quality and brand loyalty). Cobb-Walgren et al. (1995) built up on Aaker's concept and treated consumer-based brand equity as a set of four dimensions, namely brand awareness, brand associations, perceived quality and brand loyalty. Yoo et al. (2000) on the other hand, treated consumer-based brand equity as a three-dimensional construct, combining brand awareness and brand associations into one single dimension. Additionally, Washburn and Plank (2002) highlighted the need to refine the dimensionality of consumer-based brand equity. They also advocated that researchers' focus on the distinction between the dimensions of brand awareness and brand associations. While these two dimensions are conceptually different, (e.g. Aaker 1991), several studies (Yoo et al. 2000; Washburn/Plank 2002) suggest they should be combined into one. Similarly, evidence confirms these are distinctive dimensions of brand equity (e.g. Sinha et al. 2000; Sinha/Pappu 1998).

Finally, in the past decade several authors addressed the issue of building a strong brand in the new, online environment (deChernatony 2001; Page/ Lepkowska-White 2002; Christodoulides/de Chernatony 2004; Christodoulides et al. 2006; Kollmann/Suckhow 2007; Horppu et al. 2008; Rios/Riquelme 2008). Page and Lepkowska-White (2002) were among the first to research the topic, introducing web equity (i.e. brand equity for online businesses) and stating that the former can be defined similarly to offline brands' equity by relying on image and awareness, and treating loyalty as an outcome rather than a driver of equity. This line of thinking that claims brand equity models for online and offline brands are essentially the same, has been supported by other authors as well (Na/ Marshall 2005). Some authors, however, pursued a different line of thinking and proposed alternative models that build upon the traditional one(s). In their research, Christodoulides and de Chernatony (2004) defined new, internet-specific brand equity measures to complement Aaker's brand equity ten (1996), while in 2006 Christodoulides et al., comprised a new model of retail brand equity for internet companies called ORS (Online Retail/Service) based on components specific to the online environment such as emotional connection, online experience, responsive service nature, trust and fulfilment. In recent years, authors have turned their attention to examining online brand relationships, i.e. the linkage between satisfaction, trust and loyalty (Horppu et al. 2008), brand image, perceived risk and loyalty online and offline (Kwon/Lennon 2009) or brand associations, brand awareness and loyalty (Rios/ Riquelme 2008). Consequently, an even newer body of marketing research has emerged, that mainly focuses on Social Media and its impact on marketing strategy (Singh/Veron-Jackson/Cullinane 2008; Kaplan/ Haenlein 2009), with little or no reference to the impact of the former on brand equity.

New social media metrics

With a variety of new digital technologies available to everyone across the globe, consumers now, more than ever before, have the power to influence the media and content to which they are exposed (Singh/Veron-Jackson/Cullinane 2008). It is the world of Social Media, defined as the set of tools, services and applications that allow people to interact with others using network technologies (Boyd 2008;

Turow 2009; Evans 2008). Conversational media is made of web-based applications that make it possible to create and easily transmit content in the form of blog posts or comments, spoken words via podcasts, video presentations and votes on Social Media sites (Blossom 2009; Postam 2008; Gillin 2008; Safko/Brake 2009). Collectively these social technologies have enabled a revolution in user-generated content (Cook/Buckley 2008; Smith 2009). Internet-based messages exchanged through these Social Media systems have taken off with the turn of the 21st century. "They have become a major factor in influencing various aspects of consumer behaviour including awareness, information acquisition, opinions, attitudes, purchase behaviour, and post-purchase communication and evaluation" (Mangold/Faulds 2009). The increasing importance of Social Media is also due to the fact that it is "perceived by consumers as a more trustworthy source of information regarding products and services than corporate-sponsored communications transmitted via the traditional elements of the promotion mix" (Foux 2006).

For some authors like Chaffey and Smith (2008), this means that clusters or collectives of customers with similar tastes and interests are connecting with each other to form new global niches, segments and electronic tribes (Adams/ Smith 2008; Cova/Cova 2002). The act of "listening" has become an important part of every business model. This allows for increased product development and better marketing communication between customers and companies (Smith 2009). Engaging customers in Social Media has become a strategic element in building long-term advocates of the brand. As the system catches on, the ideal customer for companies will no longer be the one who buys the product, but the one who continues to contribute to a service or product over time. These actions will include sharing information and becoming a partner, exchanging useful feedback and contributing to the brand project, in a continuous process of distributed value production.

Social media or "Web 2.0" is putting consumers closer to companies so they can be perceived as part of the organization (Mandelli/Vianello 2009). If the customers of a firm spend significant amounts of time online, interacting with the company and with other customers, it will create an unexpected and unprecedented opportunity for businesses to empower the traditional customer information systems and to enrich the consumer online research methods (Fielding 2008). Social Media has inspired an environment where sharing opinions and content through the web is now interesting for the consumer as well as the company, creating a natural and spontaneous form of research. Authors such as Cook and Buckely (2008) have already stated the importance of Web 2.0 for the future because of its ability to streamline market research (Casteleyn/Morratt/Rutten 2009).

Listening to customers is the most common technique, which has been employed in market and consumer research. In the Social Media environment, the mechanisms and the operations for market and customer data collection offer some relevant improvements. Li C. and Bernoff J. (2008) identified two relevant listening strategies on the web. One is to set up a private online community to facilitate discussion. The other involves brand monitoring in blogs, micro-blogging, social networking, video sharing, etc. In fact, many web resources are available to help firms monitor messaging and editorial coverage in Web 2.0. The topic of Social Media measurement, also called "Social Media Analytics," is still in its infancy, but it enables, for instance, a company to evaluate whether conversations on a topic are increasing or decreasing in volume or whether the number of participants in a particular conversation compared to others is bigger or smaller.

The newest linguistic models allow one to analyse the content and the tonality of a discussion, even revealing whether the speaker is male or female (Breakenridge 2008). However, there are significant limits to these models. Both are technical and conceptual and therefore suffer from problems like privacy issues, incomplete raw data, oversized information, abstractions and assumptions, semantic complexity, network analysis pitfalls, etc. Despite the flourishing of all these new platforms and tools for researching and measuring conversations online, what is missing is a robust conceptual framework within which these measures can be developed.

Murdough (2009) was among the first to analyse the Social Media measurement process that consists of five consecutive phases, with their respective activities and outputs (Table 1).

Table 1 Social Media measurement process

Phase	Activity	Output
Concept	1.Maping measurement objectives 2. Identifying key KPIs 3.Establishing performance benchmarks	1. Goals 2. Objectives 3. Metrics
Definition	1.Itemize insight questions 2.Illustrate the analysis approach 3.determine the frequency of performance evaluation and timing	1. Reach 2. Discussions 3. Outcomes
Design	1.Establishing performance data sources and/or methodologies 2.Enumerating specific technical tracking hooks and manual interventions 3.Set up, configure or customize performance reporting tools	Samples of Social Media insight tools and data sources to be used
Deployment	1.Conducting quality assurance of data collection methods 2.Validation of performance reports 3.Building data infrastructure	
Optimization	Reporting and insight	

The concept phase focuses on defining what brands want to accomplish through advancing their relationships with customers via Social Media. Depending on the identified goals (e.g. deepening relationships with customers, learning from the community, driving purchase intent) he proposes a set of metrics (e.g. # of advocates and comments posted, rank of topics discussed or deciphering positive versus negative sentiment and, finally, leads to economic partners and product brochure downloads). He continues by arguing that Social Media monitoring and measurement quantifies the impact of consumer dialogue, and identifies three pillars in the Definition phase, that serve to organize around and navigate the complexity of Social Media performance, namely:

- Reach (monitoring the quantity of mentions and quality of authors)
- Discussions (understanding chatter topics and sentiment composition)
- Outcomes (diagnose behavioural engagement indicators of intent i.e. leads and purchases)

The third, Design stage lays out the specific tactics and venues most appropriate for a brands' active Social Media presence. The two final phases focus on meeting the previously set expectations, reporting and giving insight to evaluate the social program performance against the KPIs determined in the first phase of the process. Although Murdough provides a detailed overview of the Social Media measurement process, he suggests the usage of existing internet metrics that have been adapted to the Social Media landscape (e.g. site analytics solutions, text mining partners etc.). It is important to note that these measures correspond to a certain degree to the internet-specific brand equity measures identified by Christodoulides and de Chernatony (2004) concerning online and offline brands' composite equity.

Concluding remarks

In this paper we addressed the issue of how metrics are changing, considering the impact of new communication technologies and Social Media on brand-customer relationships. We reviewed the relevant literature on the concept of brand equity and the metrics most appropriate for measuring it. We then described the process of change, which is challenging brand management in Social Media, where consumers' conversations and user-generated content build a sense of brands and influence product choice. Literature is starting to become available on general principles of Social Media branding, but not so much on how we can develop new sets of metrics for listening to and researching Social Media. The first endeavours in this area set an agenda of research, which calls for a deeper effort in developing new conceptual principles of Social Media brand equity, and a robust program of empirical exploratory research for uncovering the practices in the field.

References

Aaker, D.A. (1991), *Managing brand equity*, The Free Press, New York, NY

Aaker, D.A. (1996), 'Measuring brand equity across products and markets', *California Management Review*, Vol. 38, No. 3

Adams, T.L./S.A. Smith (2008), *Electronic Tribes,* Austin/TX, University of Texas Press

Blossom, J. (2009), *Content Nation: Surviving and Thriving as Social Media Changes Our Work, Our Lives, and Our Future,* Hoboken/NJ, John Wiley & Sons

Boyd D. (2008), *Taken Out of Context: American Teen Sociality in Networked Publics,* Berckely/CA, University of California-Berkeley (Phd Dissertation)

Breakenridge D. (2008), *PR 2.0: New Media, New Tools, New Audiences,* Upper Saddle River/NJ, Pearson Education Inc.

Calderon, H./A. Cervera/A. Mollo (1997), 'Brand assessment: a key element of marketing strategy', *Journal of Product & Brand Management*, Vol. 6, No. 5, pp. 293-304

Casteleyn J./A. Morrart/K. Rutten (2009), 'How to use Facebook in market research', *International Journal of Market Research*, Vol. 5, No. 4, pp. 439-447

Chaffey D. /P.R. Smith (2008), *E-marketing excellence*, Burlington, MA, Elsevier Butterworth

Chaudhuri, A. (1995), 'Brand equity or double jeopardy?', *Journal of Product & Brand Management*, Vol. 4, No. 1, pp. 26-32

Christodoulides, G./L. de Chernatony/O. Furrer/E. Shiu/T. Abimbola (2006), 'Conceptualising and Measuring the Equity of Online Brands', *Journal of Marketing Management*, Vol. 22, pp. 799-825

Christodoulides, G./L. de Chernatony (2004), 'Dimensionalising on- and offline brands' composite equity', *Journal of Product & Brand Management*, Vol. 13, No. 3, pp. 168-179

Cobb-Walgren, C.J./C.A. Ruble/N. Donthu (1995), 'Brand Equity, Brand Preference, and Purchase Intent', *Journal of Advertising*, Vol. 24, No. 3, pp. 25-40

Cook, M./N. Buckley (2008), 'Web 2.0, social networks and the future of market research', *International Journal of Market Research,* Vol. 50, No. 2, pp. 267-292

Cova, B./V. Cova (2002), 'Tribal marketing: The tribalisation of society and its impact on the conduct of marketing', *European Journal of Marketing,* Vol. 36, No. 5/6, pp. 595-620

De Chernatony, L. (2001), 'Succeeding with brand on the Internet', *Brand Management*, Vol. 8, No. 3, pp. 186-195

Eherenberg, A.S.C./G. J. Goodhart/T. P. Barwise (1990), 'Double jeopardy revisited', *Journal of Marketing*, Vol. 54, No. 3, pp. 82-91

Evans, D. (2008), *Social Media Marketing: An Hour a Day,* Indianapolis/IN, John Wiley and Sons

Farquhar, P.H./J. Y. Han/Y. Ijiri (1992), 'Brands on the Balance Sheet', *Marketing Management*

Farquhar, P.H. (1989), 'Managing Brand Equity', *Journal of Advertising Research*, Vol.1, pp. 24f.

Fielding, N.G. (2008), *Handbook of Online Research Methods*, London, Sage Publications

Foux, G. (2006), 'Consumer-generated media: Get your customers involved', *Brand Strategy*, 8 (May), pp. 38-39

Gillin, P. (2008), *Secrets of social media marketing,* Fresno/CA, Quill Driver Books

Horppu, M./O. Kuivalainen/A. Tarkiainen/H. Ellonen (2008), 'Online satisfaction, trust and loyalty, and the impact of the offline parent brand', *Journal of Product & Brand Management*, Vol. 17, No. 6, pp. 403-413

Kaplan, A.M./M. Haenlein (2009), 'The fairyland of Second Life: Virtual social worlds and how to use them', *Business Horizons*, No. 52, pp. 563-572

Keller, K. L. (1993), 'Conceptualizing, Measuring, and Managing Customer-Based Brand Equity', *Journal of Marketing*, Vol. 57, pp. 1-22

Keller, K.L./D.A. Aaker (1992), 'The Effects of Sequential Introduction of Brand Extensions', *Journal of Marketing Research*, Vol. 29, pp. 35-50

Kollmann, T./C. Suckhow (2007), 'The corporate brand naming process in the net economy', *Qualitative Market research: An International Journal*, Vol. 10, No. 4, pp. 349-361

Kwon, W.S./S. J. Lennon (2009), 'What induces online loyalty? Online versus offline brand images', *Journal of Business Research*, Vol. 62, pp. 557-564

Li, C./J. Bernoff (2008), *Groundswell: winning in a world transformed by social technologies,* Cambridge/MA, Harvard Business Press

Lassar, W./M. Banwari/A. Sharma (1995), 'Measuring customer-based brand equity', *Journal of Consumer Marketing*, Vol. 12, No. 4, pp. 11-19

Mahajan, V./V. R. Rao/R. K. Srivastava (1990), 'Development, testing, and validation of brand equity under conditions of acquisition and divestment', in E. Maltz (ed.), *Managing Brand Equity: A Conference Summary Report*, No. 91-110, Marketing Science Institute, Cambridge/MA, pp. 14-15

Mangold, G. W./J. D. Faulds (2009), 'Social Media: The new hybrid element of the promotion mix', *Business Horizons*, No. 52, pp. 357-365

Mandelli A./S. Vianello (2009), 'Consumers involvement in organizations in the era of social media: open research questions', in G. Cardoso/C. Angus/J. Cole (eds.), *World Wide Internet Book*, University of Macau Publishing, July 2009

Meerman Scott, D. (2007), *New rules of marketing and PR*, John Wiley&Sons, Inc., Hoboken/NJ

McEnally, M. R./L. de Chernatony (1999), 'The Evolving Nature of Branding: Consumer and Managerial Considerations', *Academy of Marketing Science Review*, Vol. 99, No. 2

Murdough, C. (2009), 'Social Media Measurement: It's Not Impossible', *Journal of Interactive Advertising*, Vol. 10, No. 1, pp. 94-99

Na, W.B./R. Marshall (2005), 'Brand power revisited: measuring brand equity in cyber-space', *Journal of Product & Brand Management*, Vol. 14, No. 1, pp. 49-56

Page, Lepkowska/E. White (2002), 'Web equity: a framework for building consumer value in online companies', *Journal of Consumer Marketing*, Vol. 19, No. 3, pp. 231-248

Pappu, R./P. G. Quester/W. R. Cooksey (2005), 'Consumer-based brand equity: improving the measurement – empirical evidence', *Journal of Product & Brand Management*, Vol. 14; No. 3, pp. 143-154

Pappu, R./P. G. Quester/W. R. Cooksey (2006), 'Consumer-based brand equity and country-of-origin relationships – Some empirical evidence', *European Journal of Marketing*, Vol. 40, No. 5/6, pp. 696-717

Park, C.S./V. Srinivasan (1994), 'A survey-based method for measuring and understanding brand equity and its extendibility', *Journal of Marketing Research*, Vol. 31, pp. 271-288

Postam, J. (2008), *SocialCorp: Social Media Goes Corporate,* Berkely/CA, Peachpit Press

Rios, E. R./H. Riquelme (2008), 'Brand equity for online companies', *Marketing Intelligence & Planning*, Vol. 26, No. 7, pp. 719-742

Safko, L./D. Brake (2009), *The Social Media Bible: Tactics, Tools, and Strategies for Business Success*, Hoboken/NJ, John Wiley & Sons

Simon, C.J./M. W. Sullivan (1993), 'The measurement and determinants of Brand Equity: A financial approach', *Marketing Science*, Vol. 12, No. 1, pp. 28-52

Singh, T./L. Veron-Jackson/J. Cullinane (2008), 'Blogging: A new play in your marketing game plan', *Business Horizons*, Vol. 51, pp. 281-292

Sinha, A./R. Pappu (1998), 'Parcelling of the sub components of consumer-based brand equity using factorial survey: an empirical investigation in the New Zealand consumer electronics sector', *Proceedings, Australia New Zealand Marketing Academy Conference (ANZMAC)*, University of Otago, Dunedin, pp. 2433-8.

Sinha, A./P. P. Leszeczyc/R. Pappu, R. (2000), 'Measuring customer based brand equity: a survey-based methodology using hierarchical Bayes model', in G. T. Gregory/P. E. Murphy (eds.), *Enhancing Knowledge Development in Marketing*, Vol. 11, AMA Educators' Proceedings, American Marketing Association, Chicago/IL, pp. 156-7

Smith, T. (2009), 'The social media revolution', *International Journal of Market Research,* Vol. 51, No. 4, pp. 559-561

Turow, J. (2009), *Media Today: An introduction to mass communication*, New York/NY, Taylor & Francis

Vianello, S./A. Mandelli (2009), 'Beyond Knowledge and Branding: the Impact of Online Consumer Communities on Buying Behavior', Special issue a cura di S. Castaldo, Finanza, Marketing e Produzione, *Le nuove frontiere della ricerca sui temi distributive*

Washburn, J. H./R. E. Plank (2002), 'Measuring Brand Equity: An Evaluation of a Consumer-Based Brand Equity Scale', *Journal of Marketing Theory and Practice*, Vol. 10, No. 1, pp. 46-61

Winters, L.C. (1991), 'Brand equity measures: some recent advances', *Marketing Research*, Vol. 3, No. 4, pp. 70-73

Yoo, B./N. Donthu/S. Lee (2000), 'An examination of selected marketing mix elements and brand equity', *Journal of the Academy of Marketing Science*, Vol. 28, No. 2, pp. 195-211

Yoo, B./N. Donthu (2002), 'Testing cross-cultural invariance of brand equity creation process', *Journal of Product & Brand Management*, Vol. 11, No. 6, pp. 394f.

Chapter IV

Tourism

Božena Krce-Miočić – Krešimir Žnidar – Vinko Bakija

Perspectives of Nautical Tourism in the Adriatic

Introduction

Tourism represents one of the largest and certainly one of the most diverse activities in the world. Its influence on the economy of the country in which it develops is remarkable. According to World Trade Organization (WTO) results tourism brings 10 per cent of GDP to the world economy while in countries with highly developed tourist trade it brings over 20 per cent of GDP.

However, this is simply one of the aspects of the influence of tourism. A great impact on the social and cultural elements of society can be examined as well. Tourism enriches both the locals who learn new things in contact with tourists, and tourists who prosper when they visit new places and meet local cultures and local people. This type of influence can be extremely positive when each party involved takes only the best from the other but it can also be negative especially when one of the parties feels jealous or envious or even when various forms of deviant behaviour occur; for example, drug or alcohol abuse or prostitution. Tourism is a global phenomenon which can be seen as a fundamental link between different cultures that should in their unity represent the global European context. Tourism has undergone various changes in its development and it has progressed in different directions creating a variety of types and subtypes. One of the basic subdivisions of tourism is mass tourism on the one side and the specific types of tourism on the other, and these have actually appeared as a result of problems that mass tourism has generated.

Nautical tourism is one of the types of tourism which includes an extremely large number of other industries and precisely in this way it contributes to the development of a country's economy. Nautical tourism by definition stands for navigating and staying on board on various types of vessels (such as yachts, boats, small crafts etc. either in private property or vessels used for economic activities) as well as staying in ports of nautical tourism both for leisure and recreation[1]. There is some discussion whether or not nautical tourism is a part of mass tourism. Some researchers say that a relatively large number of customers is situated in specific places (agglomeration) which is a characteristic of mass tourism. However, the majority agrees that the number of nautical tourists among the total number of tourist lies below the point which would classify it as mass tourism.

Nautical tourism is certainly a type of a tourism which ensures high consumption per tourist and therefore we can say that it is definitely an

[1] Narodne novine No. 68 (2007), Act on rendering services in tourism.

exclusive type of tourism. In nautical tourism the mobility of tourists is a significant factor which enables them to change destination rapidly, for example passing through the whole Mediterranean in no time. The consequence of mobility is easier access to less developed tourist destinations where tourists and the locals can meet before other types of tourism make their way to these places. If we consider the example of islands, we come to the conclusion that nautical tourism is in a slight advantage before any other type of tourism due to the mobility of nautical tourists as well as the possibility to avoid the usual problems of access to these destinations. Social and cultural phenomena which the tourism implies are strongly expressed in nautical tourism. In some destinations the interaction between tourists and the locals is on the level of the beginning of tourist development.

In this paper we will examine some of the aspects that the future holds for nautical tourism on the Adriatic Coast, the trends of its development and its future ranking in the development of tourism in general. The Adriatic forms a natural bay of the Mediterranean Sea and cuts deeply into the European continent on the southern side. Its position creates a natural link between the Middle East and the north coast of the African continent. This paper is based on the research conducted on available secondary resources and on research conducted during 2008 and 2009 in Croatian marinas. The method used for this research was a structured survey questionnaire. The number of marinas included in the survey questionnaire was 31 of a total 50[2] and they own 78 per cent of berths in the country.

Nautical tourism in the tourist system

The negative aspect of mass tourism, the biggest fear of most tourist destinations of high quality, is attributed to seasonality and to ecological insensitivity towards the environment in which it develops. Precisely these two aspects lead to the biggest problems and contradictions in tourism such as the degradation of the environment in which the tourist trade takes place and which is in fact the main reason why tourists choose a certain destination. It is precisely the human need to escape from the devastation caused by urbanization to nature that leads to a stronger and faster development of tourism. Faster access by boats to areas that are usually hardly accessible was the main reason for a bigger sale of all types of vessels. In 2004 Italy, the second country in the world for boat production, sold boats worth 862 million Euros or 61 per cent more than in the year before. It is therefore understandable that such a high level of production

---

2 According to the data released by the Ministry of Tourism on 2nd July 2008 we have 50 categorized marinas in Croatia with 13,971 sea berths and 4,320 land berths/storage. [http://www.mint.hr/UserDocsImages/080702-ukup-marine.pdf] retrieved on 30.8.2008.

and sales stimulates the development of the nautical sector, and especially the construction of new marinas. (Srzić 2004: 66-73)

Today in Scandinavian countries (Sweden and Finland) every seventh person owns some kind of vessel[3], and almost half of these vessels are motor-boats or sailboats for leisure or recreation. In Italy every 66th person owns a vessel while in other countries the average is one vessel per 100 or 200 inhabitants. In 2006 the shipbuilding industry made over 6370,000,000 Euros from construction and servicing boats for sport and recreation, which is 30 per cent of the total income of the shipbuilding industry in EU-27.

The market for small boats for the purpose of fun and recreation has grown rapidly due to the increase of spare time. There has also been a boom on the cruising tourism market and that is the reason why there is a need for cruiser and luxury yacht construction[4]. Therefore, it is to be expected that the number of vessels for leisure and recreation will grow as well as the standards of luxury and comfort that these boats offer.

Figure 1 Overnight stays in marinas in the Republic of Croatia by months

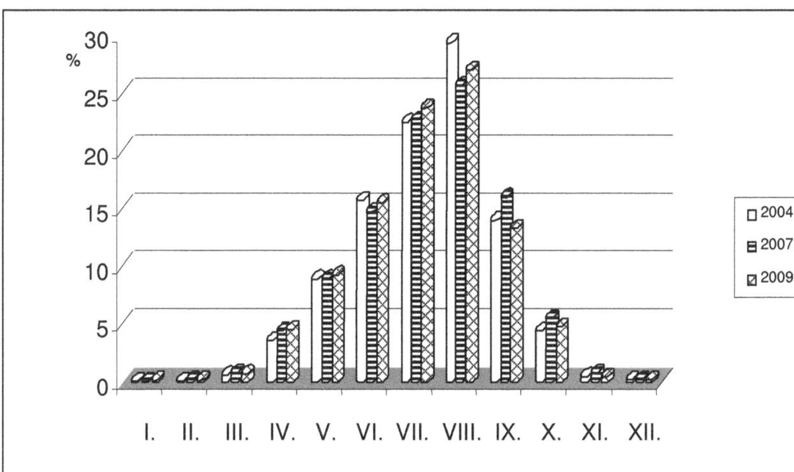

Source: according to the data by The Central Bureau of Statistics – Tourism in 2009 and TOMAS – nautika 2007[5].

3 According to [http://www.ibinews.com/ibinews/index.html].

4 Vekeman, Guy (2008) Shipbuilding and repair: From tankers to pleasure boats. Statistic in focus: Industry, Trade and Services. Vol. 16/2008.

5 Marušić, Zrinka; Horak, Sinša, Tomas (2008) Nautika 2007- Stavovi i potrošnja nautičara u Hrvatskoj, Institut za turizam, Zagreb.

Figure 2 Use of transit sea berths by months in 2007[6]

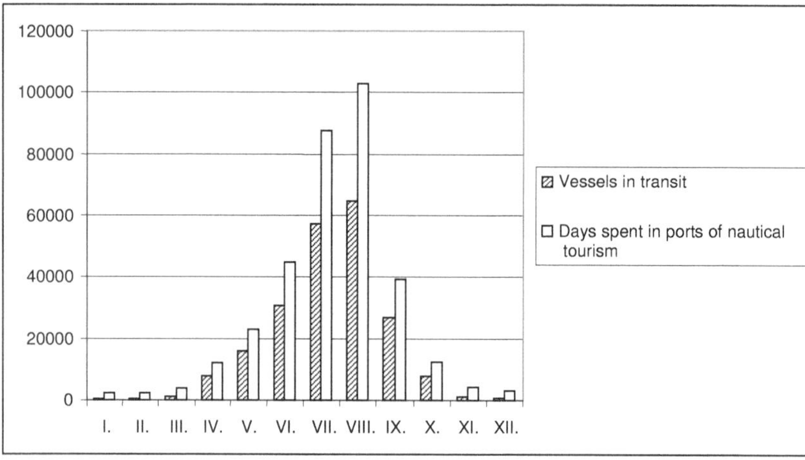

Tourism science and practical experience often confirm that navigation is characterized by short seasons because its primary product is in fact the berthing in marinas. However, nautical tourism also shows that its disadvantage is seasonality. Although the vessel is docked in a port offering nautical tourism, which is the primary accommodation of navigation, it does not have a real purpose unless there are tourists on it.

Trends in the development of nautical tourism

When dealing with the problems of seasonality new trends in the development of nautical tourism are being set. The first trend is to meet requirements for bigger and better equipped ships which will make the stay on board safer and more comfortable even in the worst weather conditions. One of the indicators of such a development is the construction of larger boats. In the 1980s the average length of a boat in Croatian marinas was 21 feet (6.4 m); in the second half of the Nineties the average length increased up to 31 feet (9.45 m). The results of our research show that today the average length of a vessel on an annual berth is 40.35 feet i.e. 41 feet or 12.30 m. Therefore, the length of a vessel has doubled and thus safety on board is increased and more comfortable accommodations are provided.

6 Communication released by The Central Bureau of Statistic on 19th March 2008. *Nautički turizam – kapaciteti i poslovanje luka nautičkog turizma u 2007.* [http://www.dzs.hr/Hrv/publication/2007/4-4-6_1h2007.htm] retrieved on 28.4.2008.

There has also been an increase in the number of mega yachts (vessels over 80 ft/ 24.38 m) which do not represent the majority but their respective value makes a difference to the percentage. The average increase of this segment was 14.3 per cent per year; in 2000 there were 317 vessels and in 2006 the number increased up to 688[7]. One of the major problems which the increase of mega yachts carries with it is their accommodation. Marinas are built according to the demands of the market for vessels at a specific time with 30 years of amortization period. However, as we have seen, the market fluctuates and it is not unusual that berths and thus the whole marina needs to be reconstructed after only 10 years, simply because berths no longer satisfy the requirements of the vessels.

Seasonality regarded as a problem depends on various social influences for example the school break, the season of low business activity; the need to identify oneself with others and so on. Therefore, marinas need to put a lot of effort into keeping guests at the destination for as long as possible. Tourism in general shows that there is an on-going trend of taking shorter holidays (from 3 to 7 days) instead of longer holidays (from 15 to 21 days) under the condition that spare time is increasing and that the prices of transport are falling. This trend is expected to pass to navigation. It is also possible that the guests will navigate for shorter periods of time but more frequently. Marinas are making serious efforts to create new products which would keep tourists there for longer and to draw them to navigate in periods when navigation is favourable and the temperature of the sea is too low for bathing. The regattas are one of these products with which marinas try to draw tourists to their destination even outside the main season while at the same time they serve as one of the marketing strategies for this type of tourism.

Over 90 per cent of Croatian marinas have recognized the need for an on-going season in order to provide services outside the main season. At the same time they are turning to markets that have a tradition of navigating but do not have conditions for it in their own countries throughout the year, such as Scandinavian countries for example. Unfortunately, although there is a small increase in overnight stays outside the main season, we can affirm that navigation is exclusively seasonal.

One of the trends that stand out not only in nautical tourism but in tourism in general is expanding the tourist offer by adding new services or simply by raising the standards of the existing ones. From the Eighties when nautical tourism started developing in earnest on the north shores of the Adriatic, there has been a constant growth of the quality of services which can be seen from the number of marinas and berths with higher categories. The research has shown

---

7 [http://www.nautica.it/superyacht/533/mercato/report.htm]

(Table 1) a relation between the years of doing business and the category of the marina. Testing differences using the Chi square test we found that there were significant differences ($p < 0.00$) and we can conclude that marinas which have been operating for longer tend to have a higher category.

In time, Croatian marinas have recognized the need to increase the standards of their services and to adjust to the need of the so called "new guest". "The new guest" or "The tourist of the future" is experienced, knows what he wants and is aware of the quality standards; he has created a sense of environment, he does not buy the journey or the object but a way of living. (Magaš 2000: 41)

Table 1 Relation between the years of doing business and the category of the marina

			Category of a marina		
			1st category	2nd category	3rd category
Years of doing business	<10	Count	990	230	1355
		%	38.4%	8.9%	52.6%
	11 - 20	Count	1464	3313	180
		%	29.5%	66.8%	3.6%
	>20	Count	584	4384	1729
		%	8.7%	65.5%	25.8%
	Total	Count	3038	7927	3264
		%	21.4%	55.7%	22.9%

Chi-Square Tests

	Value	**df**	**Asymp. Sig. (2-sided)**
Pearson Chi-Square	4062.971	4	.000
Likelihood Ratio	4842.660	4	.000
Linear-by-Linear Association	142.776	1	.000
N of Valid Cases	14229		

This rise in quality demonstrates that Croatian marinas show a serious intention to include other services in the basic nautical offer which consists of the berth itself. In this way the marinas are trying to satisfy the guests' requirements. To satisfy a guest, tourism today must create the synergy of various types of tourism taking the advantages of natural attractions of a destination in order to supply a complex tourist product.

Table 2 Number of different services in marinas by their category

Number of different services that they offer	The category of a marina		
	1st category	2nd category	3rd category
<= 10	*12.8%*	*22.2%*	*37.1%*
11-12	*19.2%*	*49.2%*	*56.8%*
13+	*67.9%*	*28.6%*	*6.1%*
Total	*100.0%*	*100.0%*	*100.0%*

Figure 3 Number of different services in marinas by their category

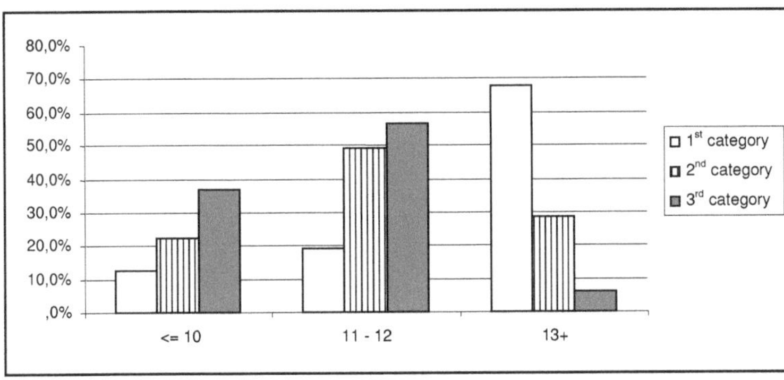

The research has shown that marinas with a higher category offer more services, therefore, 67.9 per cent of the 1st category marinas offer over 13 different services while only 6.1 per cent of the 3rd category marinas offer the same number of services. In this way, by supplementing the basic services and by changing the image of exclusively berthing boats, marinas stand out from their competition. Most of the marinas nowadays want to become event locations: a small tourist destination which guests choose for the services they provide and a safe dock for their boats. By the expression *destination* we mean an optimally combined and market-adjusted space which meets the necessary prerequisites by developing important and dominant capacities in a destination which will ensure good long-term results in comparison with the competition. The main goals of a tourist destination are the following: to provide quality for the guests and a long- term source of profit for the locals. (Magaš 2008, p. 4)

A guest today demands more, he does not travel only for the sun and the sea: he needs the extra activities; he wants to learn more, wants to encounter the culture of a destination and he wants to communicate with the locals. According to the research by Tomas nautika 2007 (Marušić/Horak 2008) the average age of a nautical tourist is 44 and he is slightly more educated than a stationary guest (over

50% have higher education while only 29% of stationary guests are highly educated) and monthly earnings are also much higher. For these reasons the demands of these guests and those of stationary guests differ significantly.

According to our research, in relation to the year 2004 there is a significant number of nautical tourists engaged in various activities. Over 80 per cent of them go to restaurants, to pastry shops, shopping and excursions. From 60 to 80 per cent go for a nature walk , go sightseeing or visit local festivities, they do all sorts of recreational activities (especially diving), they go to concerts and theatres, they go fishing. Marinas have therefore enriched their basic offer in order to please their guests; 77 per cent of them also have a gastronomical offer, 29 per cent of marinas recognize a strong connection between navigation and active tourism and this is the reason why they have included these elements into their offer. Unfortunately only 26 per cent of marinas realize that nautical tourists are similar to guests who pursue cultural tourism and they include these elements accordingly. The situation is even worse with the offer of wellness services (16%), ecologically tested products (10%) and agritourism (6%).

Table 3 Additional activities in marinas

Offer	yes			no		
	berths	marina	% marina	berths	marina	% marina
cultural activities	4351	8	26%	9878	23	74%
gastronomy offer	11260	24	77%	2969	7	23%
sports activities	4255	9	29%	9974	22	71%
wellness	1922	5	16%	12307	26	84%
shops with organic products	1969	3	10%	12260	28	90%
visits to agritourism households	1385	2	6%	12844	29	94%
other	4684	9	29%	9545	22	71%

The following trend that will make the difference in nautical tourism is certainly environment concern, implementation of elements of sustainability in business in marinas and nautical tourists' behaviour starting from their choice of a vessel up to their behaviour in navigation. According to a well-accepted definition the development is possible if the natural ecosystem serves as a resource of the constant growth of production and consumption without the changes and damages to the quality so that the following generations could benefit as well.

In its early beginnings nautical tourism aspired to expanding capacities and creating new offers and therefore it demanded the space to develop in. However, besides the need for space, this type of tourism led to a series of negative consequences such as: the noise that the boat engines produce, transport of plant life from its natural habitat, huge consumption of non-renewable resources of energy in motorboats, pollution of the sea with organic and other waste, waste elements in boat services which include oil, paint, coating etc. The first response to awareness of the environment is the Blue Flag which is awarded to marinas. The Blue Flag Program for beaches and marinas is an international ecological program for the protection of the sea and the coast. The Program's main goal is sea and coast management. In Croatia 21 marina have been awarded the Blue Flag while in the year 2009 only 620 marinas in the world were eligible for it[8]. A total of 68 per cent of berths included in the research were given the Blue Flag.

Figure 4 The Blue Flag awarded and in force

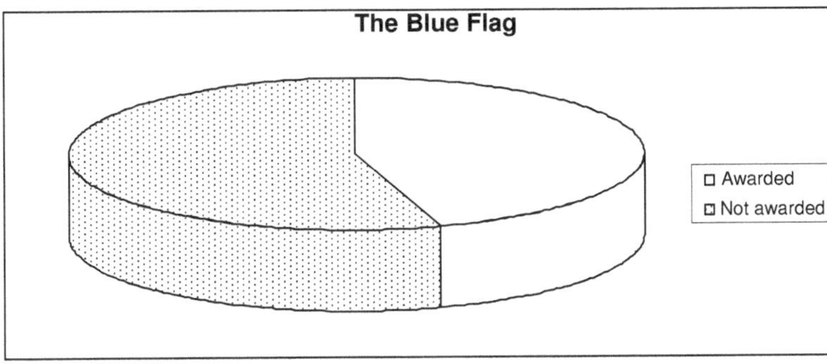

The marinas that have been awarded the Blue Flag can therefore put a higher price on their basic offer as supposed to those that do not have that 'eco-label'. If we take a look at the annual sea berth which is actually the basic product of Croatian marinas, we will see that marinas that do own the 'eco-label' increase the price by 7.35 per cent.

Table 4 Relation between prices and owning the Blue Flag

	The Blue Flag	Number of berths	The average price in Euro	Standard deviation	Standard error
The price of the annual sea berth (€)	yes	*9469*	*4721.42*	*698.28735*	*7.17599*
	no	*4458*	*4398.35*	*985.01194*	*14.75270*
The price of the sea berth per day (€)	yes	*9469*	*56.14*	*6.89965*	*.07090*
	no	*4760*	*53.51*	*3.96331*	*.05745*
The price of the annual marina berth (€)	yes	*9079*	*3295.68*	*857.11639*	*8.99541*
	no	*3577*	*2967.12*	*638.61449*	*10.67774*

8 [http://www.blueflag.org/blueflag]

Naturally, the sustainability of development includes the least intervention possible in the environment and minimal environmental exploitation and great respect for ecological standards. It is precisely the natural beauty that makes Croatia stand out from its competition (France, Spain, Greece, Italy and Turkey). In the strategic document on the development of nautical tourism Croatia claims that by the year 2018 it will have built 15, 000 new berths. One part of berths should be constructed in already existing ports and small harbours, the other part in the existing marinas and finally the third part in completely new untouched coves. This kind of capacity growth would lead to a number of difficulties such as environmental degradation, landscape alteration, problems with the local community who will lose berths for their own boats in the case of these huge changes in their living environment. Needless to say, this also means that the number of vessels on our coast would double. It would be crowded even in destinations that do not have marinas and the pollution would worsen due to more waste produced by nautical tourism. Therefore, it is necessary to expand the existing marinas first and to adjust berths according to nautical demand so that 15 per cent of berths are intended for vessels up to 12 m long, 60 per cent for vessels from 12 to 16 m, 15 per cent for vessels from 16 to 25 m and finally 10 per cent for mega yachts over 25 m.

The optimal size of a marina should range from 400 to 800 berths, bearing in mind the capacity of the cove in which marina is located. As we can see from table 5 half of the marinas researched are within the category of 400 berths. Therefore, it is expected that in the future development of accommodation capacities the existing marinas will be reconstructed and broadened which is economically the best solution and only then will new marinas be built.

Table 5 Marinas according to the number of berths

Marinas by number of berths	Total berths	%	Marina	%
200 or less	1.122	7.9%	7	22.58%
201 to 400	2.553	17.9%	9	32.26%
401 to 600	5.324	37.4%	10	29.03%
601 to 800	1.450	10.2%	2	6.45%
801 or more	3.780	26.6%	3	9.68%
TOTAL	14.229	100.00%	31	100.00%

It is interesting that the marinas holding from 600 to 800 berths charge the highest prices for sea berths and marina berths while smaller marinas have significantly lower prices.

Table 6 Relation between size of marina and price

Number of berths	Price of the annual the sea berth (€)	Price of the annual marina berth (€)	Price index of the annual sea berth	Price index of the annual marina berth
	average	average	100=max.price	100=max.price
200 or less	4,055.65	2,186.97	84.23	57.63
201 to 400	4,222.29	2,285.55	87.69	60.23
401 to 600	4,789.12	3,292.57	99.46	86.77
601 to 800	4,815.07	3;794.55	100.00	100.00
801 or more	4,690.69	3,369.31	97.42	88.79

Therefore, when the possibility of expanding the existing marinas is used up to maximum capacity, only then it is expected that small ports and anchorages will be converted and new marinas will be built.

Conclusion

Nautical tourism is one specific type of tourism and the Adriatic Sea which is like a deep bay in the European continent has a number of advantages for its development because of its moderate winds and sea currents, preserved environment and its closeness to emissive markets. Two problems occur in practice and these are seasonality and the negative impact on the environment. The solution for these two problems can be found in the increasing number of marinas (over 90%) that are open all year around and in the construction of bigger vessels which provide comfortable navigation even under bad weather conditions. At the same time marinas are working to improve the quality of the offer and fulfil it by implementing elements of other types of tourism in order to satisfy the needs of "the new" more demanding guests. One of the demands set for marinas and nautical tourism in general is certainly the reduction of the negative impact on the environment by implementing the principle of sustainable development in their business. The first step to this goal is to be awarded the Blue Flag which in fact proves that the business management is in accordance with the international ecological standards. Marinas with the Blue Flag achieve a higher price for their basic offer. In order to intervene as little as possible in the environment in the future, it is necessary to expand the nautical offer in existing marinas always considering the capacity of a certain micro location from 400 to 800 berths and only then should small ports and anchorages be reconstructed and new marinas be built.

References

Magaš, Dragan (2008), 'Destinacijske menadžment kompanije', Priručnik za razumijevanje poslovanja i uspješni marketing, UHPA, Zagreb

Magaš, Dragan (2000), 'Razvoj hrvatskog turizma', Koncepcija dugoročnog razvoja, Adamić, Rijeka

Marušić, Zrinka/ Siniša Horak (2008), *Tomas Nautika 2007 – Stavovi i potrošnja nautičara u Hrvatskoj*, Institut za turizam, Zagreb

Srzić, Marin (2004), 'Prva fijera Unije', *More,* No. 115 (November), Fabra, Zagreb

Vekeman, Guy (2008), 'Shipbuilding and repair: From tankers to pleasure boats', *Statistic in focus: Industry, Trade and Services*, Vol. 16/2008

[http://www.blueflag.org/blueflag]

[http://www.dzs.hr]

[http://www.ibinews.com]

[http://www.mint.hr]

[http://www.nautica.it/superyacht/533/mercato/report.htm]

[http://www.nn.hr]

[http://www.unwto.org]

Jurica Šimurina – Aleksandar Bogunović[1] – Milivoj Marković

The Airline Industry in Croatia

Introduction

The airline industry has been and still is a very dynamic industry with especially high demand volatility. Though the decades of hefty growth in international markets occurred in the 1970s and 1980s, over the last 15 years, some markets in have revealed that soaring demand is still very much present. Altogether, the airline industry has shown remarkable long-term growth in comparison to other industries. Developed countries (US, Canada, Western Europe) recorded the highest growth rates between the 1940s and the 1970s, with growth slowing down in the 1990s but still remaining in the double figures and well above other industries (O'Connor 2001, p. 7).

One long term characteristic of the airline industry, until recently, has been the heavy regulation by the governments or various agencies, making the airline industry one of the most regulated industries. Starting from the 1970s, plans for deregulation began to emerge and tight regulations were gradually relinquished, leaving business decisions increasingly influenced by the market forces of supply and demand. The most recent initiative of this kind is called "Open skies" and came into effect on March 30th, 2008. In essence, it allows European airlines as well as US airlines to fly freely to any destination in the US and the EU respectively, without restrictions on routes, pricing and number of flights. This marks an enormous step toward the creation of a single air transport market between the EU and the US, with a huge global impact, bearing in mind that these two markets comprise 60 per cent of the total world traffic (EU - US Open Skies in effect, 2008).

As of 2005 the EU is made up of 27 countries, many of which are transition economies. Their history of air transport is mostly characterized by state-owned airlines with relatively low domestic demand for air travel, for business or leisure activities alike. The aim of this article is to explore and account for major factors affecting the supply and demand of passenger air travel, taking special regard of developments in Croatia.

Background

The European history of aviation has witnessed a significant level of regulation by highly restrictive bilateral air service agreements between countries. Traditionally, each route was served only by the two national flag carriers that used to jointly set a

[1] Author deceased 2011.

single price and evenly split the demand. This situation provided no incentive for efficiency improvements of the industry. Deregulation followed and some improvements were made in this respect (see Table 1) (Marin 1995).

Table 1 Deregulatory measures introduced by some European countries

Deregulatory measure	*Entry*	*Frequencies/ Capacities*	*Fares*
1985 UK-Netherlands Liberal Bilateral Agreement	Freedom of market entry to any UK or Dutch airline designed by its government	No restrictions on frequency or capacity	Freedom to offer any fare unless it is disapproved by both governments
1987 EC package of measures	Multiple designation on the busiest routes	Less restrictive capacity sharing agreements (either country could operate up to 55% of capacity in 1988 and 1989 and 60% in 1989	Limited freedom to compete on cheap promotional fares
1993 EC package of measures	Multiple designation and freedom for the EC airlines to operate any cross-border services	No restrictions on frequency or capacity	Freedom to offer any fare unless it is regarded as either too high and, therefore, harmful to the consumers, or so low that it produces losses for all the companies involved

Source: Marin 1995, p. 143.

Beside the regulatory problems that limit competition, there are further problems with competition with hub-spoke networks. Competition and hub-spoke networks may pose a deterrent for the entry of regional carriers. As stipulated by Hendricks, Piccione and Tan (1997), this is due to the fact that hub operators can credibly threaten to maintain a hub's presence in the spoke market even when incurring losses in the market with increased competition. The result is that regional carriers do not have a cost advantage and are forced to exit the market.

Given the costs associated with the industry, post-deregulation effects need a long time to settle. As the process of deregulation continued in the 1980s and 1990s, workers in the airline industry remained highly compensated. This is, however, attributed to job characteristics. Wage premiums did remain but they seemed modest for most airline employees with the exception of pilots. A large part of maintaining wages in the industry is attributed to the labour unions as a key institutional force (Hirsch/Macpherson 2000).

Given the issues of competition, privatization and efficiency in the airline industry Ng and Seabright (2001) stipulate that state ownership has a large upward impact on costs, the effects of competition have an overall downward impact on rents and costs, while merely losing market share to existing competitors has the opposite effect.

In terms of the effects of exchanges of cost information in the airline industry, Armantier and Richard (2003) reveal, on the basis of a multimarket model of competition with entry, incomplete information and demand complementarities, that exchange of cost information increases profits, only moderately lowers the consumer surplus, and actually benefits consumers in a majority of markets.

Supply side of air transport

It is the general opinion that managers prefer to tackle the supply side of the airline business rather than the demand side. The rationale behind this is somewhat easy to comprehend. Costs are mostly under the control of the managers and a whole array of cost-based indicators has been derived to help managers keep track of airline performance.

Various types of reported costs in airline business reports depend on the accounting principles of the home country of the airline. There are, however, certain costs that are airline-specific due to the nature of air transport as well as with regard to their contribution to the total costs. Managers are concerned with these kinds of costs due to their role in decision-making. The two main costs related to airline operations are crew and fuel costs. These costs can be grouped in the common class of direct operating costs since they are directly related to operating the aircraft. On the other hand, indirect operating costs include ground and terminal costs as well as overhead expenses. Furthermore, ground and indirect costs are sometimes used as synonymous, since there is very little real difference between them. Terminal costs are related to the amount of traffic but not to the mileage travelled. They encompass costs such as air traffic and traffic servicing, reservations, sales etc.

It is evident that the average terminal cost per passenger drops (we can use the term cost per passenger mile) as the distance of the trip increases. It is a known fact that airplanes use more fuel on take-off and landing, hence fuel costs per passenger also have a downward slope as the length of the trip increases. It can be concluded that, *ceteris paribus*, longer trips have lower costs per passenger mile.

In airline economics we further encounter some specific ratios concerning cost and passenger capacity. The so-called seat-mile marks the physical output of the airline. If an airplane carries 100 seats and the trip is 100 miles long, then the airplane has a physical output of 10000 seat-miles. This indicator is commonly used in combination with the passenger-mile to calculate the load factor. The passenger-mile indicator is easily calculated by multiplying the number of fully paying passengers with the length of the trip, in miles respectively. The ratio of passenger-miles and seat-miles is known as "load factor". If the airplane boards just enough passengers to cover its costs for a specific trip then the breakeven load factor is reached.

Another issue that airline companies face when matching supply with demand on the short-route trips is the high elasticity of demand. Alternative ways of transport have become more acceptable to travellers since the costs for trips of roughly the same length, no matter what the means of transportation, and time *en route* using different modes of transport, are roughly the same. Transition economies are known to invest substantially in their infrastructure, both roads and railways, which does not help airlines in the long run. Some countries, in order to stimulate development or regional airports and short-routes, have offered subsidies for passenger airlines.

The fuel price is another major cost that causes airline managers increasing problems, in some cases even leading to the decision to leave the market. Advances in modern airplanes have increased efficiency in fuel consumption relative to miles travelled but external factors still account for the major increase of fuel cost in the overall costs. Data for the US show a substantial increase in fuel costs over the last few years, as can be seen from Figures 1 to 3. The labour cost trend over the last 16 years can be seen in Figures 3 and 4.

Figure 1 Total cost in gallons ($ millions)

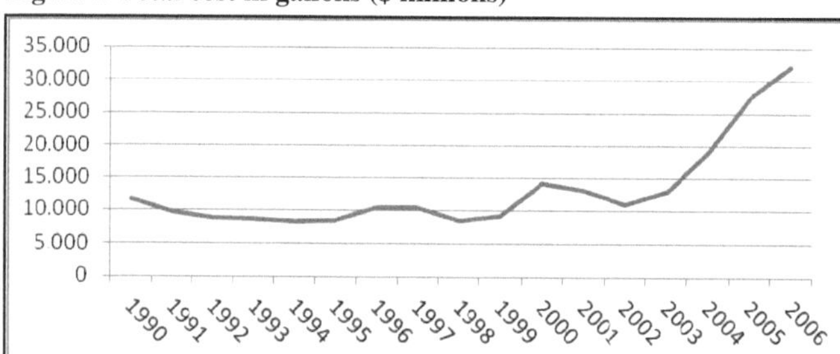

Source: ATA 2009.

Figure 2 Fuel cost as share of total operating expenses

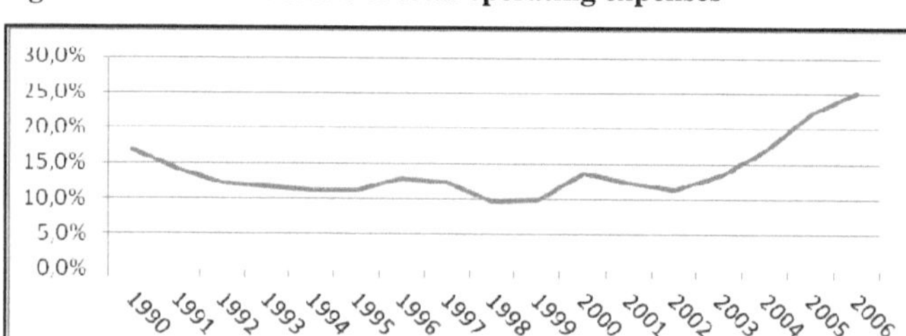

Source: ATA 2009.

Figure 3 Cost of labour (Full time employees only) ($ millions)

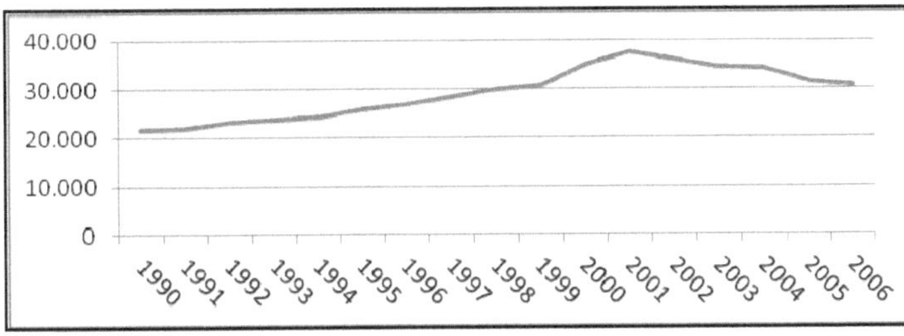

Source: ATA 2009.

Figure 4 Cost of labour as share of total operating expenses

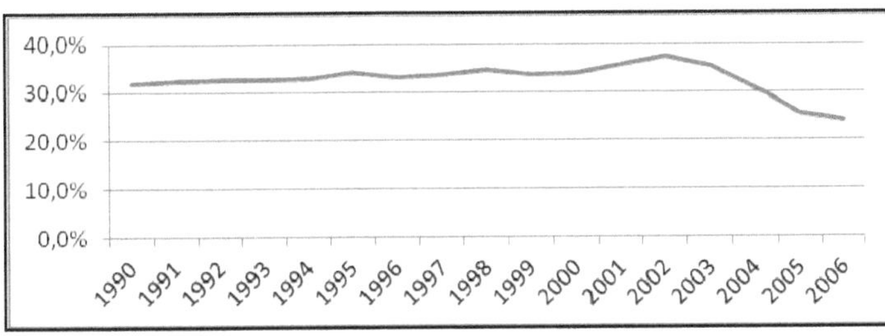

Source: ATA 2009.

Data from the figures clearly indicates the great influence fuel and labour costs have on overall costs. Transition economies have one distinctive advantage in that the influence of the trade unions is generally lower than in developed countries, so the labour costs can be lower but not significantly. Analyses have shown that despite lower input cost (including labour), Latin America airlines had lower operating results due to the better management of the load factor in the US.

Demand for airline transport

The service of airline transportation is very specific. It is defined as intermediate service, which means that airline transportation is merely a means to achieve some other goal. In other words, people do not just fly for the sake of flying. Various types of passengers can be categorized in the few broad market segments depending on the reason of the trip. Four categories, for example, could include tourist, business, friends and family, and miscellaneous travellers. Some characteristics of demand from certain types of business and tourist travellers are listed in Table 2.

Managers in airline companies are greatly concerned with important economic indicators. These indicators are the price elasticity of demand and the income elasticity of demand. Each has an unique influence on a particular type of traveller.

Looking at tourist travellers it is sound to conclude that they are much more income elastic than business travellers. Why? Let us take as an example two countries, one with a high level of real income per capita and one with a low level of real income per capita. If real income increases in the rich country, it is fair to presume that a larger proportion of that increase will be spent on luxurious goods like travelling (by air, naturally) than in the poor country. Business travellers tend to be more inelastic since the nature of their trip is somewhat more of a necessity than anything else.

Table 2 Market segmentation by trip purpose and passenger needs

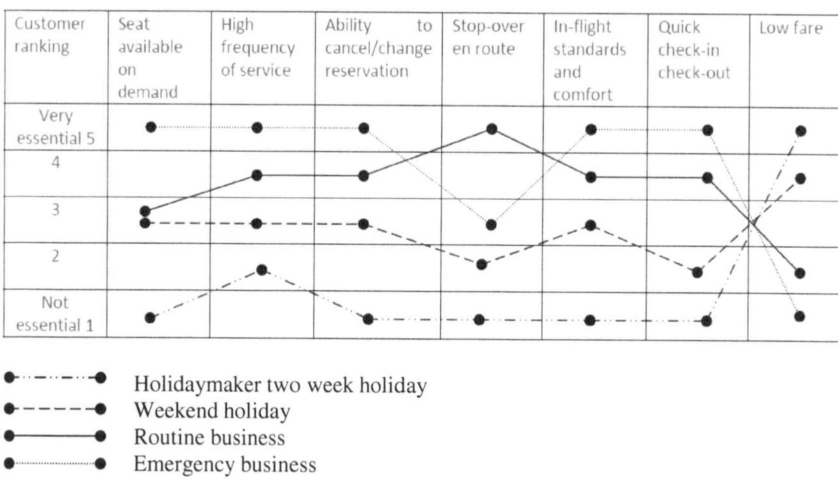

Source: Doganis 2002, p. 189.

Price elasticity is reflected in the same way. In the case that airlines increase their rates it is reasonable to expect that the tourist segment would be the one to show a greater decline in the total number of passengers, since tourist travel is a sort of luxurious good. With an increase in air rates, *ceteris paribus*, tourist travellers are poorer than before and their spending on luxurious goods would inevitably decline.

Another characteristic of passenger demand is the substantial level of variability. Seasonal variations due to holidays are well known and have recently been more pronounced due to the rise of pure discount airlines, which particularly conform to highly elastic customers such as tourist travellers. On the other hand, some markets may show a decline in passengers carried over the weekend, which could be a definite signal that the market is dominated by business travellers and vice versa.

Management has several methods at hand in its attempt to estimate the potential demand for air travel. It can pool the on-board passengers or prospective passengers, or it could analyse time series in order to derive a useful model of estimating demand etc.

A number of contemporary factors that influence demand could be pointed out. The relative depreciation of the US dollar in relation to the Euro or Yen has increased the relative income of European and Japanese citizens measured in US dollars. It is much cheaper for citizens of those countries to travel to the US than it was a few years back.

Airlines in Croatia

Recent airline history in Croatia starts with the foundation of Zagal (Zagreb Airlines) in 1989. The company went into operation with the Cessna 402 C, which was employed in the transport of UPS shipments. After the elections in 1990, on July 23, Zagal officially changed its name to Croatia Airlines. In the following year, Croatia Airlines signed an agreement with Adria Airways and started flying with a leased MD-82 aircraft. The first flights were between Zagreb and Split. In 1991 (last quarter) and 1992 operations were interrupted due to the War of Independence. During 1992 Croatia Airlines acquired two used Boeing 737 from Lufthansa. In the same year, with new aircraft, the number of passengers increased and Croatia Airlines became a member of the International Association of Air Transport (IATA). In 1993, Croatia Airlines continued its expansion with new Boeing 737 and ATR-42 aircraft, steadily increasing the number of passengers carried. The following years marked a further increase both in the fleet and the number of passengers carried. In 1997, Croatia Airlines took into operation the first ordered Airbus A320, which marked the beginning of a big change in the fleet, where all the old Boeing 737 aircraft were replaced by new Airbus A320 and A319 aircraft. In 2000, the rejuvenation of the fleet using Airbus aircraft was complete. In the following years, the number of passengers carried increased even further and in 2004 Croatia Airlines became a regional Star Alliance member. By 2010 Croatia Airlines was leasing several aircraft and changed the ATR-42 fleet, introducing new Bombardier Dash 8 Q-400 aircraft.

For the past 20 years, Croatia Airlines was the national carrier and other companies that service scheduled flights did not emerge. However, there are several start-ups that managed to stay afloat in the charter and cargo area of the business. The first one to be mentioned is Trade Air, which was registered in April 1994. The company was registered for passenger charter flights and cargo operations. Furthermore, they specialize in carrying dangerous goods. In 1999 Trade Air acquired a Let L-410 aircraft and in the following year two more Let L-410 aircraft were added to the fleet. These aircraft are designed to carry up to 16 passengers or cargo. In 2004 Trade Air introduced two Fokker 100 aircraft, which can carry up to 109 passengers. These aircraft are designed for medium range charter flights.

The other carrier that managed to stay afloat is Dubrovnik Airline. Dubrovnik Airline started flying in April 2005 with its first aircraft in the fleet, a MD-83. Dubrovnik Airline is also a charter company and its fleet today consists of three MD-82 and two MD-83 aircraft, which can carry up to 167 passengers.

There were other start-ups as well but they did not fly for long. Entry barriers are very high in airline business, thus we have not seen many developments in the network airline business in Croatia. The national carrier Croatia Airlines has a firm grip as single domestic network operator. The other two established airlines ventured into charter flights and cargo. In the meantime, low cost carriers are taking over the sky in Croatia. This kind of development is similar to the rest of Europe, however, there are no domestic low cost start-ups. In the past couple of years we have seen an increase in passengers, but mostly due to foreign competition. Even though Croatia Airlines considers itself a network operator, which has been the backbone of Croatian aviation for quite some time, the airline business has changed. It has changed for the better for consumers, however, airlines did not follow suit, thus Croatia Airlines today is posting a loss in excess of 13 million Euro. Even when all the problems with fuel costs, strikes and unforeseen events e.g. volcanic eruptions, are taken into consideration, operations of our national carrier have come under a question mark (see Figure 1). Even though the number of passengers grew almost every year up to 2009, the real issue here is the passenger load factor. In the past years, more planes meant more passengers, however, those new planes were not filled to capacity. Passenger load factors are below 60 per cent for most of the period with a declining tendency in 2009 and 2010.

Recent developments that involve the Slovenian national carrier Adria Airways and the possibility of a merger, which seems to be beneficial for both carriers, look like a possibility to escape bankruptcy. However, this possibility is on the drawing board and might be considered in coming years.

Figure 5 Croatia Airlines – passengers and load factor

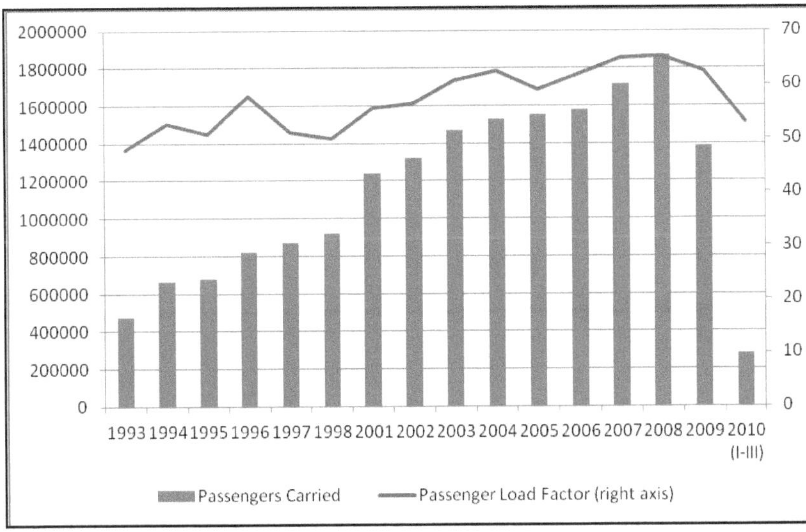

Source: IATA 2009, Croatia Airlines 2010.

Airport infrastructure in Croatia

Given the size of Croatia, it has an impressive number of airports open for commercial aviation. The geography of the country plays a major role, thus rendering the spatial distribution of airports. Roughly we can divide airports in Croatia into several groups. First, there are major airports that carry the majority of passenger traffic (Zagreb, Split, Dubrovnik). The second group consists of airports with infrastructure capable of accepting even wide body aircraft, but they have modest passenger numbers (Zadar, Osijek, Pula, Rijeka) and the final group are airports with shorter runways, capable of accepting only smaller aircraft (Mali Lošinj, Bol).

Even though one might think there are quite enough airports to service all the needs of the airline industry in Croatia, there are some further possibilities that can be explored. New airports are being planned, but their realization is probably far into the future. Croatia invested heavily in road infrastructure while other means of transportation were neglected including air transport. Given the number of passengers carried by Croatia Airlines along with the financial troubles of the airline one might think there is no need for further development of airports in the future. However, on the other hand, low cost airlines are carrying ever more passenger to and from Croatia every year. It may be that some things are better left to the market forces rather than obscure and aimless government intervention. For possible future airports in Croatia see Figure 2.

Figure 6 Present and possible future sites of smaller airports

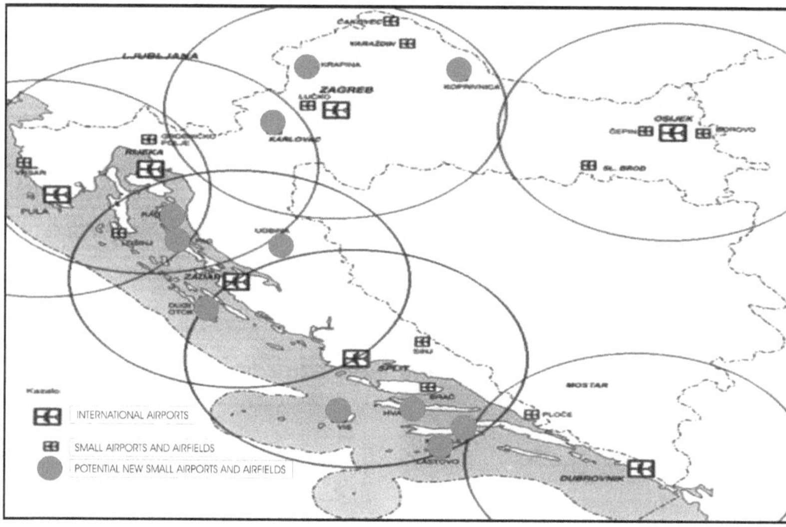

Source: Ministry of the Sea, Transport and Infrastructure 2009.

As we can see in Figure 7 below, the data for the three largest airports in Croatia reveals several facts: Zagreb is the largest airport in terms of passengers and, furthermore, has roughly double the volume compared to Dubrovnik and Split. While the runways at all three airports meet the current demand, the same is not the case with the terminal buildings. Zagreb airport was designed to handle roughly two million passengers annually. Even two troublesome years (2008, 2009) saw numbers in excess of two million. While there is a lot of talk about the construction of a new terminal building, there are no serious developments on this issue. If Zagreb airport does not construct a new modern passenger terminal it is not likely that the number of passengers will grow at the present rate and any possibility of introducing intercontinental flights is out of the question. The two other airports share the same problem; however, Dubrovnik airport is undergoing major reconstruction, which will be completed in 2011. Even though the passenger numbers are in decline all over Europe – due mostly to lower GDP – income is likely to bounce back in coming years, when we can expect further increase in passenger numbers.

Figure 7 Number of passengers (Dubrovnik, Split, Zagreb)

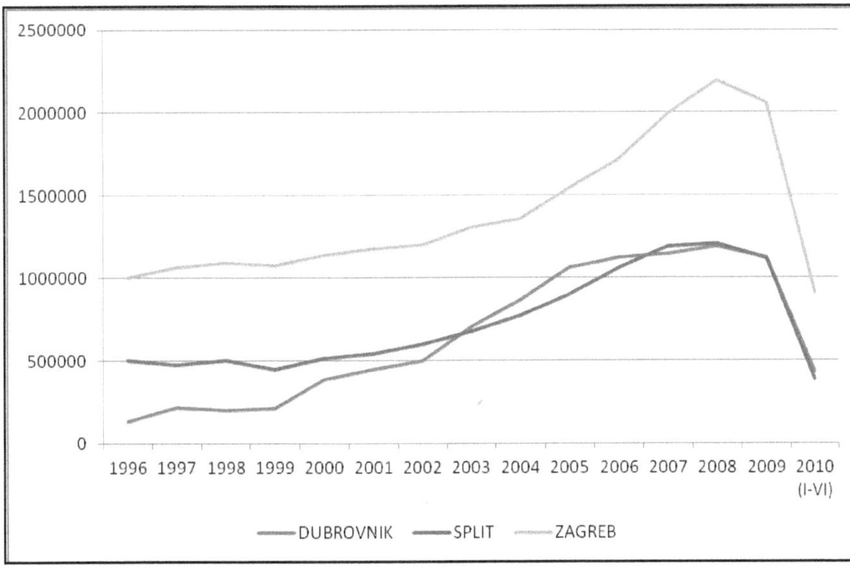

Source: IATA, Ministry of the Sea, Transport and Infrastructure.

Figure 8 Number of passengers (Bol, Mali Lošinj, Osijek)

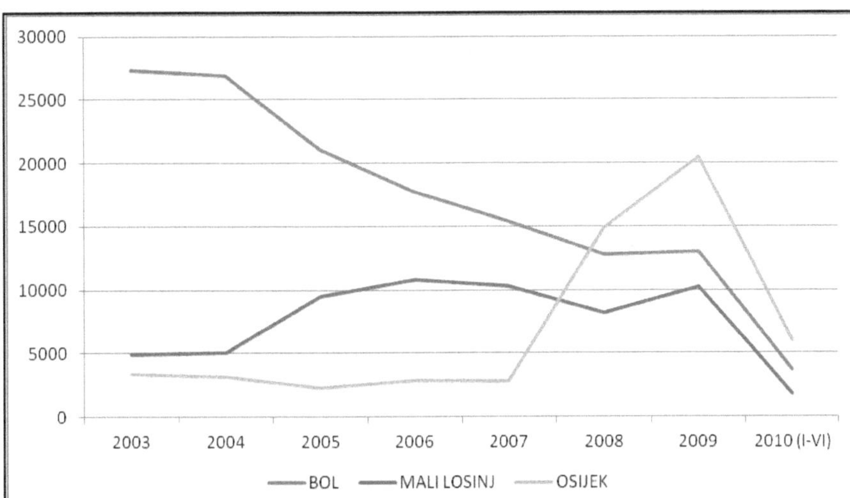

Source: IATA, Ministry of the Sea, Transport and Infrastructure.

In Figure 8 we can observe the airports from the third group, with limited runway and other capabilities, to which we added Osijek on the grounds of rather low passenger numbers. As an airport with technical capabilities close to larger airports, Osijek has seen some developments in recent years. As of 2007, passenger numbers went through the roof. This may be attributed to the introduction of flights by Germanwings, Ryanair. Croatia Airlines introduced seasonal flights to Split and Dubrovnik. We can expect further developments at this airport mostly at the low cost end of the market. Bol airport has seen a huge drop in passenger numbers even when all others grew at an exponential rate. The reasons may lie in charter traffic that brings tourists to the island of Brač. On the other hand, Split airport, which serves a number of scheduled seasonal and all year lines is nearby. However, low cost airlines contributed to the rise of small airports and they are now flying to Bol. On the other hand, Mali Lošinj does not have any charter flights (we may see some developments during 2010) or low cost flights. Limitations of infrastructure (short runway) do not allow mid-size airplanes, mostly flown by low cost airlines, to land in Mali Lošinj. However, passenger numbers are closing in on Bol. Mali Lošinj is an airport with a rather large number of landings and take offs compared to similar sized airports, but the airplanes are small, mostly private planes from the region and some air taxi services. Again, there was a lot of talk about extending the runway in Mali Lošinj but nothing materialized. Mali Lošinj can be connected to the closest larger airport in Pula with a 10 - 15 minute flight (on a single engine piston plane). On the other hand, the same journey by car is an expedition lasting several hours that involves a ferry ride. This is the airport with the most potential since it would serve a developed tourist destination and the largest island city in Croatia. Thus there is a potential in seasonal and year round scheduled flights.

In Figure 9 we can see the data for Pula, Rijeka and Zadar airports. Pula is the airport with the largest numbers; however, they are declining while Zadar is on the rise and slowly closing in on Pula. Pula has several year round flights on Croatia Airlines and many more seasonal flights on network operators, charter flights and low cost flights. On the other hand, Rijeka airport is in decline since it lost some of the low cost flights. In the years to come we can expect more low cost flights and hopefully we will see a new Croatia Airlines policy, which is more open to smaller airports since so many low cost flights end up at these airports. That simply means there are enough passengers for these destinations if the price is right.

Figure 9 Number of passengers (Pula, Rijeka, Zadar)

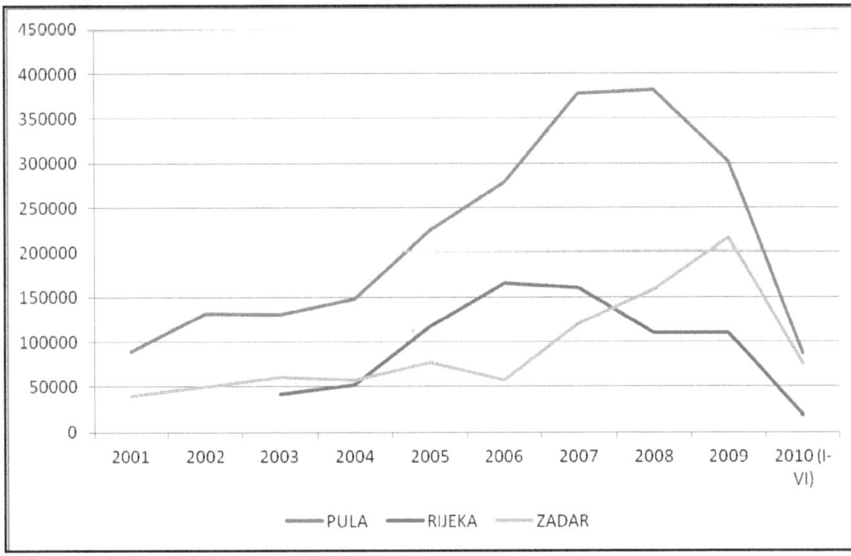

Source: IATA, Ministry of the Sea, Transport and Infrastructure.

Conclusion

In the past 20 years the aviation industry has passed through a lot of new regulations, deregulations and re-regulations on the one hand, and several shocks related to unforeseen events e.g. swine flu, bird flu, terrorism threats, increased airport security (yielding a lot of dissatisfied customers), increased oil prices for some time, and in the end the global economic crises. All of this happened over a fairly short period, thus airlines have not yet had the time to recover fully. On the other hand, low cost airlines have managed to provide lower prices and have pushed network operators to lower their prices on short haul flights. A few low cost airlines went bankrupt, but this is after all a market economy. Customers largely benefited from these developments and there were more of them.

Croatia in the last 20 years went from war and independence and the creation of the national carrier Croatia Airlines to another period of troubled markets with the world crisis. Croatia Airlines is in financial trouble and much of the air travel in Croatia is dependent on this company. On the other hand, Croatia Airlines did not see the threat and the potential of the low cost market and smaller airports as points of interest for air operations. Other carriers did see this potential, especially connected with tourism-oriented travellers. In the future we can expect to see more air passengers at more airports in Croatia through the increasing relevance (and further investment in infrastructure) of small and big airports, which can serve as growth and development boosters of airline business and overall transport potentials of the country.

References

Armantier, O./O. Richard (2003), 'Exchanges of Cost Information in the Airline Industry', in *The RAND Journal of Economics*, Vol. 34, No. 3, Autumn, pp. 461-477

ATA (2009), Air Transport Association, [http://www.airlines.org.]

Croatia Airlines (2010), Quarterly Report

Doganis, R. (2002), *Flying off Course: The economics of international airlines,* Routledge, New York

Hendricks, K./M. Piccione/G. Tan (1997), 'Entry and Exit in Hub-Spoke Networks', in *The RAND Journal of Economics*, Vol. 28, No. 2, Summer, pp. 291-303

Hirsch, B. T./D. A. Macpherson (2000), 'Earnings, Rents, and Competition in the Airline Labor Market', in *Journal of Labor Economics*, Vol. 18, No.1, January, pp. 125-155

IATA (2009), International Air Transport Association, database

Marin, P. L. (1995), 'Competition in European Aviation: Pricing and Market Structure', *The Journal of Industrial Economics*, Vol. 43, No. 2, June, pp. 141-159

Ministry of the Sea, Transport and Infrastructure (2010), [http://www.mmpi.hr]

Ng, C. K./P. Seabright (2001), 'Competition, Privatisation and Productivity Efficiency: Evidence from the Airline Industry', in *The Economic Journal*, Vol. 111, No. 473, July, pp. 591-619

O'Connor, W. E. (2001), *An Introduction to Airline Economics,* Praeger Publishers, Westport

WDI (2008), World Development Indicators, World Bank, database

Goran Pavelin

What will it be? A Vision of the Social and Economic Development of Europe with a Special Reference to Cultural Tourism in 2030

Introduction

The people of Europe and European countries have, each in their own specific way, played throughout history a very active role in the creation of what we call the present. Due to a lack of detachment and objectiveness, it is very difficult to distinguish footholds in today's world when forming a vision of the future.

Nevertheless, the variable of cultural tourism should not be left out, as history confirms that that was one of the first forms of tourism to appear in human history. Initially inspired by religious motives, today cultural tourism includes the realization of an active interaction with the local population, providing that it is able to communicate the cultural dimension of its heritage.

However, in twenty year's time, there will have been numerous changes in Europe. Therefore, the first part of this contribution will discuss partial projections in the context of the political and legal environment, then economic social and societal images as well as the influence of technology on socio-economic and cultural development.

Vision of general environment

Political and legal environment as a moderator of European culture

European history provides for very dynamic reading matter. Revolutions and changes on an international level are still evident today on the geographical map of Europe: territorial factionalism and the shape of borders between countries have been marking the disunion for centuries. Today in Europe, there are more than 80 nations in 49 countries between the Atlantic and the Urals. Besides, there are 307 national groups, that is ethnic or language minorities with more than 103 million members in the European countries. (Pan/Pfeil 2000)

Viewed in retrospect, even in the second half of the 20th century, majority communities were mostly indifferent or had a negative attitude towards minority groups and only in a few cases did the majority communities have explicitly positive attitude towards minorities. On the other hand, if the minority groups were in danger or existentially threatened, they themselves were not ready for the evaluation of their minority status.

With the implementation of a certain degree of integration, on the territory of Europe, a democratic environment was gradually created from both a political and a legal standpoint. However, the expectations that the democracy would automatically solve the issue of minorities did not bring any major results. The only thing that imposed itself was the obligation to find a way to solve these issues.

In the Nineteen Nineties numerous unresolved issues escalated on the Eurasian continent. With the breakup of Czechoslovakia, Yugoslavia and the Soviet Union new states were formed, mostly on the basis of ethnical criteria. It is worth mentioning that many critics predicted that the integration of European states into a united Europe would not be entirely successful, mainly due to the inefficiency in resolving certain minority issues and interests.

On the other hand, the unstoppable process of integrating the states into the European Union has a direct impact on the need to review other issues as well, on a political as well as on a legal level. In other words, the process of the integration of a certain country into the European Union starts with the standardization of legal regulations and in that way it directly influences politics, the economy and social environment, security and foreign policy, cooperation and the administration of justice, external affairs, etc.

In that sense, the freedom of individuals becomes a general standard of behaviour and activity, which considerably moves criteria in the countries whose heritage was differently organized in earlier stages. It is expected from countries, whose political and legal platform was in many ways different, or is different in comparison to a political and legal heritage of the European Union, to have a period of adjustment not only on an infrastructural level, but also in segments of implementation of new standards. Generally speaking, the political and legal environment in European countries in the future can be evaluated as positive, because in that way the preconditions for long-term peace are created, which is also an aim of every individual. However, it needs to be emphasized that Europe's future also depends on the success of securing a status for all peoples, nations and all denominations as a balance to previous periods of neglect of the multicultural European continent.

Economic environment

The second guideline in predicting the general European environment in 2030 refers to the economy. In a common political and legal environment, which supports a peaceful solution on an international level, the economy can make progress with a dynamic and in a direction that is characteristic for every country. Apart from that, on the territory of Europe there has been a lot of integration, which has also influenced the economic progress of certain countries. Consequently to that, an equal development of all countries has not been achieved in Europe today. That legacy has been making the gap between the developed countries, developing countries and transition countries wider, especially when one takes into consideration the fact that the countries that want to join the EU have to meet the imposed economic requirements. The promptness of the stabilization and joining measures leads to the effect that we have today and that is the financial crisis, which manifests itself through an economic crisis that is transmitted from developed countries to developing countries and countries in transition. However, with the introduction of a new economic order, the opening of the market and the establishment of private ownership, the countries in transition are going through an internal crisis on all levels. These changes are mainly evident in the countries of former socialist system. The result of that is the decline in the citizens' standard of living, higher unemployment, liquidation of uncompetitive businesses, lower market values, etc. Stronger economies are resisting the crisis, while the weaker ones and insolvent national economies need a much longer period of time to recover. All this leads to a wider gap between the economies and the solutions are to be found in the introduction of a higher level of economy specialization and that is the prevalence of the competitive industrial branches and the closing down of insolvent and uncompetitive systems.

In that sense, the Republic of Croatia has a very demanding task. All of these changes affect the formation of new knowledge and new business activities, which contributes to the general development of social and economic behaviour and working culture. The image of the economy is very broad and that is not only on the EU level and on the level of each country. Today, it is seen globally because the factors of an economic system are able to connect without much restrain. The evidence of that are corporations, which have driven out private ownership with the introduction of a dispersed ownership structure i.e. stock ownership. From that viewpoint, share capital is networked and on EU territory all the assumptions of undisturbed circulation of not only capital but also people, i.e. knowledge, goods and services, have been realized.

The globalization of economic activity is followed by waves of cultural transformation in a way that affects the question of identity, life style, etc. This however, shows itself on local levels, so local identity and culture are rooted out and replaced by symbols of global trade marks.

Social and societal environment

Social and societal reality in Europe in 2030 can be predicted by the analysis of demographic indicators. Generally speaking, twelve per cent of the total human population is in Europe (60% of the world's population lives in Asia). The population is not evenly spread across the territory of Europe so, for example, there are 16,000 inhabitants per sq.km in Monaco, whereas in Iceland there are 2.5 inhabitants per sq.km.

Another significant indicator is the natural movement of the population. This indicator is influenced by a migration variable and growth variable influence. Migration implicitly includes spatial movement of the population and it is observed through the immigration and emigration of people, while natural growth can be positive or negative, all depending on the number of new-borns in relation to the number of people who die. The natural growth is predicted based on the share of adult population, but also on a specific quality of a certain environment or even tradition.

Apart from the mentioned variables, demographic transition should be taken into consideration. It indicates the changes in population which happened, which are happening and which will happen in all countries in the world. It is about changes from high birth-rates and mortality rates to low but constant birth-rates and mortality rates. These stages are evident in the following: The first stage is a high and changeable birth-rate and mortality. Then, in the next stage, mortality decreases due to better conditions, standards, improvements in medicine, etc. The birth-rate is still on a high level for some time, but after a certain period of time the mentality changes, so the birth-rate decreases. In the third stage both birth-rate and mortality decrease, but they remain, indicating the continuously less important growth or natural decline. From the viewpoint of demographic transition, every country in the world is specific. For instance, Croatia entered the demographic transition in the first half of the 20th century. It entered the second phase in the Nineteen Sixties and that lasted until the Nineteen Nineties. The third phase is in progress, but with negative natural growth. With the backward movement on the time scale, developed European countries have gone through a demographic transition, taken into account that in some, minimal differences of natural growth and natural decline have cyclically been repeated. However, population policy influences the duration of certain phases. It is about stimulation or restrictive policy regarding natural growth.

The variable of spatial population movement has already been mentioned as being one of the factors of a population's demographic structure. The most frequent causes of migrations are economic issues and that is when people from passive and poor regions move to the attractive ones that offer a better standard of living. Inner migrations include populating cities and depopulating villages. However, causes of wars, religious and national intolerance, climate, natural disasters, etc. also influence the movement of the population. Immigration, i.e. the moving in of people from other countries, changes the population's age structure of the country, which accepts these immigrants. The movement of population can be permanent or temporary. The permanent kind means that people do not return to their country of origin, while temporary movements are linked to work, education and similar. Seasonal movements need to be mentioned as well, which are mostly connected to tourism, agriculture and similar.

If one takes into consideration that Europe has largely entered the third stage of demographic transition, the predictions for 2030 are not optimistic. It is expected that the territory of Europe will be mostly populated by an ageing population, so countries have opened their borders in order to compensate the negativity that would follow that. European countries are even today facing the deficiency of the age group of the mature population, which leads to the need to import the working force. Eurostata keeps records of this and other data, where the influences of demographic transitions on each European country's level can be seen. The developed countries are under the pressure of immigration, whereas the countries with a lower level of development register emigration.

Demographic changes in 1997 and 2005 in relation to 2008 point to the fact that countries in Europe create politics differently, which directly or indirectly influences demographic change. In European countries in most cases these are in direct correlation with net migration.

The question that imposes itself is where most immigrants, who come to Europe, are from and which groups they belong to. If the closeness to religious groups is taken into consideration, it can be concluded that the highest inflow is from Islamic countries. Therefore, it can be assumed that in 20 years or more, the members of Islamic religious groups will have become a significant part of Europe's population.

Technical and technological platform

What needs to be emphasized as the last but not least significant point of prediction, is the technical and technological platform, which has in a very short period of time rise to a higher level, thus integrating methods, patterns and forms of communication channels and at the same time decreasing language barriers.

The phase of economic transformation on the territory of Europe needs to be taken into consideration from a technical and technological aspect. The developed regions are in a post-industrial phase, whereas there are still important regions which are in a transition from industrial to post-industrial phase of development. This disparity also has an impact on the ecological component, which is becoming a very important factor and prerequisite to viable development. With the implementation of integration on a European level, ecological standards are becoming more important. However, these issues are still left incomplete on local levels where the local culture of living and working contributes mostly to it together with the flexibility in terms of exploiting natural resources for commercial purposes. On this issue, there are important differences in Europe. The protection of natural reserves, the protection of the natural environment and other essential questions are in direct correlation with the level of culture and environmental awareness. What contributes to that is the introduction of new technologies, which reduce the negative effect on the environment, for example the use of biogas, wind or solar power for the production of electrical power and similar. These initiatives have not been entirely recognized in developing countries and the introduction of new technologies is also being slowed down by the corporations which supply the market with conventional energy forms.

Finally, in 20 year's time, there will be a shortage of water on a global level. But then, Europe is not directly under the influence of these tendencies and that is mainly because of the effort that is being put into the protection of nature, the preservation of river flows and the quality of lakes.

The culture of Europe and cultural tourism in 2030

After having predicted the changes on a political and legal level and then in terms of the economic, social and societal environment, as well as on the level of technical support, culture can be taken into consideration as a specific future product on the European continent. In accordance with that, culture still remains one of the most deliberated, defined and redefined terms. Haralambos gives the following concept of culture (Haralambos/Holborn 2002, p. 589):

1. culture is a state of mind when people aspire to the idea of perfecting individual achievement,
2. culture is connected with the civilization in the etatistic sense, therefore the culture of a certain society can be superior to other societies,
3. culture in the, most general sense is also a high culture since it is at the same time a collective set of artistic and intellectual works within a certain society.

According to Ralph Linton, the culture of a society is the way of life of its members; a collection of ideas and habits learned, shared and transmitted from generation to generation. (Haralambos/Holborn 2002, p. 883) According to Maurice Duverger, the term culture has a large and narrow sense. In a narrow sense, culture includes belief (ideology, value systems, legitimacy and myths). In a large sense, culture includes special forms according to which all elements that make a society group are combined: collective notions, beliefs, ideology, institutions, technology and even geographic and demographic elements.

Culture can be seen as an entire cultural heritage, in other words as a system of learned patterns of thinking, feeling and acting. Generally speaking, culture can be observed through three interrelated sets of phenomena. These are (Fanuko et al. 1992, p. 23):

1. behavioural patterns
2. shared values, beliefs, rules and
3. tools and techniques (technology).

Behavioural patterns are learned from the earliest age and result in forms, which are today seen as equal to life styles. This influence appears on many levels, and family, as a fundamental social institution, has the biggest influence. Preschool and school curriculums, the education system taken as a whole, religious institutions, the working environment and the influence of other factors, which can also include the media, all influence the creation of culture in the most general sense. This order covers the entire *diapason* of available forms of influences on culture, and the tools used for that implementation work in a transnational way. Media platforms, e.g. cable TV, the Internet, films, etc. have an impact on the creation of an individual's perception of the world and milieu, which is to the biggest extent adjusted to the commercialization of culture in the sense of a universally accepted value systems formed through the pattern of supply and demand. In this way, culture becomes a commercial good with a targeted consumer category. On the other hand, local culture, under the influence of global marketing, is neglected, not only from the standpoint of the communicators of offered values but also from the standpoint of the media as a channel by whose means certain ideas are launched to the public. It can be said that in this way, a universal devastation of cultural values of micro locations is carried out.

Society, to a certain extent, represents a set of concepts which its members have about it. Every society group is to some extent a cultural whole which creates history. Nation is the strongest fundamental cultural whole and tribes, peoples, towns and nations gather within broader cultural entities, which are commonly known as civilizations. (Duverger 2001, pp. 107-123)

As stated in the beginning, there is a great number of minorities living in Europe and when the category of subcultures is added, we can talk about a very wide span of cultural manifestations. Besides, globalization does not mean that the world is becoming culturally more homogenous, because globalization includes more than just the emphasis on local. Therefore, there are two contrary processes within the same phenomenon; on the one hand there is versatility and on the other hand there is concentration. In this respect, the future of Europe lies in versatility and the acceptance of differences and intercultural tolerance. Though, one must take into consideration the factors which influence culture and that would also include the perception of identity. This perception has also been through its phases of evolution. At first, the focus was on the enlightening subject, then on the social one and finally on the postmodern one. The enlightening subject appeared with the period of Croatian Literary Modernism between the Sixteenth and Eighteenth centuries. In this concept, an individual was not a part of anything that was bigger than himself or herself, but was considered to have his or her own attitudes and opinions and in accordance with that of his or her own identity. The social subject appeared in the 19th century, when bigger changes in society occurred. Industrialization and urbanization made the complexity of the society greater and structural forms prevailed. It also came to a redistribution of wealth, mainly through the influence of the stockholding institution, which brought together citizens through the bureaucratic administration of modern institutions and a modern state. In that way, the individual lost importance and became one with interest groups and the identity was linked with class, profession, place of origin or nationality. We still have that influence today, however, the process is moving in the direction of individualization. In that sense, the identity of an individual is fragmented because people are complex in their nature. Fast changes that are predicted for the future will continue to influence the redefining of an individual through various prisms of personal experience and perception.

During the previous century, group approaches towards studying identity issues were developed and what emerged from that were paradigms based on gender, class, race ecological and similar concepts, whose escalation was evident in different movements and a lot of them exist still today. This means that the identity, considering a wider span, has become a part of the political issue of today. Globalization followed the processes inherited in the past, which influenced the fragmentation of the individual's identity. The mobility of people and the improvement of communications manifested itself in the aspect of tourism, through the creation of the identity of tourist destinations, entire regions as well as continents. In this sense, identity becomes a framework for creating an image in public, which is no longer local but national and global.

However, the growing convergence of cultural contents and information as a part of concentrated tendencies on the world's media markets does not automatically lead to partial and one-dimensional globalization but it gives an advantage to the local level. In this connection, a vision of future cultural tourism, as a segment of common civilization progress, can be created.

Taking into account what has already been said, the question of the viability of authentic location identities arises as well as the one of the preservation of historical and cultural heritage and tradition, and that is the preservation of the immaterial and material cultural basis of a certain destination.

In other words, cultural tourism is one of the oldest motivations for traveling, whose origin is to be found in pilgrimages. After that period, the cultural identity of a certain tourist destination developed in accordance with local attractions, in other words in accordance with the concentration of certain offers of cultural contents. However, culture assumes numerous variations in view of the networking of the influences of subcultures. In this way, cultural events are manifested in movements which are united by music, sport, fashion, science, technology, health, etc. In doing so, interaction becomes the main goal: joint action, acquiring new knowledge, i.e. an active relationship between objects and subjects as well as a transformation through an experience in which both parties achieve cultural expansion. So, the emphasis is precisely on the interpersonal way of communication By doing so, a reflection on diversities, their understanding and acceptance, i.e. the increase of the level of general tolerance, is encouraged.

In that sense, cultural tourism in Europe has a very big influence on the future. The differences can become advantages when accomplishing common prosperity through cultural tourism. However, in order to have a positive progress on this level, a series of adjustments need to be made. These adjustments are slow because the culture of a certain climate changes slowly. This means that the tendencies, which could even be called prejudices, about the identity of certain cultural groups are still present. Generalization is namely the result of the ignorance of numerous facts about the observed set. However, modern communication and information technology enables an individual approach to a global audience, so it can be expected that the changes concerning the improvement of the public perception about culturally specific qualities will go in that direction. That is also the way towards the growth of cultural tourism, which can be developed in urban centres as well as in rural parts of European countries. The issue of balancing urban and rural culture is just a matter of time, because in accordance with a shared agricultural policy of the EU, the countries that will join the Union are adjusting by supporting the settling of rural areas and the development of rural tourism. Within that scope, an essential characteristic of the tourism product comes out of the culture of living, i.e. living in a natural ambiance, consuming naturally produced food, becoming acquainted with the natural environment and similar.

Conclusion

What prevails in the formation of a general vision refers to the level of communication technology development. What is created in that manner is an assumption about a higher level of knowledge about a certain culture and prevalence of cultural diversities with an increase of the tolerance level. On the other hand, the culture of today points to the cultural heritage from the past, so the changes in the future can be expected only along with the acceptance of new visions of the present.

To sum up, cultural tourism represents one of the strategic preconditions for the realization of Europe, mainly because of the creation of space for an equal status for all cultures of our multicultural continent.

References

Duverger, M. (2001), *Politička sociologija*, PanLiber, Osijek-Zagreb-Split
Fanuko, N. , et al. (1992), *Sociologija*, Školska knjiga, Zagreb
Haralambos, M./Holborn M. (2002), *Sociologija*, Golden Marketing, Zagreb
Pan, C./B. S. Pfeil (2000), *Die Volksgruppen in Europa*, Braumüller Verlag, Wien

INDEX